Dynamic
Competitive
Strategy
& Product Life Cycles

Chester R. Wasson

A Revised Edition of
PRODUCT MANAGEMENT:
PRODUCT LIFE CYCLES & COMPETITIVE MARKETING STRATEGY

CHALLENGE BOOKS
ST. CHARLES, ILLINOIS

Library of Congress Catalog   ISBN: 0-9600352-4-9 clothbound
Number 73-93479   0-9600352-5-7 paperbound

Contents

iii

Preface

When experience dictated expansion and revision of my original PRODUCT MANAGEMENT: PRODUCT LIFE CYCLES AND COMPETITIVE MARKETING STRATEGY, it also became clear that the title really ought to be reversed, to better reflect the broad and fundamental content of this work. Although the basic focus is still on product strategy and pricing tactics, these concepts must be defined so much more broadly than they generally are that all phases of competitive maneuver must be included (as they were and are). From a marketing vantage point, product can only be defined as perceivable value, and value is the result of the effective working of all elements in the marketing mix, of advertising, sales and sales promotion, and of the efforts of those in the various levels of the distribution channels. Likewise, any realistic view of price must take into account much beyond mere monetary considerations. From the buyer's point of view, price includes other inhibitions to acquisition of the values offered: time costs, search costs, design negatives, restrictions on distribution, etc. For this reason, what I had labelled as product management encompasses every aspect of product design and marketing strategy.

The new title, DYNAMIC COMPETITIVE STRATEGY AND PRODUCT LIFE CYCLES, would be basically redundant were it not for the static stereotype of competition inculcated by traditional economic disquisition. As my discussion makes clear, the only possible kind of competition is dynamic. Any equilibrium achieved is that of the bicycle--maintained only by constant forward motion. For this reason, no reference will be found in these pages to such terms as monopoly, duopoly, oligopoly and other such labels of equilibrium economics whose only relevance, if they ever possessed any, are to the dead world of pure commodity trade. In the modern world of mass production of finished consumer and capital goods, monopoly is a delusion which leads those who think they have one to early somnolence and death. Likewise, even an elementary knowledge of modern psychology precludes any belief in the possibility of the kind of direct competition which most elementary economics texts are constructed around--no two sellers can hope to succeed in the same segment of the market.

Because any useful understanding of the true nature of competition and of strategy must rest on the best available knowledge of the fundamentals of human behavior, this new edition includes a specific chapter outlining the key concepts of well-established modern psychology which are basic to such an understanding. For the rest, this edition utilizes additional illustrative material and includes some other expansions, as well as some reorganization of the original materials. Because the term "product life cycle" is frequently used interchangeably for both product category life cycles and for mere brand life cycles, it was felt wise to devote some space to a specific discussion of brand life cycles and both their likenesses to product category cycles as well as their divergencies. Otherwise, I have found no need to make any changes in the viewpoints which led to the encouraging reception of the first edition in both the academic and business worlds.

Geneva, Illinois   C. R. W.

Part One. Product Life Cycles and the Basic Behavioral Factors Shaping the Outcome of Their Management

Competitive strategy must be shaped to the forces of the product life cycle and to the underlying psychology, both individual and social, which give rise to such cycles.

All products and ideas introduced to society pass through some kind of life cycle--some form of initial build-up in adoption and acceptance pointing toward some plateau, then some eventual decline and death. The market response to any given competitive maneuver will differ drastically at different phases of the cycle.

Not all product life cycles are the same, however, and initial acceptance and growth patterns can be completely opposite for two superficially similar introductions, requiring entirely different introductory strategies. The difference lies in the built-in learning requirement--in whether or not product use requires a change in motor habits, habits of thought and perception, or habitual social roles.

We can best plan for success if we first absorb the lessons of a few well-established principles and concepts of individual and social psychology, and of the sociology of new product diffusion. Only then will we understand why competition can never be direct, why some products take off from the moment of introduction while the sales of others grow slowly only through years of hard promotion, and why fashions of all kinds come and go, and must be taken account of in our designs.

THE KEYS TO STRATEGY PLANNING: PRODUCT LIFE CYCLES, PRODUCT USE-SYSTEMS, AND USE-VALUE SEGMENTATION

Rational planning of successful competitive strategy must start with a sound understanding of the phenomena of product life cycles and a wise assessment of the place of each offering in its own cycle. Successful management of every aspect of marketing strategy involves the appropriate match of marketing plans to the current stage of the market life cycle. Products and ideas of any kind have a finite life cycle very similar to the life cycle of the animate humans who originate and consume them. Conceptually, the full cycle proceeds through eight stages which can be described in biological terms: conception, gestation or pre-introduction development, infancy (market development), an adolescent period of rapid growth in sales, a settling-down period of maturization characterized by competitive turbulence, a greater or lesser period of relatively stable maturity, a decline, and finally death. Each of these phases calls for a different pattern of management, and the appropriate marketing mix changes radically with changes in the stage of the cycle.

Like biological growth and decline cycles, the course of product life cycles can be modified by careful management but not side-tracked. Unlike the biological cycle, the product life cycle can skip some of the initial development period naturally or it may go through several successive periods of rapid growth as well as an indisputable reincarnation implicit in the fashion cycle. Thus there are many types of product life cycles, not just one cycle.

Since each stage of the life cycle requires a substantially different marketing and management mix, the appropriate marketing strategy at any given stage requires advance recognition of the character of the next developing stage and the way buyer perceptions of product and value change with the changes in phase. Advance recognition of the probable character of introductory acceptance is espe-

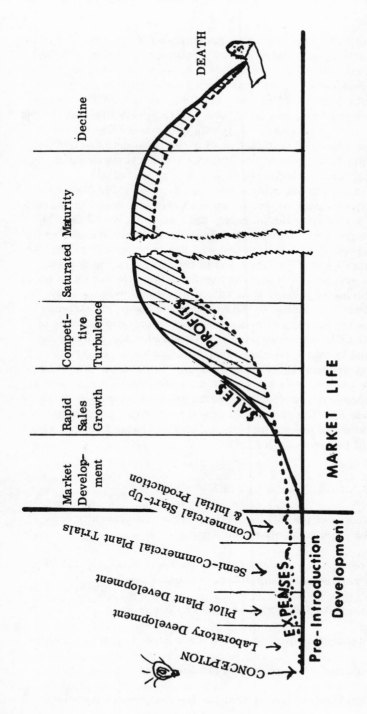

FIGURE 1-1. The Full Product Life Cycle

3

cially crucial, since the two basic acceptance patterns require completely opposite product introduction strategies of design, pricing, distribution and promotion. Prediction of the acceptance pattern rests on an understanding of what the customer will really be buying--not a physical offering, but a bundle of perceived services which come as close as any he is aware of to completing and making possible a ritual use-system. It is this use-system which is perceived as the source of satisfaction of a complete set of active desires. People differ both in the kinds of satisfactions they value, and seek, and the degree of satiation of these satisfactions. Thus both the desire-set content and the personal value placed on the satisfaction of each desire in the set varies from one individual to another, segmenting the market. Each segment would thus be composed of groups of individuals whose desire-sets are in about the same degree of satisfaction and who are seeking approximately the same mix or set of satisfactions in the total offering design.

Initial acceptance of an offering depends on the extent to which the total offering is perceived as fitting into some existing use-system and will be inverse to the need for the buyer to learn new motor use-systems, learn perceptions of new types of sources of satisfaction, or learn to perceive new levels of value of some key service in the bundle adequate to justify the price necessary to undertake its production. Price is simply the obverse side of perceived value and involves any kind of sacrifice which might inhibit a desire to possess the offering. Price should thus be defined as any avoidance characteristic built into the offering or its terms of sale. The kinds of price which are or can be charged change with the phases of the product life cycle.

THE BASIC LIFE CYCLE PATTERN

The stages of the full theoretical cycle are generally considered to be eight in number (See Figure 1-1):

1. Conception of a performance package capable of fulfilling a related set of unfulfilled consumer desires.

2. An incubation period of product development

3. Introduction of product and market development (infancy)

4. A period of rapid growth (adolescence)

5. Maturization (young adulthood)--competitive turbulence

6. Stability and saturation (full maturity--middle age)

7. Decline

8. Death and replacement

STAGES OF THE LIFE CYCLE

Conception

Products have been born, developed, and matured by accident, or even by mistake. Such accidents and mistakes have become less the rule as modern organizations have become increasingly aware that competitive innovation of new product development is the only assurance of continued vitality. To the extent that creation of any kind can be guided, most new product programs, like most healthy families, are planned. Whether planned or fortuitous, the start of any product is the mating of a set of conceptual product attributes with a set of conceptual market needs. As in any mating, the potential future health and success of the offering is limited by the quality of the match between the product attributes contained in the initial concept and the unfulfilled desire-sets it is intended to satisfy. The values inherent in both sides of the mating need to be carefully evaluated in terms of the market which is expected to be the outcome of the birth.

The concept needs also to be evaluated in terms of the ability of the organization to develop the concept into a viable product introduction and to nurture the infant introduction through a period of early market development. If the organization lacks the resources or ability, then the idea probably should be turned over to foster parents better equipped--to organizations with the strength to carry the concept through the incubation period and the market development phase. The mere act of a successful mating of product concept and market need does not lead inevitably to a thriving market introduction. The offering can withstand the rigors of the marketing environment only when carried through a period of wise development. The prematurely born mammal or product offering lacks independent vitality.

The Product Development Gestation Period

Like any other mortal organism, products start existence as a mere germ of their eventual form. At conception, they are usually either a simple performance attribute without form or substance

5

or some physical item whose perceivable performance attributes are imperfectly perceived. Market life is possible only when a suitable physical form has been developed which can fulfill a set of physical or psychical satisfactions desired by some substantial set of potential buyers, and delivered into a marketing environment capable of developing the desired potentialities. If the starting point is some service concept, some substantial marketing intelligence must be carried out to determine the nature of the total physical performance specifications needed to fit the highest valued desire-sets and the nature of the marketing segment perceiving the highest value in the potential offering. While research and development is attempting to come as close as possible to the desired attribute combination, a marketing plan must be prepared to facilitate favorable birth conditions. Every precaution must be taken to prevent premature introduction, to avoid exposure of the product to the market before either the product or the market are prepared.

Insight into a marketing need is not the only starting point of a product mating. Successful products have been evolved from newly discovered physical forms and concepts of technological possibilities whose satisfaction attributes were not clearly definable at the time. Nylon did not even start with the search for a fiber, but with a delving into the possibilities of building giant molecules such as nature produces organically. The hosiery market was not even a visible target when the first crystals of the new resin came out of the test tube. In cases such as this, research and development consists first of determining the performance characteristics of the new item, and marketing intelligence looks for unsatisfied desire-sets such attributes could fulfill.

Whether the starting point be an insight into an unfulfilled need or into some possible physical item, development must proceed to the point where the product has the optimum chance for continued life after introduction, and the easiest possible birth pains of market development. Otherwise, premature introduction to the world may lead to a crippling of the future potential, or to early death. Even when well carried out, research and development do not alone insure success. The target market must be well pinpointed, and the market itself must be taught the value of the product in meeting a desire-set which may not have been previously perceived as a related set of needs. A market preparation or development period precedes every successful introduction in some way.

The Market Development Period

Most really new products start life slowly, fail to generate

6

enough immediate sales income to match development expenses because the public must be made aware of the satisfaction bundles available and be educated in their use. Quite usually also, the potentialities for user satisfaction are not clearly defined at the time of birth, and the introductory period is also a period of learning of the possibilities for satisfying needs and of the market niche the new offering can earn. An alert watch for product weaknesses and defects needs to be kept during this phase and corrections made as quickly as possible to prevent an early death or crippling of the demand, and also to fortify against a take-over of the developed market by perceptive competitors when the later growth period arrives. Both the design of the product and the design of the distribution should be such as to attract the market segment most highly interested and to raise the least obstacle to its acceptance.

Relatively direct competition is never a real problem during a true period of market development because of the lack of profits and because the major potential is among those not yet familiar with the offering. Profit itself is low because promotion expenses are relatively high in comparison with sales, and the most expensive and intensive kinds of promotion--usually the personal forms-- must be relied upon. Both the promotional needs and the lack of substantial sales volume imply limitation of distribution to a few selected, aggressive distributive outlets.

If the introduction proves viable and the development period well managed, a time arrives when the acceleration of acceptance and the volume of sales become noticeable and returns get past the break-even point. The period of rapid growth has arrived, and with it aggressive competition which can be forestalled only if adequate preparations for it have been made in advance.

The Period of Rapid Growth

All sales curves manifestly start at point zero. They can no more go to full volume immediately than you can start your car at 50 miles per hour. As with any other dynamic phenomenon, full momentum takes time to reach, requires a period of acceleration. Curves of acceleration are typically what the mathematician recognizes as exponential functions--that is, they tend to increase at a relatively steady rate of gain, which may be slow or speedy. Whether the rate be low or high, all exponential functions sooner or later develop a steeply rising curve, and the sales curves of successful product introductions are no exception. They reach a point when public acceptance tends to be as widespread as the nature of the offering permits, and sales start ballooning. Promotional deficits of the initial period then normally turn into ever-widening and

7

attractive profits.

The sales volume and accompanying profits are just as visible and just as attractive to potential competitors as to stockholders. It is not then long before others attempt to carve out a piece of the market with innovatory variations. The initial innovator can protect the investment he has incurred in pioneering the market only if he has well-developed plans to fill all the market demand he can cover, both in terms of product availability and in terms of product variations to meet the now diversifying desire-set variations. Distribution needs to be transformed from the selective to the intensive. The rapid growth of sales itself is proof that potential customers are now aware of the benefits available and need no longer be sold on the product concept. The promotional emphasis thus needs to aim at solidifying the preeminent place of the introducer, to insure that he will be able to maintain his niche when the inevitable shakeout of a maturing market arrives. Unless the original producer is well entrenched in the affection of both the buyers and of distribution by the end of this period, the first on the market may not live to be the last.

The Competitive Turbulence of the Maturization Phase

All sales growth sooner or later slows down. No product can hope to gain an ever-increasing number of new customers at ever-increasing volume. The supply of potential buyers runs out. The slowdown which signals the approaching market maturity normally uncovers some degree of overcapacity and initiates a competitive battle for permanent market position. Unit profits diminish despite continuing sales increases. The time has come to entrench established market positions and prepare for the even thinner profits of the saturated market period. The time has also come to shift the creative and development sections of management to bringing promising new products along to the growth stage. To use the phrase popularized by Peter Drucker, the offerings are now beginning to pass out of the role of "today's breadwinners" and about to be "yesterday's breadwinners". The distributive network needs to be tightened, and ties with distributors strengthened, for the product differentiation is now beginning to diminish in perceived value and distribution will more and more be the key to sales volume. The product line itself will need intensified review, eliminating line elements which gain no preferred position for the organization, adding variations and design flexibility to make certain that the segment actually being served gets an ever closer fit to the needs of the individual buyer. As the saturation level approaches, promotion should more and more be aimed at reduction of the cognitive dissonance of buyers, at convincing the already converted of the value of the choices, reminding them of the values they are getting.

The Plateau of Market Saturation

All markets sooner or later become saturated. New customers are largely offset by the disappearance of the old, except for population growth, and an increasing proportion of sales is for mere replacement. Profit margins become thin as the keenness of the initial value appeal is dulled. Production cost reduction becomes the principal means of sustaining net returns. Lacking new potentials to tap, all aspects of marketing strategy must of necessity be aimed at market maintenance, at defense, as creative talents are shifted to newer lines whose profit prospects are brighter and a close watch is kept for the onset of a period of market decline.

The Declining Phase

Products, like everything else mortal, come to some end of the line. Life may be measured in decades or even centuries, but the history spans less than a human generation for most products, for many only a year or two of profits, and for many a brilliant fad, the end is measured in months. Once the market for a product is clearly on the skids, the only wise course is to use every device to milk it dry of profits, then give the product a quiet burial.

THE COMPLEXITIES OF REAL-LIFE PRODUCT CYCLES

Like all useful concepts, the above description of an idealized product cycle exposes the basic underlying pattern but ignores the complex variations we meet with in everyday life. The characteristics of each stage are essentially the same whatever the total cycle, but there are many kinds of cycles and not all cycles go through all stages outlined above. Basic inventions seem to tend toward a series of pyramided product cycles as the combination of technical advances and marketing imagination develops new satisfaction attributes and combinations attractive to new and wider segments. Other potentially useful offerings perish in infancy because of inadequate product development, or unwise market planning, or both. Some survive such a premature birth, but often at a loss of potential which might otherwise have been achieved. The market for some is much less extensive than had been supposed, and the looked-for ebullient growth phase never appears. Others take off on a rapidly

9

accelerating growth phase without any substantial period of market development, and of these, some attain a long life while some of the rest collapse at the moment of peak success. Figure 1-2 depicts some of these more common variations. Clearly, the product life cycle concept alone does not furnish us with an easily read roadmap of an automatically unfolding highway to profitable strategy. Rather, it provides us with a framework of expectations--a set of patterns of the kinds of developments to which we need to be on the alert and for which we need to plan in advance. Prediction of the timing and nature of the unfolding developments necessarily demands an understanding of how adopters perceive product value and of the bases for market segmentation necessary to gain competitive advantage.

WHAT IS A PRODUCT?

The term product is probably one of the most deceptive concepts in our language. It bespeaks a tangibility which few other aspects of management seem to have, yet is actually the most elusive intangible an organization deals with in its planning. The physical entity to which we gain possession in any purchase is really simply a necessary nuisance, merely a requisite bit of evidence that we have acquired a key element of a system needed to satisfy a group of desires. Consider, for instance, a set of key performance specifications for the ideal transportation vehicle:

Immediate transport to any desired destination at the moment the wish arises, with no element of discomfort of any kind, without need for any kind of road, with no learning required for its operation.

An unlimited capacity for whatever luggage and cargo we may wish to take along.

Clearly perceived evidence, visible to all, of our possession of this marvelous device.

Complete freedom from any need for service or care of any kind--no repairs, no cleaning, no storage requirements between moments of use.

Complete freedom from any kind of operating cost.

No depreciation, no need for parking.

10

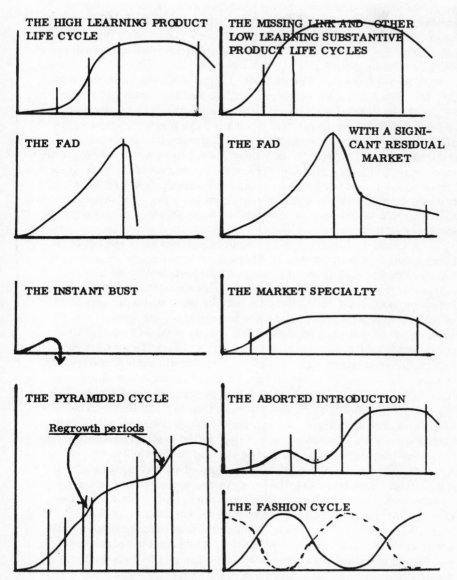

FIGURE 1-2. Common Variants of the Product Life Cycle

11

Note well two aspects of this list: the need for the product to serve, simultaneously, a complete set of desires, and the negative value of everything tangible about the product. The product we have labelled a transportation vehicle really must promise to satisfy a whole bundle of desires which the user perceives as related--a desire-set--all at one and the same time. And the physical side of the product simply gets in the way of complete fulfillment of this desire-set.

The only vehicle ever conceived by man which came close to this set of desires was the magic carpet, and that probably needed an occasional cleaning, existed only between the covers of a book of fairy tales. As with all real products, the more mundane vehicles we can and do buy require learning of complex motor habits for their use, work only in the context of a complicated use-system involving many other kinds of products--roads, fuel, service garages, maps, parking lots, etc. And they always require us to compromise between speed and cost, between cargo capacity and handling characteristics or required parking space, and many other elements of the desire-set.

A product, then, is simply a perceived cue to some set of buyers that they will be able to complete a learned use-system which is perceived, in return, as yielding satisfaction of a set of active desires. Some, but not necessarily all of the physical performance potentials of the product may be part of the perceived values, but only part, at most, and may only be incidental or not even relevant. A good perfume really ought to have an attractive odor, but if this is all it offers, its sale is certain to be limited and the price modest. Even what is attractive is defined partly by the society of which we are a part. To justify the price of any leading fragrance, it ought to connote glamor, or more bluntly, romance. The chemist does not create this key attribute. The culture does, as the barbers became painfully aware when a shaggy neckline on a man switched from being defined as bad grooming to being the mark of "in" grooming as the end of the 1960's approached.

Perhaps the most dramatic example of the cultural origin of much value is instanced by the story of frankincense and myrrh, ranked with gold as an offering to kings and gods at the birth of Christ. Products of two trees growing only in South Arabia and Somalia, production and trade in these two powerful essences built a wealthy and flourishing civilization in South Arabia from about the 14th century before Christ until the triumph of Christianity in the 4th century A.D. destroyed the practice of cremation and with it the market for frankincense in the Roman empire. The market value of their principal exports destroyed, five kingdoms vanished, leaving behind only archeological remains testifying that once there existed a prosperous and highly developed merchant culture where

12

today there are only the impoverished feudal countries of Yemen and the South Arabian Federation of the Trucial Coast (Van Beek, 1969).

From the buyer's point of view, then, the valuable attributes of the seller's offering is a bundle of potential services with many elements in addition to those inherent in the physical object which is the immediate object of the transaction, and some of these elements may even originate \outside of the seller's control. The coat or dress my wife buys may protect her from the weather, but if this were the only function, she would not shop so frequently. The one she picks must have a pleasing design, and this, in turn, is only incidentally built-in performance. What she considers pleasing is defined for her by the culture to which she belongs at the moment. She buys where and when she does because the garment is displayed in a convenient place--a distribution service created by the dealer, not the manufacturer. And she goes to the particular dress shop she does because the salesclerks there know what she wants (perform a sales-aid service), and because the store will let her return goods she finds are not quite what she wants (a consignment-and-trial service). The value of the actual style she buys is dependent on the acceptance of that particular fashion--at that moment in time--something completely outside the control of the seller. We buy the automobile we do for many reasons, but among them are certain to be consideration of the service network the manufacturer has created, although not mentioned on the bill of sale, and the expected trade-in value later-- something created by relative acceptance by other consumers of that particular model and make. If we purchase one of the "prestige" makes, we pay for that prestige--something every manufacturer would like to create for his design, but which the public, not the stylist, confers. We may not have any special preference for the make of gasoline we have pumped into the tank, and several brands have stations convenient to us, but we buy one special brand because of the quality of the periodic servicing and lubrication we get at its nearest outlet and find the advice of the mechanics there especially helpful in diagnosing minor troubles.

Moreover the mix of satisfactions we desire is quite likely somewhat different from the mix desired by our next-door neighbor, and almost certainly quite unlike that of the fellow on the other side of the tracks, whichever side we live on. Markets are not homogenous. They are "segmented" in myriad ways, so the offering of competitors must be differentiated to meet differing desire-sets.

The bundle of services we desire and the values we assign to the desired attributes are a highly personal package. Our neighbor's wife buys different dress designs, perhaps at a shop quite differently merchandised, drives a different car, decides on her gas station because it handles the trading stamps she is saving.

13

Both what is bought and the reason for its purchase vary from one purchaser to the next. Different buyers may be seeking quite divergent desire-set satisfactions from the identical physical product. Thus the same prestige make of automobile may be purchased by one buyer because its possession spells "arrived", while another may hesitate to get it because he does not want that attribute, but nevertheless purchases because he sees the same automobile as the finest creation of automobile engineering, and he appreciates fine mechanisms. A third buyer may simply see the vehicle as an extremely durable vehicle which is very economical in operation under the hard usage he must give a car. The same prescription may be given one patient to alleviate symptoms of arthritis, to another to suppress allergic reactions. The values we see in an offering are thus dependent on the use-system in which we desire to employ it. All products have value only as a means of facilitating a use-system—a set of habitual procedures which produce the satisfactions we are seeking. Quite often, full product success requires the development or even invention of accessory elements and services to complete this use-system, and full acceptance lags without them. In addition, as noted above, even the distribution outlets can be important elements of value. Since a product can only be defined as a set of values in some use-system, the term "offering" will be used to comprehend all the related values, and the term "product" will be used synonymously with offering except where qualified as the "physical product".

THE USE-SYSTEM AND PERSONAL ROLES: DETERMINANT OF
VALUE AND KEY TO ACCEPTANCE

Satisfactions result as the end-product of an habitual set of procedures involving the products we seek, never from mere possession of the product alone. An automobile has extremely limited utility unless we have acquired a complex set of driving habits, have available a road system and maps or other guides, know where we can fuel the tank and get mechanical service, and of course, have some place to park at home and at our destination. Even the simplest of personal products--such as a cake of toilet soap or a pack of cigarettes--generate satisfaction of some desire set only in the context of an habitual use-system involving other products and a set of learned motor reactions.

Consider a cake of toilet soap. We may say we buy it to clean our face, but the soap, either in the store or sitting on the washstand, does not itself do that job--it is merely an inanimate solid chemical, a product of the toiletry industry. To get a clean face, we must have some kind of wash basin and some warm wash water,

14

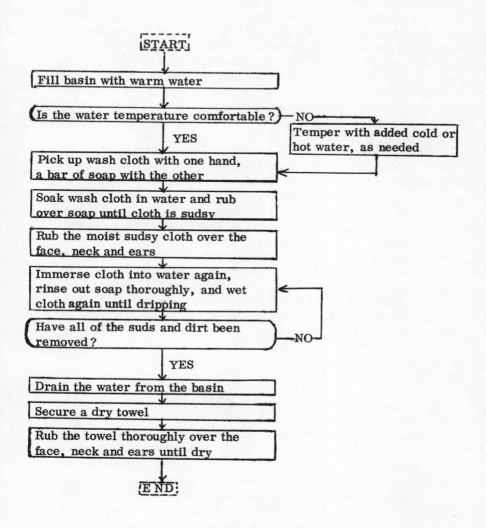

FIGURE 1-3. Use-System for Soap-and-Water Cleansing of the Face

15

at least, and really would like a washcloth and towel also. To achieve the desired end result, we go through a set of procedures outlined in the flow diagram of Figure 1-3. For most of us, this ritual was learned so long ago that it seems simple, but the mother of any young boy can testify that the learning process is neither simple nor instantaneous nor lacking in pain for the learned. Furthermore, while we may think of achievement of a clean countenance as the end sought, a little reflection will indicate that we really are expecting a complex of satisfactions: the comfort of cleanliness, the social approval generally accorded those who are clean, and perhaps, in addition, a softer beard for shaving, to achieve even greater social acceptance and comfort.

As complex as they can be shown to be, the use-systems involving such minor personal products are much simpler than most of those around which our continued existence is organized. One source of simplicity is the fact that the system normally involves only one person--ourselves. Most of our spending for personal consumption, and virtually all other kinds of spending, is to facilitate completion of consumption systems involving more than one person, each in one or more of the necessary roles in any system. Any consumption system is a mechanism for producing a set of intangible benefits. It is a production system, whether consumers be in the home, be merchants buying from a factory, or citizens voting for mayor. Designing products for any system requires an understanding of the well-structured roles people play in such systems, the differing motivations of the people in each role, and the need to adapt design to the systems in which it will be used. The key roles are:

Designer and gatekeeper: The individual or individuals who specify the specific inputs and the physical form the output will take. These are the people who make the final choice of brand and product type for each element in the system, constrained by the limits set by those putting up the funds and by the known tastes and desires of the end users who are their consumers. In the case of the evening dinner at home, for example, this is the role of the housewife; in the factory, the design engineer; in the symphony, the conductor; in the medical situation, the prescribing physician. It is the key positive role. The roles of all others are negative--they exercise a veto, or a modifying influence--but in this they can obviously be important.

Financier: The person or persons who determine the budget and disburse the funds to acquire the system inputs. Those in this role inevitably limit the inputs in terms of the amount allocated and may exercise a more direct veto on the specific input, but do not, in their finance role, prescribe the inputs themselves. In the traditional one-worker family, this has been, of course, the wage-earner family head. In the factory, the controller governs the expenditure level; for the Community Chest, the Board; in a governmental consumption unit, the Appropriations Committee.

Producers: The person or persons who carry out the production procedure itself. In the case of the family dinner, the housewife usually doubles in this role, doing the cooking and serving up the meal. In the factory, of course, this is the work of the production organization itself--foreman, workers, etc. The producers can and often do exercise a substantial role in modifying the choices made by gatekeeper, whether by outright rejection, by sabotage, or by mere protest and social disapproval.

Disposers of the output, or consumers: These receive and dispose of the product. In the case of the family meal, this is all members of the family, of course, including the housewife who planned and produced the meal, father who paid for it, and Suzy and Pete who did little more than gulp it down. For the community organization, this is the role of the case-worker's client; in governmental services, the ordinary citizen for much of the effort; in the medical situation, the patient. The factory, too, has its group of consumers--the customers who buy the output to devour in the production of what they expect to sell, either as another factory further along the line to final consumers, as merchants building an assortment to meet the needs of their customers, or as institutions (such as schools, hospitals, governments) utilizing the output to develop a set of directly intangible services. Even this is not a completely passive role. The final consumer can reject, and even mere protest brings social pressure to bear.

It should be noted that some or all of the roles can be combined in one person, or may be entirely separate. Thus the physician may be the designer when he prescribes the infant's diet, mother be the producer but not the gatekeeper-designer, father may supply the purchase funds, and baby play no other role than that of consumer. Quite obviously, too, the consumer may simply be another consumption-production system, building a different set of satisfactions for another set of customers down the line who may physically consume the product itself or simply incorporate it into their own products. If the latter, the producer may have to design

17

with more than one set of disposers in mind--for his immediate customer and his needs, for the customer of his customer and his needs, and for the customer of the latter and his needs. Even though the consumption system be another industrial system, however, the immediate customer may dissipate the output or so alter it that the immediate customer is the only one who must be satisfied.

From the viewpoint of those selling to him, the designer is a true gatekeeper. His specifications determine whose products may be incorporated in the product he is designing, and which ones barred. He thus plays a key role in any selling situation, and he must be identified and his tastes and desires planned for, even though he may never directly purchase any of the product or sign the purchase order itself. The tastes and prejudices of the architects must be kept in mind when designing building products although they may purchase nothing that goes into the structures they design. The perceptions of instructors in an academic area must be kept in mind when designing a textbook, although they will never buy a copy themselves.

But the designer-gatekeeper's choices are not completely free from the influence of the others in the consumption system. They must be within the cost restraints set up by the financier of the system and also within what he considers a proper kind of design. When the Production Department is separate from the designer, the department is operating a consumption subsystem of its own. The design is just one ingredient in the production system for the physical end product for which the Production Department is responsible, and it will desire to fit it into a system with which it is familiar. Finally, since the sole purpose of the whole system of systems is the satisfaction of final consumers, the desire-set they perceive as being granted by the design must fit their expectations as well as possible. Even the dog food must be attractive to dogs if dog owners are to buy it.

Any established role in any organization implies an established set of behavior patterns--a set of habits of thought and action which define the status of each individual member in the group. Anything which requires that this role be downgraded is likely to meet resistance. Housewives proud of their role as family chefs did not initially accept instant coffee, which allowed no leeway for individual skill differences in the making of their favorite beverage. Likewise, typesetters and printers have resisted the introduction of computer typesetting which renders typesetting little more difficult than mere typing.

On the other hand, any introduction which fits easily into established motor and perceptual habit patterns is speedily adopted. Black-and-white television changed no person's perception of his role and required no change in entertainment habits. It was an overnight success.

Since any consumption system is just such a series of linked perceptual and motor habit systems, the acceptability of any product offering is dependent on its fit into established systems, and the resistance met by any new product will be proportional to the extent that its use requires reorientation and learning of habitual patterns of thought, action, and role and value perceptions.

The problem of product design and promotion is further complicated by the fact that any physical product normally fits into several different use-systems, the system varying from consumption system to consumption system because of the differing tastes, habit patterns, and value systems of the people playing key roles in each. This is why almost no product ever captures the whole or even a major part of the "market" for a given functional product category, why markets are segmented, and why successful competition can never be a form of direct conflict.

MARKET SEGMENTATION AND PRODUCT COMPETITION

No product offering is likely to completely satisfy all of the desires in the set which lead to its acquisition by any one individual because of the inherent conflicts present in every desire-set. Likewise, no product ever satisfies equally all of those who are attracted by it because of the different values placed on each component attribute by those who are interested. For some people, the physical transportation attributes of a new automobile (comfort, speed, ease of handling, dependable service, roadability, economy) may be the most important and thus most valuable, and they will pay highest for the vehicle which comes closest to meeting these needs. Others may stress flamboyance, status symbolism, or stylistic characteristics and place little value on the strictly transportational virtues. A third group may look for precision workmanship, acceleration, and racing characteristics and be willing to sacrifice dependability and ruggedness, have little interest in changing styles, and care nothing for mere economy. Different buyers of the same car will vary in taste and levels of evaluation placed on each characteristic.

This combined variability in desire-sets and in the valuation placed on each element in the set means that each individual prospective buyer is in essence a different market segment and that the only way he can get the closest possible compromise to that set is by some form of custom production. For most products of mass consumption, such custom production would be so expensive that buyers must generally settle for a somewhat less valued compromise, at a much lower price. The gap between what buyers get and

19

the offering nearest to their desired ideal will vary greatly from one individual to the next, with some coming close to full realization and others obtaining so little satisfaction that they have a substantial incentive to search further for greater fulfillment.

Any offering thus serves an ill-defined market segment, or most likely, a group of related market segments for a category of physical offerings. Within each segment are groups of consumers with somewhat divergent desire-sets. Some are so close to getting what they desire they have no incentive to search for greater satisfaction and thus are unlikely to pay attention to any possible competitive offerings. Others will have different degrees of noticeable dissatisfaction of divergent kinds and thus a significant degree of incentive to search for greater satisfaction. These latter offer the opportunity for profit for the perceptive potential competitor.

Competitors succeed when they put together an offering coming closer to satisfying the needs of poorly served fringe segments of (usually) several sellers (often including themselves, when they are wise). They fail when they succeed in coming very close to duplicating the offering of some one competitor. The really "me-too" product is aimed for segments who are not searching for some alternative. In such a case, the target segment will not, psychologically, pay any attention to the offering because it promises no satisfaction to any active desire or drive and, at the same time, is new and untried and thus involves a risk, or extra price.

The secret of successful competition is thus always the offering of some quite substantial perceived differential value. The source of differential value may be in physical performance or external to it. When the difference is in physical performance, it may consist of adding product attributes for which some market segment will pay a substantial premium of some sort, or may go in the other direction and subtract attributes in which some major segments see less value than the cost is worth, and thus seek a low-end product. Non-physical differentiation may consist of service tie-ins, as with the repair and maintenance networks which every mass automobile manufacturer must provide, or the engineering advice which may accompany a major industrial purchase. It may consist of emotional expectations and associations derived from imaginative promotional communications and smart merchandising or created by the culture itself and simply exploited by the seller. It may simply be more convenient availability derived from skillful logistical planning or an excellent and extensive distribution network. For the latter reason, or for others, it may be a matter of timing on the market. The first design to be purchased and yielding an adequate measure of satisfaction thereby has an almost insurmountable lead over closely similar introductions which hit the market later. Even if attention to them is somehow forced, purchase of them involves a perceived risk that they will not be as good as the first and therefore will be worth less. Perceived risk is itself a basis of differentiation, whatever its source. For this reason, a believable guarantee can alone make the offering more valuable.

Whatever its nature, the difference must be quite substantial in added value to a group of market segments--mere difference is not enough. All differentiation is in value and in the relation of the latter to the buyer's cost--that, is in the relationship between perceived value and perceived sacrifice to obtain it. Price is the negative side of every offering.

PRICE: A RATIONING DEVICE WHICH CAUSES PRODUCT AVOIDANCE

Every economic good must have some kind of built-in price or the demand will always outrun adequate supply. Without price, consumers will waste the offering and suppliers will withdraw from the market. The laboratory pigeon who can get a grain of corn any time he pecks a specific button will eat until gorged and unable to peck anymore. His gluttony can be kept in check by a simple price mechanism, however--by so positioning the release button that the pigeon must step on a plate imparting an electric shock in order to reach it. The shock received causes the pigeon to avoid the corn until his hunger reaches a level (causes him to perceive a value in the corn) greater than the negative value to him of the shock.

Similarly, humans will overuse and waste any resource-- water, minerals, soils, and freeways, for example--whose use entails no perceived sacrifice. When charged a price of some kind, they will cut back on that use to the point where the sacrifice approximates the perceived value received. The sacrifice may be monetary, as in traditional economic theory, but usually involves perceived costs of other kinds as well, and may be limited to the latter. The motorist may have to balance the charge of a tollway (and the monotonous scenery) against the time cost of the parallel free road, and its greater interest and variety.

Among the more important non-monetary costs are design compromise, search effort, source loyalty, time, and learning requirements. For purposes of marketing decision, then, price must be defined very broadly, must include every avoidance characteristic built into the offering and into its terms of sale.

Every offering exacts a design-compromise cost. No automobile can be engineered to grant both extreme acceleration and fuel economy simultaneously, ease of parking and high cargo capacity at the same time. No dress designer has ever found a way to give high accent to a woman's physical femininity and grant complete ease and freedom of body movement. Furthermore, the desire-sets whose satisfactions we seek are generally quite complex and enforce a multitude of compromises. The necessity to make such multi-dimensioned compromises is what segments markets. Different buyers find divergent avoidance values in specific compromises.

Every purchase involves at least some slight degree of <u>effort to search</u> out a source, and the effort involved must always be commensurate with the perceived net value of the satisfaction desired. For this reason, so-called convenience goods are always those with relative low value and relatively little differentiation--soap, cigarettes, beer, low-end goods in general, but not quality wines, formal ball gowns, or handblown glassware. A major consideration in the design of the distributive network for any product must be the search-effort price the prospective customer would be willing to pay to obtain the offering as compared with some lesser substitute.

A great deal of industrial selling, in particular, involves a <u>source-loyalty price</u>, but many other kinds of selling exact such a price also, particularly professional services. The guarantee of a continued supply of many kinds of industrial raw materials is contingent on a commitment to continue buying from the same source, written into contracts. When the developer of hybrid chicks was requested by one large purchaser to supply partially reared stock (20-week-old pullets), he demanded and received a binding seven-year contract of supply. Many overworked physicians hesitate to take on new patients. Better department stores customarily promote special sales first to their charge-account customers before the general public is let in on the news, and tickets to the choice seats at the symphony in many cities are available only to subscribers to the series in former years. Buyer loyalty is often a complete monetary substitute for many raw materials in short supply. Rather than raise price, sellers will ration customers on the basis of purchases made in previous years when supplies were easier.

<u>Time and convenience</u> are sometimes the overriding price considerations in the consumption of many goods and services, with monetary costs relegated to the point of near insignificance. Despite the demonstrably lower cost of mass surface transit systems as compared with the private automobile, the regular bus and trolley systems have been driven almost to the wall in most American cities by the automobile because they were less convenient and took more time, being caught up in the same traffic jams. Subway systems and commuter railroads, on the other hand, have been able to make a comeback because their privileged rights of way permitted faster travel than the jam-packed expressways, and more conveni-

ence for some. The profits of many a food processor have been boosted by the growth in "convenience foods" which take less of the working housewife's time, even though often of lower flavor quality. The growth of complete self-service in the food markets unquestionably resulted from the delays occasioned by reliance on personal service at the meat counter. Customers were ready to sacrifice some of the custom-fitting of meat cuts to be able to get in and out of the store quicker.

Finally, the initial usage of any really new product exacts some learning-price: some need to acquire a new set of motor habits as well as new perceptions of value and of sources of satisfaction. As will be shown later, the acceptance of new products tends to be in direct proportion to the learning-price exacted by their adoption. The breadth of many markets is limited by the need for learning, and many markets have been broadened by the introduction of methods of reducing the learning. There is little question that the growth in the use of automatic transmissions in automobiles was directly related to the growth of the family chauffeur role among women, large numbers of whom abhor any kind of mechanical learning. Similarly, IBM's dominance in the computer industry was due largely to their aggressive development of program libraries and program service, minimizing the need for trained programmers.

Price reactions, product perceptions, and all the various phenomena of product life cycles are the result of buyer psychology. We need to understand a few key basics of this psychological structure to plan sound competitive strategy.

SUMMARY

1. All ideas and offerings which gain acceptance by society pass through some kind of life cycle roughly analogous to the biological cycle of growth and decay.

2. The theoretical basic life cycle can be conceptualized as passing through 8 possible life stages: conception, product development, market introduction and market development, rapid growth, maturization and competitive turbulence, mature stability and saturation, decline, and death and replacement.

3. Actual life cycles take on many and diverse forms, however. Not all pass automatically through all eight stages, and some exhibit a pyramided series of growth periods. To understand these diversities, we need to comprehend the psychological meaning of product, from the user's point of view.

4. The product is every aspect of the firm's offering which gives it value in the customer's eyes. The physical entity which is the subject of the transaction is only part of that value, and then only

23

to the extent that the performance of that entity is perceived as rendering some of the satisfactions in the sought-for-desire-set. Indeed, the same physical product may be a number of market products, depending on the use-system for which it is purchased.

5. The end result for which any product is purchased is a set of internal satisfactions rendered by an habitual use-system in which the offering purchased is perceived as playing a key role. Usually, this use-system involves other products and an established set of learned procedures.

6. For most market offerings, the use-system involves more than one person, each playing one or more well-defined roles. The roles played are those of system designer and gatekeeper, of financier, production, and disposers or consumers. The designer role is a key positive one, determining the components which will be purchased and their value. All of the other roles are negative, or veto in nature, limiting the choices open to the designer, but not specifying them as a rule. The consumer of the end product of any use-system generally utilizes it as an input into another use-system, except the very ultimate of personal products. Thus the entire economic system is an interlocking set of use-systems.

7. The desire-set which each product is intended to satisfy differs between individuals, and the value and importance placed on each satisfaction obtained also differs in level and relative importance. Therefore no product satisfies everyone in the market for that particular category of item, and many who do purchase are relatively unsatisfied, some well-satisfied. The less well-satisfied can be attracted by competitors who design an offering coming closer to the needs of those on the fringes of a number of market segments. Those at the core of the segment are too well satisfied to pay attention to competing offerings closely similar to those in use, and such offerings cannot hope to succeed. Effective competition must be differentiated in some manner.

8. Competitive differentiation of the offering may be in terms of physical performance, either through added attributes or through omission of some, or may be external to the physical entity. Nonphysical differentiation may be in the form of external service components in the offering, of emotional associations developed by the buyer or by society at large, of better distribution or logistics, or of lessened perceived risk in purchase. All differentiation is some form of relative value for some set of market segments.

9. Price is the negative side of that value. It is the sacrifice of any kind which is exacted in order to acquire the desired satisfactions. The monetary price of traditional economics is only one aspect of this sacrifice, and often not the determining one. All offerings exact a design-compromise cost--the need to trade off some desired satisfactions in order to gain a greater measure of others.

24

Search effort, source loyalty, and time are other important prices. Some kind of learning requirement is always involved in the initial use of any product and thus is a major factor in acceptance.

2

THE MARKET AND ITS PSYCHOLOGICAL STRUCTURE: THE CONSTANTS AND THE UNIVERSALITIES OF BUYER REACTION

Product life cycles exist because the people who constitute a market are not puppets set to dance at the whim of the seller. They are, instead, a rather refractory lot who shape the market far more than they are shaped by it. The diversities of their psychological makeup determines to whom a specific offering can appeal, what in that offering potentially appeals to them, and when and how individuals and the different market segments accept an offering. It is this market segmentation which permits not only new entrants, but all competitors of any sort, to gain some degree of success. Marketing segments themselves exist because buyers differ widely in their congenital makeup and personality, in their conditions of life and developmental background, and in the degree of satiation of their motivating desires.

On the other hand, the existence of any kind of predictable demand is due to certain constants in the psychological reaction of human beings. Rational plans for fulfilling that demand can work out because of certain universalities in the way buyers' needs express themselves in some kind of market demand.

Marketing strategy plans therefore need to be based on an understanding of certain universalities of psychological response and also the universal existence of diverse responses due to diversities of personality, background, and condition.

Although we tend to speak of markets as though they were some sort of tangible entities quite separate from the individuals who make them up, markets are not much more than the sum of these people. Their reactions to the would-be sellers' attempts to get them to buy are readily understood in terms of some very simple but quite important psychological concepts.

To the psychologist, people in these markets can quite definitely not (as sometimes viewed) be manipulated as desired. They are selection-making entities who respond only to those offerings

FIGURE 2-1. How Customers Respond to Stimuli (Offerings Proferred or Advertised by Sellers)

NOT as Puppets To Be Manipulated at Will

BUT

As Individuals Whose Inner Drives Select Out
Those Stimuli Promising Desired Satisfactions

which promise satisfactions they desire. To plan for success does not require a graduate course in psychology. It does require a thorough understanding and deep appreciation for a few basic fundamentals of psychological and social-psychological knowledge, knowledge of both the constants and universalities of buyer reaction and the diversities of final response between buyers.

THE UNIVERSALITIES OF PERSONAL (AND BUYER) BEHAVIOR

The Stimulus - Response Reaction

Let us look at the purchase situation as a psychologist would interpret it. In this situation, a would-be-seller--a person or a firm--presents a stimulus to a person he considers a potential buyer in order to elicit a response from that buyer. In marketing terms, a potential seller makes an offering hoping to get some person or group of persons to purchase that offering (or more likely to start a series of purchases of such offerings). In other words, when, we use the word "trade" to designate what happens, we are being literally correct. The transaction is a two-way process requiring the seller to modify his own behavior if he is to get a desired response from the buyer. Even so, he must understand that the process is far from either simple or foreordained.

As psychologists long ago learned, the stimulus does not itself necessarily determine the reaction. In fact, a stimulus is merely a promise or a cue. In mechanical terms, it is a trigger which activates certain mechanisms (in psychological terms, certain drives or tensions) within the possible buyer. These mechanisms are what determine the response. The response may be one of four separate types:

1. Most of the time, there is no response at all. No corresponding drive exists. The mechanism is not cocked or the chamber loaded, and so the trigger releases nothing.
2. There may be no immediate response but a delayed response later, as a result of this and further additional stimuli later on.
3. There may be a positive response of the nature sought by the would-be-seller--the customer may make a purchase.
4. There may be a negative response. The very offering itself may cause him to draw back and to seek satisfaction in some other way.

To put it in elementary psychological textbook language, the process cannot be diagrammed as S→R, (as stimulus elicits response). It must be diagrammed as S→O→R, with O standing for the operator, (that is the person toward whom the stimulus is being directed) who then determines the nature of the response which will

28

be elicited. The product is merely a cue or trigger. By itself it does not set off the hammer. It simply releases whatever impulse, whatever drive, is there.

The differences in personal impulses arise from the fact that action can only come as a result of some inner drive or motivation. These drives are what determine whether the response is that of complete inattention, a delayed response, or positive or negative reaction. If no related drive for satisfaction exists, there will be no reaction of any sort, since the buyer must conserve his energy and pay attention only to those cues around him which promise satisfaction of some of his desires. He is highly selective in his choice of cues for attention.

Selective Attention

The principle of selective attention applies to all sentient beings, including the very lowest in the biological scale. A frog, for example, can discern only two aspects of any flying insect: the degree of convexity and its velocity. The reason for this is very simple. He makes his way through life reaching out his long tongue to snatch flying insects from the air and would miss his meal if he spent time discriminating as to color, texture, and many of the other elements which may appeal to a biologist. To a dog, the world is made up of blacks and whites and he does not discriminate between reds and greens. But a dog can distinguish sounds not discernible by the human ear, can discover scents which the human nose completely ignores. These are the stimuli which enabled him, first as a wild animal and then as a companion of man, to pursue his hunting activities. And the consciousness of a middle class consumer, going through his day, will register no more than one or two ads of the several hundred which are immediately posed to his ears and eyes in the course of a 24-hour period, because only those advertisements appeal to drives which currently direct his attention.

Without this ability to select for attention those things which are of immediate importance to the receiver (and only those) we would have our attention too utterly fragmented to be able to act. We all live in a world of tremendous confusion, since around us all the time are a true infinity of possible stimuli to eye, ear, nose and feeling, far beyond our attempt to even number them. The housewife looking over the food store ads in the inch-thick Thursday newspaper skips over the ads for International Markets because none of these stores are near her. In the ads for Oscar's, where she can and does shop, she notes only the rump roasts and strawberry specials that fit into her Sunday dinner plans. The artichokes may be an excellent buy, but her family does not like them so she does not even see the artichoke listing.

Because of this principle of selective attention, the sellers' first problem is to attract the customer's attention with an offering which the customer feels is important to his own ends, then convey the nature of that offering in language that appeals to the drives of the people in the particular market segment he hopes to reach. Even so, the problem still remains as to how the customer will perceive both the product and the message concerning it. The message never is received in all of its intended details by the prospect. The customer interprets what he hears, omits many details, amplifying and sharpening what remains so that it assumes greater importance to him, with more motive force. His perception of what he does react to is just as selective as the attention itself.

Selective Perception

Selective perception is the tendency for the customer to interpret messages and offerings in terms of his own interests, drives, and experiences. "Perception" is different from seeing. Perception is the meaning the viewer sees or senses in what is presented to his eyes or other senses.

The old parlor game "gossip" makes use of this principle for entertainment purposes. A message is whispered to the first person, who in turn whispers it to a neighbor as he perceives he heard it, and so on through the group. When the last person makes known the story as he received it, it seldom even resembles the original. It has been selectively perceived by each person according to the points in it that appealed to his interest, interpreted in terms of those interests, then repeated, in the form in which he has assimilated it, to the next person whose own interpretation differs because he perceives different points as being important, and so on.

Much the same thing happens in the marketplace. One of the main problems of new product introduction has always been the question of how the customer will perceive the product. Sometimes, accidentally or by design, this perception can and will be shaped by the advertising to either the advantage or disadvantage of the seller. At other times the product itself may prove, as in fact nearly all products do tend to prove, to have characteristics appealing to drives of which the seller was unaware.

Thus a book written for a course in managerial economics may find its market instead as a micro supplement in a course of macro-micro economics--in this case a quite lucrative mistake on the part of the author. Conversely, a toothpaste which is touted as a major advance in effective whitening of teeth may be perceived by customers as so strongly useful in that direction that it is used only infrequently, when they begin to feel that their teeth are getting too dark with their normal toothpaste. After they feel their teeth are improved, they go back to their regular brand. In this case, of course, the seller inherits a much more specialized market than he originally intended.

That information which the consumer does admit to his senses is given a specific interpretation in the context of his own experience or observation, and he adds to this interpretation associations he has built out of past experience. Those items he chooses to perceive are those which are important to his most salient inner needs at that moment in time. He interprets them in relation to the social role he is playing at the moment, according to expectations built up out of past experience which the stimuli brought to his mind. These expectations lead him to add meanings, feelings and impressions to the original cue stimulus in order to organize the whole in some meaningful relationship to his needs at the time. The associations themselves may be even stronger than the objective realities.

One case in point is that of the sales manager who had been using chemical duplicates of expensive perfumes as advertising specialties for his line of industrial deodorants. These duplicates were blended from the same natural essences used to make well-known brands and to the same formulas. Deciding to have some fun with his wife, the sales manager took home an empty bottle of his copy and a full one. In his wife's absence, he switched contents between her perfume bottle and his copy. When she returned he asked her, with feigned innocence, "Hazel, how much difference is there between our copy and your perfume?" She took a quick sniff of both and said "a lot." "Which one smells better?" he asked. "Why the one in my bottle, of course," she said, pointing to the one which now held his copy--an item identical with her perfume in everything except container and manufacturer. This experience was, of course, not an unusual one. Beer manufacturers have long known that, when given a truly blind test between their own brand and other brands on the market, drinkers who favor the maker's brand often can consistently point out real differences and attributes they consider important to the taste. But the result can often be that the beer that they claimed tastes best when they see it with a label on comes out inferior in the blind test. The associations themselves turn out to be stronger than the initial physical stimulus.

The extent to which past experience and associations color our perceptions of products and the messages concerning them are old stories in terms of advertising and product management. Campbell's Soup Company tends to be the beneficiary of everybody else's soup advertising because of their own identification with the term soup itself. Some years ago, the Wm. Wrigley Company discovered that an intensive spot radio campaign put on by one of their competitors, in an area in which Wrigley had run no radio advertisement for a considerable period, was identified by one-fourth of the listeners as Wrigley ads.

This tendency of associating past experience with the product also has its negative aspects. A product which has been a lemon in the recent experience of many buyers almost never is able to recoup a previous good reputation. Thus, when Chrysler sought to continue the Maxwell nameplate when it started in business with a new, and for its time well designed automobile, in 1924, the recent reputation of Maxwell as a lemon thwarted success. Chrysler was forced to drop the effort and reintroduce the product a couple of years later under the Chrysler label, and still later as the Plymouth, before they could succeed.

Allied with this tendency to associate products with past experience is a tendency to associate products and messages with the context in which they are produced or distributed. Phillip Morris Company was able to successfully build a major brand position for the Marlboro cigarette by associating the cigarette in ads with he-man and western themes without the words in any way even implying that Marlboro contributed to virility. Similarly, products distributed through prestige channels and outlets, initially at least, tend to gain a prestige image. And a premium product cannot be sold in an outlet associated with low-end products. For a time, at least, "plastic" became a cue that the product was "cheap" and not well-made. So plastic boats were labelled by their reinforcement--fiber glass--which had the prestige their main plastic material did not convey.

Thus it is that associations and experience can often affect the reception and sales of a product more strongly than anything done directly by current advertising or in terms of current product itself. Purchase behavior is learned behavior, and the product as seen by the customers is a cue that he will gain certain satisfactions, the cue itself having different meanings for different individuals because of their different learning experiences and differing drives at the moment.

Some of these experiences will be positive and will move some potential customers to acquire the product. Others will be negative and tend to cause them to avoid it. As initially noted, response to any stimulus can be negative or positive as well as indifferent or delayed. And it is the nature of the individual's own internal psychological makeup, plus congenital and learned attitudes, that determines which will be the case. Thus both in politics and in the market the very word "new" itself may be a triggering cue for some people to consider what is offered. To others, it may be a cue to look elsewhere for their satisfaction. Detroit's gaudiest and heaviest monsters may be the acme of everything some buyers seek,

while to those who have learned to appreciate the sports car and
the European models, they are an instant stimulus to a violent distaste. The dress that appeals to one woman as pretty and glamorous
may appeal to another of a different social class as something she
wouldn't be "caught dead in". To one buyer the offering is what the
psychologist would designate as an approach stimulus. To his
brother in the market it may be avoidance stimulus.

Approach-Avoidance Reaction

Approach and avoidance reactions, however opposite they
seem, come combined. No product is a single stimulus, but normally a bundle of cues of various kinds, some of which cause the
buyer to wish to acquire it, others which lead him to draw back.
If nothing else, the very fact of some kind of price itself will cause
an avoidance stimulus of some degree.

Psychologists are quite familiar with this mixed approach-
avoidance behavior in their laboratories. They can, for example,
train a pigeon to peck at a button by rewarding him with a grain of
corn when he does so. This sets up an approach reaction to the
button, as a cue stimulus that the pigeon will be rewarded by being
fed. They can then modify the pigeon's desire by causing the bird
to experience a light electrical shock when it steps on a plate necessary to approach the button. Under this situation, the pigeon will
initially avoid pecking the button until hunger reaches a certain
point. At this point, the pigeon's drive to satisfy hunger will overcome his motivation to avoid the shock, and he will step on the plate
and peck the button to get his corn.

In the marketplace, the seller is always presenting the customer with one or more such mixed approach-avoidance sets of
stimuli. In order to survive, the seller must demand some kind of
price from the customer, and this will not necessarily be money
alone. This price will cause customers to hesitate in varying degrees, depending on each one's level of motivation and his interest
in the satisfaction he hopes to achieve.

Both the approach and avoidance behavior, of course, are
learned in humans as well as among pigeons. And both result in
habitual responses, because any being must depend on reflex action
for most of his satisfactions.

REFLEXES, HABITS, AND THE LEARNING PROCESS

A response to a stimulus can be automatic or reflex, or it
can be, among human beings, a considered response. Most of our

33

responses to most stimuli are reflex responses. That is, we react automatically, whether due to an inborn reflex or to a conditioned reflex (that is, to a habit). We can cope with living at all only by reducing the number of considered (thoughtful) responses to the very minimum of exceptionally important unique decisions. Taking thought before acting requires scarce time and effort. We must and do, therefore, short-circuit time-consuming thought by reducing repetitive responses to the reflex (habitual) level.

Indeed, only by reducing responses to the habitual level can we become efficient in carrying them out. The initial attempt to carry out any procedure is likely to be awkward and inefficient. Only by repeated practice can we learn to do a good job--only when we have thoroughly conditioned our reflexes to respond automatically. Thus, we conduct all of our existence, including all of our use of purchases and other outside resources to satisfy our drives, largely on the basis of habitual routines.

Establishing these routines itself exacts a price--the price of the repeated practice we call learning. Changing the routine in any major way exacts a double price, the price of unlearning one procedure and then learning a new one. For this reason, introductions which promise greater satisfaction only on condition of such a relearning process have a strongly built-in avoidance potential.

Any product use-system is obviously such a structured habit system--a complex structure of conditioned reflexes. And such use-systems can include mental and perceptual processes as well as physical-motor routines. Moreover, since use-systems can involve more than one person, as in organizational procedures, we can legitimately speak of organizational habit structures in which each participant has a set of habits corresponding to his role.

Since all products involve use-systems and all use-systems are acquired at some considerable time and effort, it should be clear that the extent of use-system change required can affect the speed of product acceptance. This will be discussed at length later.

Habits, Risks, and Search Effort

Habits and related use-systems develop because they have been found to result in the satisfaction of some inner need, of some drive. Once established, the choices faced are thus narrowed. Since any alternative use-system is not yet proved, such an alternative will be discounted in value because it represents a risk that it will not satisfy. Both sides of any market transaction are thus looking forward to repeat performance. The seller hopes that a given offering will continue attractive for a long series of purchases and thus that his sales use-system will bring in the desired returns

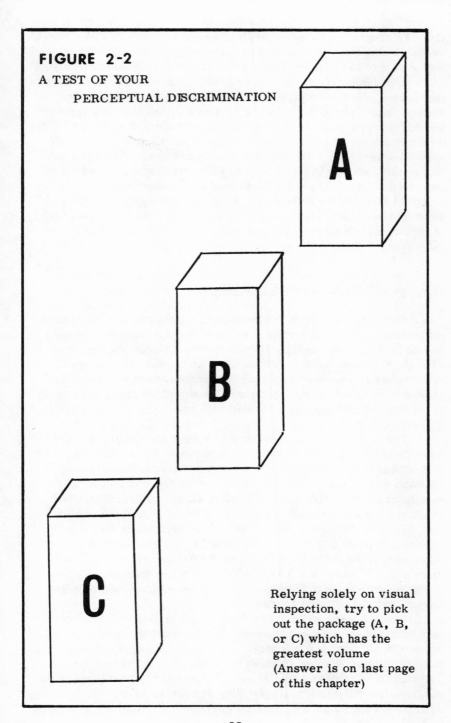

FIGURE 2-2

A TEST OF YOUR
    PERCEPTUAL DISCRIMINATION

A

B

C

Relying solely on visual
inspection, try to pick
out the package (A, B,
or C) which has the
greatest volume
(Answer is on last page
of this chapter)

(his own sought-for satisfactions). The buyer hopes to find a dependable source for a key item in some use-system and thus avoid further search and experimentation. He seeks to reduce the buying to a satisfying habit, rather than go through a series of considered purchases. He will interrupt this habit only when he perceives some substantially discriminable shortfall in satisfaction, a shortfall which some new offering promises to reduce or eliminate. That difference must be <u>noticeable</u>, in psychological terms. Only substantial differences meet the test of noticeability. Products that, technically, appear to experts to be different may be perceived by the average buyer as identical because of the phenomenon of discriminal threshholds and the <u>just noticeable difference</u> (j. n. d.) phenomenon. This j. n. d. phenomenon has to be an important part of the product design and pricing planning in order for either to be effective.

Discriminal Threshholds and the j. n. d.

More stimulus does not necessarily mean more response. In marketing terms, a lowering of price may not stimulate demand nor an increase necessarily curtail it unless either the lowering or rise is very substantial. Neither does an improvement in quality or difference in product necessarily mean different demand. The reason is the phenomenon known as discriminal threshholds, typical of all sentient beings: the phenomenon known as a <u>just noticeable difference</u> (j. n. d.).

The j. n. d. can be illustrated by a very simple experiment. Take two identical reams of paper (letter-size bond with 500 sheets to a package, for example). Subtract one sheet from one of the bundles and give them to someone and ask him which is heavier. No respondent will be able to tell the difference. Subtract a second sheet and the same result will be obtained. Subtract ten sheets, and no normal human being will be able to distinguish which is lighter. In point of fact, something close to fifty sheets will probably have to be subtracted from one bundle before someone can discriminate either that it is lighter or that the stack is shorter, in the absence of an objective measurement instrument which goes beyond that of the mere senses.

Far too many sellers of packaged goods have discovered this lack of finely-sensed size discrimination, to the detriment of the consumer and even the industry. Take a 48-ounce can of fruit juice and shrink it in all three dimensions to hold only 46 ounces. The customer, unless he refers to the fine print on the label, will not know the difference. (In the end, of course, everybody will be selling 46-ounce cans and the customer will be paying for more

36

metal and less contents without any competitor having an advantage in cost. But the first seller to do so may gain an additional share of market because of what seems to be a lowering in price.)

The j.n.d. involves every aspect of human perception: sight, sound, feeling, and even calculation. A price difference of one cent is no difference on a $5.00 item anymore than one sheet in a ream is immediately perceived as a difference in package size. It is true that the consumer will see that one that is 499 and the other is 500. But even at the industrial level of purchasing, he does not consider the difference significant.

Merchants long ago learned this without reference to any psychological textbook. They discovered that any cut in prices must be deep to stimulate immediate demand. No merchant ever holds a sale advertising cut prices, "Price special! Four percent less than normal!" If he wants to move the goods he goes well beyond what he long ago discovered by experience to be a substantial difference. He always quotes 20%, 25%, 30%, or 50% below in order to effect a clearance sale.

In the field of competitive product strategy this means that in order to get customers to try a new and improved product, perceived improvement in performance must be quite substantial--one well beyond the level of a j.n.d.

One thing generally accepted about the size of the j.n.d. is that it is relative to the size of the stimulus itself. That is, the j.n.d. is a percentage phenomenon. Whether or not it is exactly proportional may be open to doubt, but it is certainly approximately so. But what percentage? This will vary with the individual and the subject involved. It has been said that the expert wine taster, with an educated palate, is able to distinguish not only the year, the vintage, and the type, but even the vineyard from which the grapes were taken. The average wine imbiber, however, probably can tell little beyond the difference between a quality first crushing and a third-run "wine-o" drink. An unpublished study of the ability to discriminate variations in a grapefruit-orange juice blend showed that, with a 50-50 norm, there had to be more than 60 percent or less than 40 percent grapefruit juice in the blend before consumers could sense a difference.

Since the j.n.d. is a result in part of education and interest, we might expect to find major differences in taste between classes in the population, and this is indeed so. In general, those of the better educated classes tend to settle for much less contrasty types of textures and styles, for example. A study made by one of the major automobile companies, of possible vinyl upholstery materials, found that the upper classes tend to pick finer grain textures like pig-skin, as opposed to the coarser grain textures such as scotch grain favored by the lower economic classes. The middle and upper

class women tend to prefer the simpler less ornamented fashions
in dress and the lower classes like the ones much more highly ornamented and contrasty. The author's own observations of two towns,
one an upper working class town and the other a middle class area,
noted that the house painting patterns went in for heavy contrast in
the working class town as opposed to two-tone muted combinations
in the middle class area.

Thus the j.n.d. has important implications in terms of the
level of effort which must be put forward to obtain a given result.
The j.n.d. also has design implications in terms of the target market at which the product is aimed.

There is, moreover, another aspect of "more does not get
more response" that needs to be understood much better than it is
among both marketers and economists. This is the phenomenon of
satiation or satisficing.

Satisficing and the Hierarchy of Needs

Maximization is a figment of the psychologically illiterate
economist's imagination. No human being, and indeed no other
animal, tends to keep seeking more and more of any one stimulus
or cue to satisfaction. When his hunger is appeased he quits eating.
Even if a glutton, he comes to some point at which he must quit.
In other words, the concept of maximization of profit, or any other
satisfaction, does not accord with psychological knowledge or, indeed, with market experience.

The reason is simply that people have a myriad number of
divergent needs or desires at any one moment. For some of these
needs, a given person, at a given moment, has a greater degree of
drive than for others. In effect, the buyer's needs are arranged in
some kind of hierarchy, with the most salient need of the moment
at the top. But the very act of meeting this most important need
lowers its standing in the hierarchy. When the goal to which the
drive is directed is attained, the human being (or any other animal)
then begans to seek a relief of some other new, more salient drive.
Once the customer has found a product that does a reasonable job
of fulfilling a given satisfaction which he seeks (an automobile for
example, that meets the speed and acceleration characteristics
sought in his everyday driving), he does not respond to a stimulus
giving more in the same direction. His resources, time, and energy
are limited, and his needs are multitude. He must turn his attention
to devoting these resources to fulfilling these other now more pressing needs.

Thus, when a customer finds a product and a brand which does
meet his needs, his tendency is to return to this same source by

38

habit to fill these needs. He gives no attention to messages about offerings which might give him some slight advantage or even a truly substantial difference. He will institute a search for something different only when he begins to feel a substantial lack in whatever source he is choosing for his satisfaction and then discovers something else that gives him a substantial difference--a j. n. d. in that direction.

For this reason, the first brand or product that comes to a buyer's attention and passes trial satisfactorily, gets his business. The second brand, even though it may be somewhat better from his point of view, will not even attract his attention and thus not even get a chance at trial. Many manufacturers have learned the penalty of being "beat to the market". Publishers and authors are well aware of this through sad experience of getting on the market a few months after another book meeting a similar need has already come out and secured relative degree of acceptance.

Some of the automobile industry's most publicized failures are also due to this phenomenon of satiation. The greatest mistake of the Edsel was too great a similarity to the Buick, Olds, and Pontiac whose market Ford was trying to capture. Most Buick, Olds, and Pontiac purchasers already had a product they were satisfied with. They were not interested in looking at another similar product. What the Ford Motor Company needed to do, as it had succeeded in accomplishing with the Thunderbird, was to find a different kind of market among those purchasing other makes of cars--one whose owners were not fully satisfied with any offerings then on the market.

Only through exploiting the diversities of taste and needs on the market can a new competitor hope to capture a substantial share of that market. The sources of these diversities are many, and they account for the fact that half a dozen department stores on State Street in Chicago, or on Market Street in Philadelphia, can all succeed and make money and that even each of the Big Four in automobiles must have a wide variety of offerings to get any major share of market.

SOURCES OF DIVERSITY OF TASTE AND DEMAND

No greater fallacy exists, than to talk of the market. In point of fact, there are probably no two individuals whose needs, values, and desires are the same. There are too many sources of individual diversities operating in too many different ways. Some of these diversities are born with the individual. There are congenital differences in both level of ability and in type of ability, even within a given family. Psychological research has established that many

39

of these personality differences are stable throughout life without regard to environment.

Thus, Thomas, et al. (1970), in a long continuing study of 130 individuals, found that the patterns with respect to attitude toward new experiences are stable during the first fourteen years of life in which they had so far been able to follow their individuals. Some are immediately receptive to new foods, new persons, new experience. Some reject all new experiences up to the limit of what it is possible for them to do and still survive. Others in-between have varying degrees of initial rejection and then acceptance.

Nor is the pattern with respect to new experiences the only differences between individuals. There are differences between levels of ability and between types of ability. Some members of the same family are better oriented mechanically and visually, and others seem to be completely impervious to mechanical relationships. Some people are born tone-deaf, others with such a high sensitivity to musical values that they have what is known as "perfect pitch". In addition to those differences with which we are born, we are all subject to multitudes of learning experiences which result in divergent levels and types of learned values and expectations. Moreover, innate approaches to learning seem to differ, so that some people with the same experience can come out with different levels and kinds of learning.

We are all subject in addition to social influences around us, to group pressure with set values to which we adhere: forces of family, social clique, and social class. Finally there are different degrees of attention to different kinds of products and different kinds of messages about these products due to different levels of satiation.

The result is that in a market of 200 million-odd possible buyers there are probably 200 million possible discernible segments. However, mass production and sale are possible only because there can be some kind of clustering of people around a given set of satisfactions offered by sellers' designs. It is this clustering that becomes market segmentation. But segmentation is not a pigeon hole sort of clustering. Segments are created by the product offering itself--by the offering and the terms and nature and context in which the offering is made--all in relation to alternatives perceived by the buyer.

DESIRE SETS AND THE IMPLICATION OF PSYCHOLOGICAL
KNOWLEDGE FOR THE COMPETITION

As noted before, individuals are not driven by single desires at one moment, but by whole series of these at one time. These desires are so many that in order to economize, in the effort to

40

satisfy as many as possible, the individual seeks to meet a whole series of desires he perceives as related in a single purchase or acquisition of any kind. When ordering a steak, he seeks not only to appease his hunger but to acquire certain aesthetic qualities of taste, for example, and even perhaps of surroundings and the context of the total meal. When buying an automobile, he seeks not transportation alone, but comfort, cargo capacity, such competitive driving aspects as acceleration and speed, roadability characteristics such as cornering and straightness of braking effort, fuel economy, parkability, and perhaps prestige or its very opposite, lack of showiness.

Many characteristics the buyer seeks may be in direct opposition to others. In fact the number of characteristics he seeks almost always includes many that are mutually incompatible, if sought to their fullest extent in a single offering. A car cannot have high acceleration characteristics and fuel economy, large cargo capacity, and ease of parking in small spaces, for example. A woman's dress cannot be both extremely comfortable and extremely form revealing at one and the same time. A steak cannot be tender and tasty and at the same time cost less than a hamburger.

The buyer must make compromises, and it is the design compromise package which defines the market segment. Any single design will come close to satisfying only a small share of the total possible buyers. Others who are much less satisfied may nevertheless buy because no other compromise comes as close to the one offered in meeting their needs.

At the periphery of every market segment will be groups who are largely indifferent as to the choice between two or more competing but differentiated designs. These peripheral segments are the only accessible targets of competitive strategy of any kind.

A new competitor can get a niche in the market only by taking people from the fringes of several different competing products. The initial success of the Chevrolet Corvair, for example, was due to the fact that it did not take many previous Chevrolet customers but gathered its customers from many segments of the market, and thus was mostly a plus for General Motors sales volume. The Ford Falcon, on the other hand, pretty much appealed to many of the same people who had been buying Fords, so that the Ford Motor Company felt that Falcon introduction, although it got the largest single portion of the domestic "compact" market in the United States in 1960, was a partial failure. On the other hand the Mustang, its later introduction, was an outstanding success primarily because it attracted people from the various foreign car market segments, from Chevrolet, from Plymouth, and from many other sources which Ford was unable to trace, and this was a plus for the Ford Motor Company.

41

Those attracted were not from the central core of any of these markets. Such core customers are largely invulnerable to competition except when no design yet on the market really comes very close to what anyone desires, and there is a high level of dissatisfaction with all designs among nearly everyone on the market. Otherwise, the principle of selective attention means that new offerings will get no significant attention from core segments and thus cannot hope to gain sales among them by any form of advertising or other promotional gimmickry.

Another corollary of the principle of selective attention is that the true "me too" offering is certain to fail. Unless the new introduction has some difference of physical construction, terms, or manner of sale, perceivable as substantially higher than a just noticeable difference from the products currently available to the market, it will fail to attract any attention or any trials from that market.

Note that the difference must be one perceivable by the customer, not one that is technically obvious to engineers and designers. This does not mean that a product that is identical in most or all of its characteristics cannot succeed under some circumstances. A company whose line needs an item in order to be seen by customers as a more complete one can introduce a product that is no better than those on the market simply because its customers prefer to satisfy more of their needs at one time. This added item thus makes their total line (which is the product the customer really is seeking) more attractive even though that particular element is no different from similar items offered by competitors.

THE PSYCHOLOGICAL REALITY OF SUCCESSFUL COMPETITION

In sum, psychology tells us that competition cannot be anything but differentiated if it is to succeed. And it succeeds by an appeal not to an entire hypothetical market but to particular segments of these markets and by offerings values that those particular segments view as substantially greater than satisfactions currently available to them. The offering we make as an intended stimulus must be one which will be selected for attention because it is perceived as meeting an important unfilled drive for satisfaction. The advantage over competing values must be perceived as greater, by these segments, than their j. n. d. The real prospective buyer is seeking to fulfill some habitual use-system, or must learn to develop a new set of conditioned reflexes (habitual system) to gain the desired satisfactions. Once the buyer finds an offering that comes closest to meeting all of the needs he seeks to fulfill at one moment, satiation sets in. His attention is withdrawn as he seeks to fulfill

42

FIGURE 2-3. Theoretical and Actual Learning and Experience
Curves

A. Theoretical Curve
on a Standard
Double-Logarithmic Scale

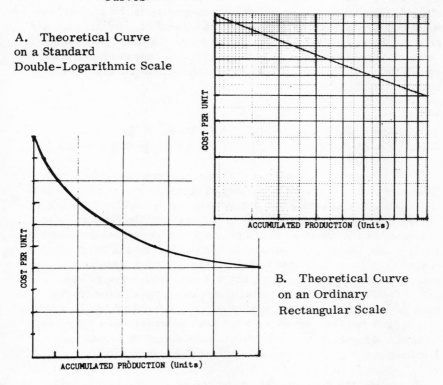

B. Theoretical Curve
on an Ordinary
Rectangular Scale

C. Actual Performance Learning Curve of a Fluid Catalytic
Petroleum Cracking Unit

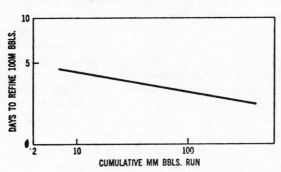

Source: Winifred B. Hirschmann, "Profit From the Learning Curve,"
Harvard Business Review, Vol. 42, No. 1 (January-February, 1964),
p. 130.

43

the next item in his hierarchy of demands.

Different buyers will have different hierarchies of demand due to innate differences, learned differences, and differences of condition. Thus there will be clusters or segments in the market, defined by those offerings which seem the closest compromise to each group's desires, with some buyers so poorly satisfied with any offering available that they will give attention to new offerings promising them a substantially greater (more than a j. n. d.) level of satisfaction.

LEARNING CURVES, EXPERIENCE CURVES, AND THEIR RELATIONSHIP TO HABITS AND COMPETITIVE STRATEGY

The learning curve and its broader application, the experience curve, are pragmatic concepts of human behavior of critical importance to competitive strategy. The concept of the learning curve grew out of practical observation, but the phenomenon is so universal that it has to be based on fundamental psychology. Indeed, its probable basis is not hard to find in the learning of habit patterns. The implications of that psychology for maintaining the gains the experience curve can bring are worth close consideration.

The concept of the learning curve dates back to the frantic pace of aircraft design and production during World War II. It was discovered that the cost of a given model decreased at a relatively constant percentage over the life of that model. Moreover, the learning curve rate of improvement--the percentage decrease in cost--was substantial. To cite figures from a later civilian aircraft model: the first Boeing 707 off the production line is said to have cost about $12 million. But on the basis of orders for several hundred, the planes were priced at $5 million each, in the knowledge that the learning experience curve would bring costs down to a level permitting a profit, at this price. As Figure 2-3A indicates, the learning curve tends to be a straight line when plotted on a double logarithmic scale for costs and for accumulated production units, since the decline in cost is a constant rate (that is, a constant percentage) for each percentage increase in experience.

But as Figure 2-3B indicates, it is a typical self-limiting logarithmic curve when plotted in ordinary absolute terms, because a constant decrease in percentage means an ever smaller decrease in absolute terms. Originally, it seemed that the rate of process improvement was closely associated with the degree of human activity involved in the process itself. But then some studies began to show a similar process and cost improvement trend in operations with a very low human labor input such as in oil refining (Figure 2-3C).

44

Consequently, some began to question whether the observed phenomenon of consistently and perpetually decreasing cost did not apply to all elements in the cost structure, not simply production labor cost. Henderson and his colleagues in the Boston Consulting Group were thus led to formulate the hypothesis they called the experience curve, and found it checked against the record of every specific product on which they could get data. As formulated by this group, the experience curve principle states that costs decline by some characteristic percentage each time accumulated experience is doubled (B.C.G., 1968). The implications of this proven relationship for R & D, for competitive strategy, and for market entry are critical, as will be seen later.

The experience curve phenomenon indicates that the old maxim that "practice makes perfect" needs restatement to "practice makes ever better." This is hardly surprising. We know that even within any highly skilled group, skill increases with experience. As has been noted, the purpose of habit formation is to reduce reaction to the reflex level. The process of habit formation normally involves far more than mere repetition. Quite usually, some kind of rhythm needs to be established, and waste motion, all errors of movement, and even steps in the process eliminated. Anyone who has ever watched a worker performing a repetitive task, as for example a roofer or a drywall applicator in building, cannot help but remember the smooth rhythm of his hammer strokes, for example, and the absence of hesitation and waste effort of any kind.

Such gains from pure habit formation are not limited to motor habits. They apply at least equally well to the mental habits involved in planning, design and execution at the management level. The skilled research analyst can often get to the heart of a problem and pinpoint an answer in hours, after some junior has mulled it over for weeks without discovering any light. Management whose experience and skills lie in highly advertised package goods can come up with an effective advertising campaign to counter a competitive threat that had taken a lesser competitor months to launch. Thus, knowledge of the process of normal habit formation should have led us to expect the phenomenon of the experience curve years before it was discovered.

However, habit formation by itself is hardly an adequate explanation for the continuing nature of the improvement. In fact, habit formation would tend to limit improvement by acting as a barrier to the more important improvements--those requiring a change in the habit pattern.

Habits, however, have an important side effect--they free the mind from concentration on the details of the process of the task in hand. They thus permit us to focus on the end result of that process. This diversion of interest can reveal weaknesses in the

45

process itself--results which are less than they could be with some change. Since change itself requires some new learning, and thus is an avoidance incentive, we might expect process improvement to come to some end whenever there is no perceived incentive to greater perfection.

In fact, we can easily find numerous examples of such limitation of the process. One such is the tendency toward competitive somnolence of any firm or individual which thinks it has as a monopoly--the railroads were an excellent example in the first half of the century.

Another is the tendency of any guild or closed trade to set maximum limits on individual output--the firing of workmen for laying more than a standard number of bricks.

The general tendency of most people to satisfice, whether assembly line workers or corporate chairmen--is an obvious barrier. They tend to set limited goals for attainment and the coasting on reputation thereafter (not unknown among professors, for that matter).

Clearly then, continued progress under the experience curve requires some constant pressure--some kind of continued incentive to change established routines.

For a rare few in this world, the incentive comes from the inside. We have an occasional Picasso of the art world who keeps experimenting and developing to the day of his death. Once in a while we have an entrepreneur who keeps seeking new and higher goals of profitable enterprise. There is an occasional corporate executive who will resist the stultifying bureaucracy to keep his firm and industry on the move, or move on to where he can do this. For all of these, we can name examples. But the names we come up with will be much the same, because few there are who have such a fiercely burning inner drive.

For the rest, the drive must come from the outside. In the marketplace, it is the threat of a successful competitor, chipping off poorly satisfied fringe market segments, who furnishes this incentive. Dissatisfaction is the prime mover toward the learning most of us undergo, with however much reluctance. The consumer is no exception, and the market growth rate will depend on the degree of learning required of him for acceptance of any new offering.

SUMMARY

1. Competitive success at any stage in the product life cycle depends on shaping strategy and tactics to conform to known laws of buyer psychological behavior, both those laws which are universal and those which make for diverse relations to the same offering or

other stimulus.

2. The most important universal law is that the reaction to any intended stimulus is determined by the individual's own make-up of desire-sets and personality, not by the stimulus itself. Most stimuli will get no response from most buyers, some will get a delayed response, some a reverse response, and only a few will respond as hoped for.

3. Selective attention is the universal major reason for lack of response. Attention is directed only to those stimuli, among the infinity bombarding the individual, which are perceived as promises (cues) that acquisition will permit satisfying a desire-set.

4. Selective perception is the universal tendency to note only those aspects of a stimulus which are perceived as relating to current important desires and interest as interpreted on the basis of past experience and associations. All of these factors differ widely between individuals. So reactions, when they do come, are as wide apart as the poles of approach and avoidance behavior.

5. Approach responses to a stimulus are those which lead to positive action toward acquisition. Avoidance responses are adverse to acquisition. Nearly all stimuli, and all offerings, are a mixture of the two--some attributes stimulating an approach reaction, some activating an avoidance or withdrawal response. The degree of drive for the approach side determines whether or not the subject (the buyer) will sacrifice the price to get it, and if so, when.

6. Most responses are automatic or reflex, due to established habit patterns. Only thus can the individual optimize his satisfactions. Learning any habit patterns, including product use-systems, is a painful, time-consuming task, and once a habit, it is not quickly or easily discarded.

7. The incentive to acquire a patronage, use-system, or any other habit is the satisfaction of some pre-existing felt need. Finding a source of satisfaction usually involves substantial search effort. Hence both buyer and seller are seeking a continuing, habitual relationship. Once established, the search for alternative sources is inhibited. If complete satisfaction is not secured, there may be some lesser residual drive which an alternative can use to get attention. But any alternative not yet tried represents a risk, and will not automatically get attention.

8. The j.n.d. (just noticeable difference) effect is a universal

phenomenon which requires that any alternative must offer a substantial difference if it is to be perceived as different at all.

9. The discriminal thresholds of j.n.d. apply to every aspect of human and consumer response--to product and other offering differences, to selling efforts, and to prices of all kinds.

10. "More stimulus does not necessarily get more response" because of the j.n.d., and also because of the principle of satiation, or "satisficing", due to the multitude of drives in each individual and the hierarchical nature of their manifestation. The buyer reacts most strongly to stimuli promising satisfaction to his most pressing drive--the drive at the top of this hierarchy. The very process of gaining that satisfaction relieves further pressure, and drops that one drive to the lower rungs of the hierarchy, giving way to what was previously the second most pressing drive. This explains the obvious difficulty of the second seller on the market, and of the true "me-too" offering.

11. All of these universalities of human behavior would lead inevitably to considerable diversity of response and to substantial market segmentation, merely on the basis of differential satiation of needs alone. But there are many other forces causing diversities of drives and thus of response: congenital differences of psychological make-up, personal abilities and sensitivity to various kinds of satisfactions, acquired differences of personal situation and condition, learned differences of all sorts, differences due to social pressures. In a very real sense, there is never a single market, but almost a different market response for each individual.

12. Segmentation is a result of mass production and product design compromise. A segment is really defined by the offering itself. The inherent compromise in any design will attract a relatively loyal core of buyers because it comes as close as possible to fulfilling their desire-sets, and other buyers because its deficiencies are less than the defects in alternatives. At the fringe of every segment will be buyers who find no one product very close to their desire-sets. These are the potential targets for new market entries.

13. All of these established psychological principles imply that only one seller can occupy a given niche in a given market. Others must develop differentiated offerings attracting different segments. The perceived difference must be substantial--well beyond a j.n.d.--if it aims for reasonably stable success. And the extra value must not exert too high a learning price to gain the hoped

48

for patronage habit.

14.   The process of habit formation, on the manufacturing side, seems to be an important explanatory element for the learning curve   and its more general formulation, the experience curve. The latter is a pragmatic formulation based on wide industry experience which finds that "costs decline by some characteristic percentage each time the accumulated production experience is doubled."

This principle has a number of critical corollaries for diversification policy and competitive strategy in general.

49

3

THE LEARNING REQUIREMENT AND ITS EFFECT ON PRODUCT ACCEPTANCE

No product sells at full potential from the moment of introduction. The reason is the need for a threefold learning process. The prospect must first become aware of and learn of the existence of the product and what "new" satisfactions the new introduction promises. The buyer must then learn for himself directly or from others what the promised "new" in the new product means to him and what its value is in his current or possible use systems. Finally he must acquire by learning some degree of change in his habitual purchasing and use patterns. The degree of that last change in use patterns is what determines the potential speed of growth and market acceptance and sales.

For a great majority of the highly touted introductions on the market, what the seller means by "new" is that he simply has a slightly different version of the already familiar--an emulative near carbon copy of some successful competitor's offering, or an adaptive variation of one of his own established lines. Such introductions may require only that some substantial market segments discover that some previously unavailable attribute they already desired, valued, and understood is available and in a form to which they are accustomed.

At the opposite extreme are those completely unfamiliar offerings combining a completely new bundle of satisfactions whose meaning and need they must learn to perceive and value. In such cases, success will hinge on an effective, prolonged and aggressive educational campaign directed at those individuals and segments most likely to pioneer the new use systems required.

In between these extremes are all degrees of variations of course, and prediction of that degree and intensity is the first prerequisite to estimating the resources required for introduction and for planning introductory tactics.

Estimating the learning requirements is not necessarily easy. What the customer perceives as really new and the degree of that perceived newness has no relationship at all to the technological novelty involved in the physical design or construction of the offering. The system of use into which the product is initially perceived as fitting will determine that. The really new product is one requiring some significant degree of learning: some learning of some new use-system, of a new kind of satisfaction source, of a new role in an otherwise similar system, or of a new level of value for some major product attribute.

The amount of learning required determines the degree of perceived newness. However revolutionary the technology which gives birth to a new offering, if its adoption exacts an insignificant learning price of any kind and it fits into an already established system with noticeably improved benefits, acceptance and sales growth will be rapid from the very start. However minor the technological newness, market acceptance must pass through the hard-won creeping growth of market development if the offering imposes a high learning price to obtain its desired benefits.

Moreover, the use system(s) the customer will perceive as appropriate cannot be completely predicted. The use system may be substantially different from the one foreseen in developing the design and in many cases will include quite unforeseen possibilities.

Three basic types of product life cycles can be distinguished on the basis of learning requirements and benefit content--the basic eight-stage high-learning cycle and two types of foreshortened low-learning cycles, the short-lived fad cycle and the long-lived cycle of the low-learning product yielding a major substantive benefit. The fad can be distinguished in advance by its lack of any major added benefit other than that of pure novelty.

The other major kinds of low-learning products are the emulative products and adaptive products which enter the market after an initial offering has proved out, and the most valuable offering of all--the systems-completing or missing-link product which makes freely available an already accepted but still incomplete system. A fourth complication, really a subsidiary component of a large portion of all life cycles, is the fluctuating fashion cycle.

The prediction of the probable course of the cycle and its basic form is important because each basic form requires a divergent production and marketing strategy for profitable introduction. The prediction itself hinges on a correct analysis of the learning content of the product use system.

Some years ago, an article by the author summed up some experiences and observations about product introduction under 14 points of newness (Wasson, 1960). Although the point of view expressed therein has received wide and apparently unchallenged acceptance, the author himself has long felt that some much simpler principle must underlie this lengthy list. Reanalysis now indicates that the list can really be reduced to two factors--the positive factor of more value and the negative factor of some learning price.

Five points, labelled positive in the original exposition, all definitely spell "noticeably more value":

1. new cost or lower price
2. greater convenience in use
3. believable performance which is better or more dependable
4. greater availability in time or place
5. perceived status symbolism

A sixth positive characteristic, all four of those classifed as negative, and three attributes whose value depend on familiarity are manifestly learning price related:

6. (positive) easy credibility of benefits
7. (negative) new methods of use
8. unfamiliar use patterns (new use-systems, that is)
9. unfamiliar benefit (the need to learn to perceive value)
10. risk of error in use

The others are ambivalent: positive or negative depending on culture climate and familiarity:

11. new appearance, style, or texture
12. different accompanying or implied services
13. new channels of sale or new market

The 14th characteristic, difference in physical construction or composition, was classified as neutral because, by itself, it has meaning only when it changes the expectations of performance.

What these 14 points say is thus simply that what is new about any new product is composed of the positive or product side which can attract the buyer's attention because of some noticeably greater value of some kind, and the obverse negative or avoidance side of some kind of learning price, or its absence. That value may not be in the physical product itself, of course, but simply its availability. New channels may make it "new" to new markets. Promotion of new uses can make it a new product.

When that learning price is not perceived as significant, the prospect does not perceive the product as "really new" and is usually ready to seek out and purchase the substantial added visible values. If, however, the extra added value is perceived as bearing a high learning price tag of any kind, his interest in acquisition will be low and his approach cautious until he is satisfied that the degree of change required of him is a less certain cost than such added values as he can immediately perceive in a new benefit.

The very fact of newness itself may take some adjustment for many prospects. Thomas, et al. (1970) have shown that a majority of people may be congenitally predisposed to react negatively to anything unfamiliar. Thus, those who will immediately accept the new are always a minor part of the total market. Since new must be defined in terms of the psychologically perceived learning price it should be clear that technical newness has no clear correlation with market newness. What the engineer may view as a spectacular breakthrough may be perceived by potential buyers (as was black-and-white television) as merely an old familiar offering in familiar form, simply an already known and desired satisfaction with a lowered avoidance content. On the other hand, what may seem to the technician to be a relatively minor technical improvement may be perceived by prospects as imposing such a high use-systems learning requirement that it should be adopted slowly and with extreme caution. Such was the case of the A. O. Smith Harvestore: basically the old familiar farm silo, but constructed of glazed steel, with a mechanical unloader at the bottom, and a vinyl inside cap which rode the contents down and prevented ready spoilage. Although the Harvestore was technically a much improved silo, at a reasonably higher price, its adoption was economic only if the farm purchaser changed his whole system of livestock management, confining his cattle to feeding pens and feeding them forage harvested periodically from the old pastures and put through the silo. When this was done, the crop yield could be increased as much as three times in volume, but at a tremendous cost in habit change. It took hard selling to establish the Harvestore market.

Similarly, the microwave oven appears to resemble any other separate oven (a simple enclosure with a see-through door and a dial to regulate cooking). Such an oven promises, moreover, a tremendous added value for many a housewife in our time-short culture--cooking time reduced by as much as three-fourths. Nevertheless, initial sales were very modest and had to be accompanied by vigorous demonstration because its use requires learning a whole new set of cooking procedures and also learning to perceive "doneness" of the item being cooked by something other than its surface brownness.

Anyone familiar with the reluctance with which all of us face any change in our motor habits and ways of thinking would not be surprised by the unwillingness of buyers to search out and purchase high learning products.

The Four Kinds of Learning

An introduction may require any or all of four kinds of learning on the part of the prospect:

1. Motor learning - a change in habitual muscular use system sequences.
2. Value-perception learning - Learning to value the improvement as greater than the cost.
3. Role-perception learning - Learning to accept a changed social role as a result of the product use.
4. Use-perceptual learning involved in crediting a new satisfaction source as a reliable and improved fulfillment of a given desire set.

In a world with so many changes in products as most of us have seen even in a period as short as a decade, there is little need to emphasize the problem of making changes in our motor habits. Anyone who has ever gone from a three-speed manual transmission car to a four-speed transmission, or conversely to an automatic transmission, will be aware of the initial learning cost of a simple functional change which requires new muscular sequences. Any office worker who has ever shifted from one make of typewriter to another knows the frustration cost implied in a few minor changes in keyboard design, like the different location of a backspace key. A housewife who has moved from one city where electricity was used for cooking to one where she has to use gas will testify to the length of time it took her to get use to different sequences of timing and muscular use in regulating her cooking.

Learning new sequences of muscular coordination is only one of the kinds of learning required by new product introductions. Many product introductions, for example, require some degree of learning to perceive value where value had not previously been sought. Probably the outstanding example of this in the last generation was the introduction of color television. When originally introduced, the industry was convinced there would be an immediate switchover from black and white. Quite the opposite proved to be the case. From 1954, when colored television was first introduced, until 1964, RCA had to plow millions of dollars a year into market development because very few prospects were willing to pay the difference in price between black-and-white and color.

The electric typewriter is an excellent example of a product that required both what might appear to be a minor change in muscular coordination and a change in value perception. Superficially, the electric typewriter would appear to be a relatively minor change over the manual form it was intended to replace. The keyboard was

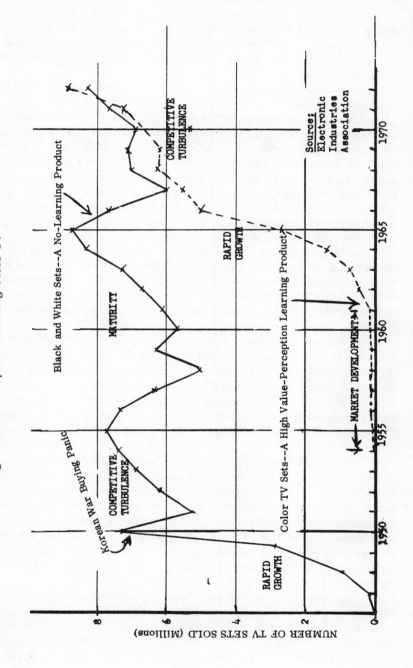

FIGURE 3-1. The Contrasting Market Growth Patterns of the No-Learning Black and White TV Versus the High Value-Perception-Learning Color TV

the same and the results were obtained in much the same manner--
by striking a key with a finger. It had some excellent offsetting
values. The copy produced was much more uniform than that normally produced on a standard typewriter by anybody but the most
skilled typist. The effort required by the typist was a great deal
less, resulting in much less fatigue at the end of the day and a consequent increase in productivity.

But the electric typewriter required a much greater motor
learning cost than would be obvious initially. It required a complete change in the muscular habits of the typist. Whereas she had
previously been trained to rest her fingers on the middle of the al-
phabetical row of keys, she now had to avoid touching any key at all
until she wanted to register it on her copy. Even a slight passing
brush of a key would cause the typewriter to print. The result was a
great deal of spoiled copy until she had unlearned a relatively simple finger position that had become habitual to her, and had learned
to be extremely careful of how she moved her hands. A learning
period of approximately two months was not unusual for a person
who was changing over from a standard typewriter to an electric
typewriter. Thus it was that only the stenographer who was in a
situation where extremely uniform copy was extremely important
to her would undertake the effort. Most other typists and steno-
graphers would prefer to work with the kind of machines on which
they had been trained to type.

Moreover, the electric typewriter was a much more costly
machine to keep in service. Not only was the initial cost twice as
high as that of a standard typewriter, but it was far more prone to
get out of adjustment and service contracts were much more expensive. Thus many office managers could not initially see the productivity advantage of an electric typewriter over a standard one.
Consequently, he too needed to learn a great deal of value perception.

Given these learning costs, it is hardly surprising that the
electric typewriter required a full generation to gain even a moderate degree of acceptance and nearly forty years to become the
major element in the market. The first electric typewriters were
introduced in the middle 1920's, and of these the Electramatic make
was taken over by IBM in 1933. Yet, as late as 1948, the electric
typewriters were only six percent of unit sales. Then electric typewriters rose to 26 percent of sales in 1955, 42 percent in 1960, and
by 47 percent in 1961.

One reason for the quicker later growth was that by this time
the electric typewriter had become standard in a good many typing
schools. The initial learning process was now with an electric
typewriter, and many typists therefore had problems in changing
back to a standard. This kind of changeback in itself can be not

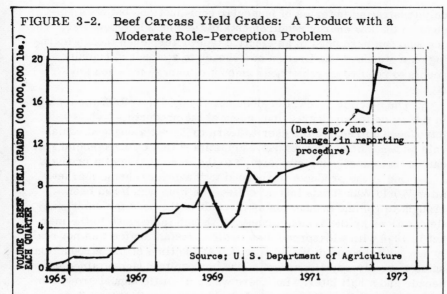

FIGURE 3-2. Beef Carcass Yield Grades: A Product with a
Moderate Role-Perception Problem

(Data gap, due to change in reporting procedure)

Source; U. S. Department of Agriculture

VOLUME OF BEEF YIELD GRADED (00,000,000 lbs.) EACH QUARTER

0 4 8 12 16 20

1965 1967 1969 1971 1973

The U.S. Department of Agriculture has long had the responsibility for developing vol-untary standards of quality for use in the sale of agricultural commodities. When re-leased for use, the department's well researched standards have proved so useful that they have gained almost universal acceptance, and carry high credibility.

One of the standards in long use has been for the eating qualities of beef--essen-tially a tenderness standard. Familiar grades of prime, choice, and utility have been the basis for sale of livestock to packers, of beef carcasses to retailers, and of retail sales to consumers. But while this system does a good job of reflecting eating quality, it leaves undone a job important to the retail butcher. It tells him what a pound of steaks from the carcass will sell for, but not what proportion of the carcass will be steaks, what part the much less valuable hamburger, and what part almost worthless trim (bone and fat.) Thus two choice 800 pound steer carcasses may vary as much as $75 or $100 in "cutability" values.

Until recent years, retailers have relied on a single standard for the carcasses they sought (such as "lightly covered 800 pound steers"), plus inspection of and choice from the individual carcasses available at the packer's warehouse. This procedure ob-viously requires highly trained judgment, and the degree of skill exercised could affect the meat counter's profits appreciably.

After some years of research, the USDA developed a system of yield grades in 1965 which defined the cutability value of a carcass in terms of 5 levels within the eat-ability grade. Using this system, a retailer could determine the value of the offerings without inspection. Moreover, he need not limit his purchases to a single yield grade, but choose whatever yield grade gave him the best net return after cutting. The stand-ards were launched with a thoroughly publicized drive, backed by the credibility of the USDA. They were obviously a much simpler and less involved system than that in cur-rent use. However, contrary to the theory that simplicity is the key to quick accep-tance, there was no rush to use the new grades. As the chart above shows, only a few innovators gave the system an early trial. There was no substantial growth in use for a year, after which expansion of use grew at a moderate pace for a number of years, reaching what may be close to saturation only 8 years later.

The probable reason for the slow growth: this system downgraded the role of the meat buyer, turning the task into one that was little more than clerical. Causing a shift in the role, it was bound to meet resistance.

57

only frustrating in terms of muscular coordination, but does emphasize the low energy requirements of the electric typewriter. To one who has been used to an electric typewriter, even though learning on a standard one first, a switchback to a standard machine seems to require a tremendous amount of energy for each key stroke.

The electric typewriter does not change the role of the typists in the office to any degree, but many of the products which are introduced do require the user to learn to accept a changed social role as a result of product use. Sometimes this changed social role can be an almost complete barrier to the introduction of a product.

One of the products introduced to the general home market after World War II was instant coffee--an item which had been brought to volume production as a result of the need for emergency field rations by the armed forces. Although introduced to the market in 1946 with widespread distribution, instant coffee was not really new with the end of World War II. At the time of its introduction sales were already 10 percent of the per capita usage attained some decade and a half later. But there was very little annual growth in useage for the first five years of post-war promotion, and it required another six years until 1957 to reach the initial market saturation stage.

The problem in this case does not appear to have been in the product itself. The 1946 product was essentially as good and as easy to handle as the 1957 product. The problem seemed to be, in fact, that the product itself was much too easy to use. It became associated in the housewife's mind with careless housekeeping. Studies had shown that women whose major business was housekeeping tended to view the person who used instant coffee as a lazy housewife. Coffee, it seems, is a product to which women attach a certain degree of skill in the making. It is probably no accident that the growth in instant coffee paralleled the growth in the extent to which women began to participate widely in the outside work force and to become themselves one of the wage earners in the family, thus lowering the importance of the home-keeping role in their place in the family.

Almost any product which tends to downgrade the skill of the user will meet some resistance. This is especially true when the product is used in an industrial setting. Paint rollers received an extremely widespread use among the home painters long before the professional painters were willing to adopt this speed-saving and productivity-producing tool. The introduction of the diesel locomotive did away with the need for the locomotive fireman, but the unions resisted the elimination of the job itself even up to the time of this writing. Computer typesetting has a great many advantages over linotype operation. But one of its greatest advantages is one which has set the unions against it: it eliminates the need for much knowledge beyond that of mere typing.

Even the automatic transmission in the automobile required a long period before it became standard. First introduced in the late 30's, it began to be an important standard element in automobiles only in the 1950's. It was probably no accident that the reason it did become important was the strong residential shift to the suburbs and the two-car family, where the woman had to become the family chauffeur. A very large portion of women are not mechanically oriented and dislike the use of the standard gear shift. At the opposite extreme were the skilled drivers who resisted the automatic transmission to the point where the "stick shift" became a prestige item worth a premium on sport cars.

A good example of a product which downgraded human skill too far for its own success was the fully automatic washer, which was intended to take all the guesswork and manipulation out of the housewife's washing work by substituting a push-button for practically every kind of possible variation of the washing cycle. It did not sell and had to be withdrawn from the market, although backed up by a firm with an extremely good reputation and extremely wide distribution. Housewives preferred to trust their own judgment about the proper variation of the various elements of the cycle, and would not buy it. It downgraded their social role in the family too far.

Finally, a great many products require use-perceptual learning. They require us to learn to perceive to credit a new satisfaction source as both reliable and an improvement in the fulfillment of a given desire-set. The small foreign sedan is a case of a product which took a rather long period to attain a substantial share of the market because a great portion of the market could not see that in some respects it was not only as good as, but even better than the larger products they had been buying from Detroit. It was difficult for a great many people to perceive that a car which had external dimensions quite markedly smaller than the cars to which they had been used could actually be more comfortable in many cases and have even more room for the riders than the obviously mammoth products they had been accustomed to buying.

Of the major foreign cars, the Volkswagen was first introduced in 1949, but it was a decade later before the sales became such that the major Big Three of Detroit felt that they had to counter the trend. Even after their 1960 introductions of "compacts", the Detroit manufacturers felt reasonably safe in increasing the size and gaudiness of their output for a considerable period. Nevertheless, when they lost experienced drivers from their large cars to the small imports, they often did not regain them. By the 1970's even the buyers of luxury cars were beginning to switch to imported luxury models.

Almost every fashion that is introduced on the market gains

ground slowly until the major part of the women in the market are convinced that this new fashion does a better job for them than the ones which they had been using. This is not true of fads, however, because a fad requires no use-perceptual learning, as will be pointed out later. A fad's main advantages is its only obvious difference: it is new.

The building material field is full of instances in which acceptance has been slow because of the unwillingness of both the building industry itself and the final buyers to perceive that the new is actually both an improved and a satisfactory substitute for what they have been using.

Since the payment of any price for any first purchase always carries some implication of risk that the results may not be worth the cost, any learning requirement involves a risk-cost. Learning itself is a time-consuming process and thus guarantees some retardation of new product adoption. The common propensity to avoid unnecessary risks would tend to restrict adoption, thus further slowing it down.

Obviously, the learning requirement of new products is highly variable and not all prospects put the same stiff price on the attainment of added attributes not previously as readily available.

Of course really new products are a minute fraction of the flood of well-advertised "New! New!" "Major Discoveries" familiar to any who can read or even listen. Many of these are new only to the seller, and most offer rather minor evolutionary increases in value at best. Others which are radical innovations technologically fit the established use systems and performance expectations so well that buyers perceive only substantially improved value levels in familiar patterns of consumption. New product adoption speeds could thus be expected to vary widely, and they do, of course. In fact, the market success of some introductions comes with such speed that the initial introducer may find it hard to keep production in pace with initial demand. Others gain favor so slowly that the marketing operations pile up substantial deficits for years before a break-even point is reached. Many, of course, fail to get off the ground at all, and of those which do, not all attain broad markets. In some of these latter instances, the introduction itself was misconceived because the potential value was never there for the customer. In other instances, the strategy and tactics of the introduction were simply mishandled, and a viable product denied a merited chance at life. Sometimes, the problem is simply that the organization introduced a product which had, under the right circumstances, a large success potential, but one not realizable within the resource limitations of the introducer.

FIGURE 3-3. The Four Basic Life Cycle Forms

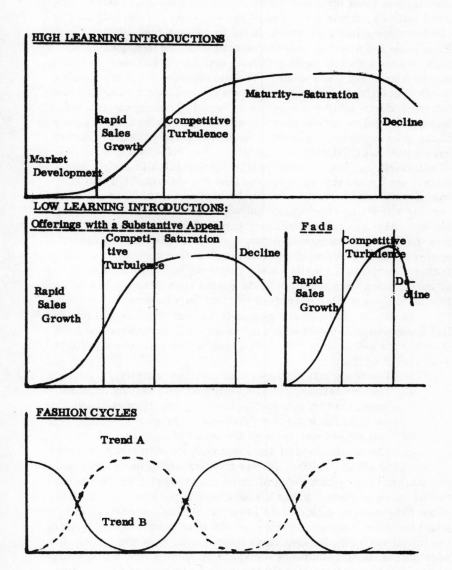

THE BASIC LIFE CYCLE FORMS

As already indicated, product life cycles take on multifarious forms. Even for those which follow the classical pattern outlined initially, the initial rates of acceleration vary greatly. The electric typewriter took two decades to reach a take-off point. Broad-spectrum antibiotics and insecticides, on the other hand, rose to peak sales so rapidly that no market development period can be perceived. For some, the saturated phase covers a relatively specialized market segment with very modest sales volume. Other products achieve something resembling universal demand. Most fads tend to die out abruptly and completely at the very peak of the growth curve, but many stop short of extinction, proving to have small residual markets for which they offer some basic set of satisfactions. Some which might seem faddish in their appeal attract such a narrow age segment that the market, like that for baby foods, is constantly renewed by new recruits. Even more durably attractive offerings go through successive fashion cycles. Many fundamentally revolutionary products are built up by perceptive marketing management through successively larger product cycles as their continuing use and development uncover new satisfaction potentials. Finally, many products fail after a brief flurry of initial sales because their basic design is in error--they do not live up to the promise perceived by their purchasers.

Basically, then, there appear to be four fundamental product life cycle patterns out of which all successful variations are built. (See Figure 3-3). Each requires a distinctively different product and marketing plan:

1. The basic full 8-stage cycle outlined initially
2. The truncated cycle of an offering with lasting substantive appeal but no substantial learning requirement, and thus no need for a market development stage.
3. The sky-rocket cycle of the true fad
4. The oscillations of the fashion cycle with opposing trends

These classifications are far from mutually exclusive, and the market history of a given offering may reveal a combination of two or more of them. It has already been noted that the sales of some fad products subside to a lower level, but not zero. Such could be conceptualized as the sum of a true fad cycle (for most of the initial market) plus that of an introduction with some kind of substantive added benefits perceivable by some small market segment. Fashion affects largely the visible, formal and thus more superficial aspects of offerings rather than the central functions: the styling of a car, not its basic conformation, the organization chart of a firm, not the dynamics of the basic interpersonal rela-

62

tionships.   Fashion fluctuations tend to be a component of major
product categories of every sort, and fashion cycles an element added
to the course of the normal life cycle.   The pyramided cycle is
really a normal fully-phased cycle augmented by additional low-
learning cycles as new design possibilities open up new use-systems
for which the public has been prepared.   The life cycle theoretically
applies to a whole category of offerings, of course, with only the
offering of the original introducer travelling full course and the
offerings of succeeding sellers entering the cycle at various advanced phases.   New products, in the usual loose usage of the term,
thus comprise several gradations between the really new pioneering
product as we have defined it and the "new only to us" emulative
product with some attractive differential.   Nevertheless, no introduction succeeds unless it offers a noticeable added value of some
sort.   Thus every introduction requires at least a slight degree of
learning of some kind   and will have its own product life cycle.

THE DIFFERING KINDS OF NEW PRODUCTS

     The basic types of product life cycles outlined above clearly
point up four basic groups of new product types: pioneering products, two kinds of low-learning products, and new (or more often,
renewed) fashions.   Fashion is less a separate group of new product types than a second order of value present in all types of life
cycles and is thus reserved for separate discussion later on.   The
degree of pioneering being attempted by any revolutionary product
is manifestly a variable, so that we have a large family of revolutionary introductions, each with a different variation of the level of
any or all of the three types of learning price.   Logically, these
grade off to the low-learning point in the scale, which we have differentiated as two distinct types of product life cycles of their own.
These two types of low-learning introductions would be worthy of
specific attention if for no other reason than the low market entry
fee involved even for the initiator of their market introduction.
     Low-learning products are the only kinds with which entrepre-
neurs with limited capital resources have much hope of success.
Once past the gestation stage, such demand little of the costly market development investment which hinders the entry of high learning
offerings.   Naturally, new offerings which are not very new except
to the introducer would require no very significant learning at the
time of their introduction.   Because the life cycle is already in an
advanced stage, products which are emulative or adaptations of
established offerings require no significant learning price.   Neither,
however, does the revolutionary low-learning introduction--the
really new product which offers very substantial, previously un-

available perceived value. These generally rocket to early success because many potential customers have already paid much of the learning price and are actively looking for something like it. Such products are <u>systems-completing</u> (or "missing-link") offerings which customers are prepared to buy as soon as they are made aware of their benefits and availability.

Computers were developed to free scientists and others from computational drudgery and make available computational tools too cumbersome for hand calculation. Few prospects could use the initial models, however, because of the mathematical skill needed to program each use. IBM released that potential promise of computational relief by developing ready-made software--the standard computer program, the programming program, and the computer library. By implementing an insight into the need for standardized software, the firm made available a technology capable of revolutionizing corporate information systems and putting some complex mathematical tools within reach of executive decision making. By adding this missing ingredient, IBM reaped the potential results of a device pioneered by others but introduced with a use-system defect.

Tractors had been around longer than automobiles, well over 40 years before the rubber tractor tire of the 1930's propelled American agriculture almost overnight into today's highly mechanized agribusiness. The auto could hardly hope to be a major part of the transportation system so long as the pavement ended in some tracks through the mud just outside most population centers. With the founding of a national highway network, the public eagerly voted for the necessary paving bonds which, in turn, made Detroit a national industrial capitol. Then in the 1930's the supermarket became the missing link which united the automobile, the mechanical refrigerator, and good roads into a food shopping use-system which obsoleted the corner market and crossroads, changing America's shopping habits and eventually her eating habits and the whole food industry.

The Systems-Completing Product

The distinction between the merely technically new and the psychologically unfamiliar can be seen in the history of the cases of the rapid acceptance accorded such products as black-and-white television, computer programming libraries and services, the national highway system, rubber tractor tires, and supermarkets. Each of these was, in its way, a quite radical departure from the preceding products available and a major technical achievement. All were outstanding market successes from the moment of full market availability and quickly replaced or caused drastic modifications in the predecessor alternatives for the same satisfactions. In each case, also, the overnight success might have been predicted by anyone with insight into the already felt needs of the prospects and the nature of the perceived benefits these products offered. Every one was a no-learning product--each added a significant missing ingredient to an existing use-system.

The public needed no learning to perceive the entertainment values of black-and-white TV and adopt immediately. It had long before learned to switch on the radio to bring comedy, drama, and news into the home. The picture tube simply added a new and highly desired dimension to radio and permitted the broadcast medium to fulfill a need previously available only through a trip to the movie theater. Moreover, it dispensed with the nuisance of the theater trip itself and the accompanying parking problem, the lineup for tickets, and the cost of the ticket itself. It also eliminated the need for a baby-sitter, and often served as such itself. Black-and-white TV thus simply combined the best parts of two previously incomplete entertainment systems and improved on both. The industry never had a major market development expenditure to make.

Clearly, the missing-ingredient product can be by far the ideal type of product introduction. If it builds on an already felt need of high value, the expensive market development phase of introduction is by-passed and early or even immediate profits result. Because it opens up the results of a wholly new approach to satisfaction, even a completely new set of already desired satisfactions, those prospective profits can be very large. However, the size and immediate visibility of those profits normally attract potential competition which the introducer must be prepared to meet right away. Sometimes, of course, the initial main product cannot even arouse a substantial volume demand without the missing link. In such a case, the seller must make the missing link available to get his initial offering off the ground.

One of the most attractive features of the systems-completing or missing-link product is the precision with which the development can be targeted. Once the need is pinpointed and the system identified, the rest is simple engineering, and seldom is any more difficult than developing a less profitable emulative or adaptive modification of an established offering. Nevertheless, such emulative and adaptive products can be profitable when correctly designed and managed. They make up the bulk of the successful items in the product mix of almost any firm.

Emulative and Adaptive Products

The decline of unit profits which accompanies the slowdown

of the growth phases is due partly to changes in customer perception of value, partly to the competitive pressures from emulative products. The novelty element in value inevitably evaporates early, and the later adopting segments come into the market late precisely because they perceive less value in the core benefits or because they desire adaptive modifications of the original offering. Some of these adaptive variations are inevitably low-end, low-margin offerings designed to broaden the market. All contribute to model proliferation and thus to some extent to costs.

Additionally, once the market development stage is passed, the rapid acceleration of sales and profit growth attracts swarms of profit-hungry competitors and some of these latter are bound to try to buy into the market with closely margined emulative designs.

Thus the established market phases see the introduction of two other distinguishable types of introductions--the adaptive and the emulative offerings. Tull (1967) has distinguished between these quite similar entries in terms of the identity of the introducer. He defines the adaptive product as a variant of some other offering of the same producer, presumably designed to broaden market share. This would include such offerings as the introduction of another nameplate or model in the automobile industry--the Ford Maverick of 1970 or the GM Vega the following year. The emulative product, on the other hand, is a new offering by some competitor (the Vega would be emulative in the illustration above, with respect to the Ford Maverick, or both, with respect to the VW). For both the adaptive and the emulative, the cycle for the individual offering plugs into the product life cycle at some advanced stage--generally the growth stage or later. Both succeed only when they include some attribute adding noticeably to the value perceived by some market segment.

Emulative and adaptive entries may come well along in the established or saturated phases of the product life cycle, adding nothing to the size of the total market, as when Procter and Gamble launched its emulative Gleem. The added value may be more perceived than physical, a mere attention-getting claim rather than a different formulation ("for those who can't brush after every meal", for example). Or it may be a better, more easily used package. It may also be a real difference in the performance-related characteristics of the basic product, as when P & G introduced its own adaptive Crest toothpaste, with a stannous fluoride additive conferring unique proven benefits.

Emulative and adaptive products are clearly competitive offsets, designs with the same aim of building new markets among those still not completely satisfied with currently offered values. The adaptive offering is an often overlooked defensive necessity-- a means of preventing the inevitable erosion of the fringes of an

66

organization's market share through the introduction of identical or similar emulative offerings by some competitor. Both succeed only to the extent that the offering design fits the needs of these fringe segments better than any offering currently available. Otherwise, they are <u>non-products</u> whose markets never materialize--the all too common "instant bust". The fad is a quite different offering whose brief success is so evanescent that it sometimes is mistaken as a failure.

The Fad: The Empty Product

The fad differs from other products in that its sole contribution to the desire-set of prospects is the element of novelty. No product succeeds unless it is perceived as promising satisfaction of some desire-set not previously felt as well satisfied. Most products simultaneously fulfill some complete configuration of several desires at one time for each of the segments attracted to them. The desire-set satisfied differs for every product, and for each of the segments using a given product. But every introduction also offers one universally desired attribute--the element of novelty. Psychological experimentation has long established that one of the drives causing all sentient animals to act seems to be something which can only be labelled as curiosity, or as a drive for new experience. Every new product, by the very fact of its newness, fulfills this drive. The fad can be distinguished from other new products by the fact that, for most prospects, it adds no other new benefit of significant value and thus bears no risk of unfulfilled satisfaction.

Novelty is by its very nature an evanescent benefit. Once large numbers of prospects have adopted a fad, the novelty disappears and the product ceases to have any substantial value for most buyers. The market evaporates.

Sometimes, however, a residual market maintains a residual demand under one of two conditions. If the fad is one interesting a very narrow age segment, successive generations may find the novelty interest there for them. Thus popular parlor games which sweep wide areas of the market seldom die out completely. Successive generations of children still find Monopoly an interesting Christmas gift a full generation after their elders have lost interest. Most such game fads share a second characteristic which can sustain a residual market: they help the user to kill time in some moderately interesting manner. Hence any game or simple armchair hobby has value for invalids and others forcibly idled. It can retain such a residual market because it meets another condition necessary to a fad--only the most minimal learning is required. Fads and fashions are sometimes lumped together as though the only difference between these two phenomena were the length of their cycles. This is a misconception. True fashions are much more substantive products which pass through the major phases of a normal product life cycle. In fact, a fashion is simply another aspect of some standard product life cycle which can be recognized as having some aspect of repetitive fluctuation, the nature of which deserves extended discussion, given later.

Because each individual life cycle has a different history and each stage quite different marketing-mix requirements, all management planning and tactics must be built around a correct appraisal of the nature of the phase to be faced next and the probable life course of the entire cycle.

RELATIONSHIP OF THE CORRECT INTRODUCTORY STRATEGY TO THE EXPECTED ACCEPTANCE PATTERN

Each basic type of initial acceptance pattern calls for a quite divergent basic introductory marketing plan. Consider the marketing and production plans needed for optimum success with a potentially widely popular offering whose expected learning requirement involves a substantial market development investment, and the contrasting plans appropriate to one which is destined to become a fad.

The producer of the development product with a lasting potential must be prepared to finance substantial promotional and even production cost deficits for a considerable period of time, not unusually five years or more. He would be wise to minimize these deficits by keeping inventory and other capital requirements to as low a level as possible. At the same time, if he foresees a long product life, he would wish to minimize long-run production costs by using permanent tooling and making provision for future expansion of production facilities. Because the extent of the learning requirement would necessitate very intensive selling effort, as personal a one as possible, he would severely limit initial retail distribution to a few outlets carefully selected for their aggressiveness and strength. For the same reason, and also because the initial market would be a narrow one, his promotional mix would accent the personal sales side heavily rather than the use of mass communications tools, but would neglect none of them, spending would be quite heavy relative to sales volume. The theme of that promotion would emphasize the product concept primarily, not the brand, the benefits and the value to be obtained, not the source.

The introducer of a recognizable fad should pursue introductory tactics which are the opposite in almost every respect. Initial production volume would be at full speed from the moment of introduction. Distribution would be as extensive and intensive as could

68

be achieved and outlets kept loaded with inventory at almost any cost. Every effort should be bent to insure that no outlet is ever out of stock during the growth phase, which starts almost from the day of first sale. Otherwise, the intense competition, which will materialize from the day popularity is apparent, will be given a direct invitation to enter the market, and receive a wide-open welcome from outlets not able to keep up with demand. Actual lasting production facilities, by contrast, should be kept to the absolute minimum which will insure market coverage. If possible, contract production should be used to the utmost, and if any proprietary facilities must be used, tooling should be of the most temporary character possible. Other than some unavoidable initial mass promotion, the communications mix should be limited to the amount and to the types best calculated to strengthen ties with dealers. Whatever promotion is used should strongly stress brand--the market is soon fully aware of the availability of the only satisfaction sought from the offering (novelty), and the only problem is brand preference. The closest possible watch must be kept on the sales curve, and at the first sign of a slowdown, production phased out while the market still has enough life to clean out remaining inventories. Otherwise, the sudden collapse which comes at the end may bounce back unsold inventories in excess of much of the profit accumulated.

A further difference is obvious in the case of sellers who do not initiate the introduction. In the case of the durable product, they can wait until well into the growth period and still capitalize on it with emulative or adaptive models. At times, even, a non-pioneering competitor can enter a saturated market and profit if the cycle is a durable one. But in the case of the fad, he who does not jump in early loses his shirt.

The total plan for the potentially lasting product destined for high initial sales acceleration should be of a still different character than for either of the above. Because prospects will be in a buying mood as soon as they are aware of the availability, initial production and distribution should anticipate an early surge of demand, just as with the fad. As with the fad, as intensive distribution as possible is important, and heavy dealer stocks urgent. But production plans should be based on the assumption of a continuing volume market and should look forward to the day when markets reach saturation and cost competition will be a major consideration. Tooling should be permanent and cost factors predicated on the long range. Promotion should be very intense during the initial phase, just as with the learning content product, but the entire emphasis should be on mass communications, and strong brand identification be the aim. In short, every phase of marketing and production policy during the introductory period of a low-learning product with a potentially durable market should be the same as for the learning-content product during its <u>second,</u> or growth phase because the market situation is the same.

Products subject to frequent fashion cycles should obviously be designed for manufacture in relatively flexible facilities. The major focus of management should be on design, promotion, and constant research into the changing level and direction of buyer preferences. Since it is virtually impossible to fully protect ownership of the superficial aspects of design responsible for fashion shifts, distribution needs to be kept as intensive as developing acceptance permits, and variants introduced as acceptance broadens. The existence of pronounced fashion cycles in a product category also implies the existence of a specialized market niche for one or a few producers--the market catering to those not caring to follow every wind of change and opting for the classical design with minimum changes.

Products which have a mixed fad and residual basic demand market offer a special opportunity to another kind of producer: one which has the resources to survive the initial shakeout of the fad collapse and exploit the much smaller residual market profitably. Normally the latter will be a maker with a long line of related products and well established distribution.

Long-range management of basic inventions capable of pyramided cycles through continuing product evolution and/or changes in social habits requires a well-organized product research and development effort, astute customer research, and imaginative insight into developing new market possibilities.

Quite clearly, management needs to recognize very early the specialized character of the demand for those products whose appeal is to a narrow market segment and tailor all plans accordingly.

The production and market planning for any product introduction thus requires making a fairly accurate prediction of the general order of eventual market size and careful analysis of the initial learning requirement of the proposed design. Since product is value, the other side of value--price--must be an important consideration from the beginning. Price is a many-factor phenomenon, and involves far more than the monetary consideration.

SUMMARY

1. Because the life cycle is inevitable, the vitality of the profit structure depends on continuous development of the right kind of new products.

2. What is new about a new product can be summed up under two aspects: the positive aspect of perceivable new value and the negative aspect of some kind of learning price. The combination

of these two determines which kind of introductory sales pattern a product can expect.

3. Although actual introductory acceptance patterns exhibit numerous variations, they fall into four basic classifications: the full 8-stage high-learning cycle, two low-learning cycles--fads and those with an extended life--and fashion fluctuations.

4. Low-learning introductions are especially attractive to those organizations with limited capital because of the low demand they make on resources of all kinds.

5. The really new low-learning introduction which gains long life from a substantive benefit is the ideal introduction. These are always systems-completing introductions rendering some already accepted technology widely available.

6. Emulative and adaptive products skip the need for learning by being introduced after the market demand has been proven. If the product is a variation of some other established offering of the same seller, we term it adaptive. When introduced by a competitor, we call it emulative. Whoever the introducer, its success depends on some degree of perceived differentiation better fitting it to the desires of some fringe market segment, and the adaptive product is thus a necessary defense of a seller's market share against the possibility of emulative competition. Both emulative and adaptive products must be differentiated in some substantive manner from current offerings or they are non-products.

7. The fad is an empty product with no substantive added value beyond that of mere novelty, and so collapses at the peak of acceptance.

8. The kind of acceptance pattern to be expected must be predicted well in advance because each basic classification of acceptance pattern requires its own unique introductory marketing and production plan. The high-learning product calls for limited commitment of capital to production at the beginning, a heavy investment in market developing personal sales promotion, and selective distribution. Low-learning products generally require intensive distribution, a heavy initial commitment to production and mass inventories, and reliance on mass communications of all kinds. With fads, however, any commitment to specialized production facilities must be avoided. Whenever fashion is an important attribute, production facilities must be kept quite flexible in order to swing with the winds of taste.

71

4

PRICE: THE OBVERSE AVOIDANCE SIDE OF OFFERING VALUE

Since any offering is merely a perceived bundle of diverse values, the obverse side of product is a statement of value to be sacrificed to obtain it--the price. No rational product policy, no product design, and no marketing strategy can be formulated without consideration of price, nor price be set in isolation of the total strategy, any more than the mint can strike a single-faced coin.

Pricing is such an important element of any system of exchange that it attracts independent study in whole areas of law, of economic theory, of the behavioral sciences, and of management science, and comprises, in addition, a large part of the rules of thumb which link business experience and practice. Since the purpose of marketing strategy is to influence human behavior, all plans must take some kind of account of any guidance available from the behavioral sciences, particularly those areas dealing with perception of value and reaction to avoidance stimuli. Quite clearly, such plans must work through existing business institutions and must accept the limitations imposed by the practices of these institutions. The legal end is important only in terms of the negative limits imposed--it gives no positive guidance. Traditional micro-economic theory, unfortunately, contributes little beyond the bare concepts of elasticity of demand and supply and the principle of opportunity costs and losses. Otherwise, it is too much focussed on a nonexistent state of equilibrium for dynamic competitive purposes and assumes a pattern of human perceptions at complete variance with what both psychological study and merchant experience have discovered. The major contribution of management science is competitive bidding theory., discussed later.

The exclusive focus on the monetary aspect of price severely limits the usefulness of both legal and economic theory. Money

72

FIGURE 4-1.   The Interrelationship of Various Approaches to
Pricing and to Practical Pricing Decisions

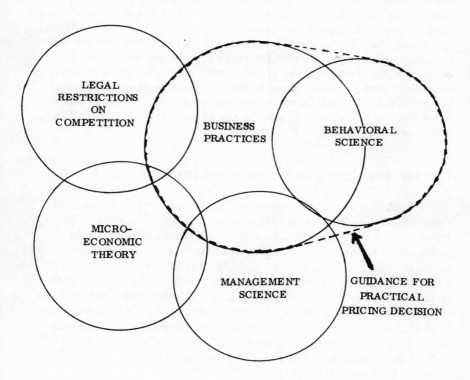

price is only one of eight interdependent purchase-inhibiting factors in the buying situation, and frequently not the decisive factor. A workable marketing strategy must take full account of the other seven avoidance factors built into the offering: time and place availability costs, risk costs, time expenditure costs, search effort costs, learning costs, and design compromise costs. The combination must be planned in terms of the ways customers perceive value and react to stimulus differences of any kind.

Both experience and behavioral science research have demonstrated that customer value perception and expectations are structured in many ways: There are clearly established noticeable difference thresholds, customers expect price lining and price slotting, they impute both quality level and the appropriate use system from the price, they see price differences in reverse under certain conditions, make judgments about correct cost-price relationships, obviously approach a buying decision with fair price reference points in mind, react to some prices in the assortments they purchase in terms of the aura cast by other prices in the assortment, and react differently to what seems to be the same price when quoted in a different manner.

PRICING THEORIES AND BUSINESS STRATEGY DECISION

Exchange and its necessary concomitant of price is such an integral part of civilization that pricing is a major subject of study from at least four disciplinary directions: those of the law, of equilibrium economics, of behavioral sciences, and of management science. Quite independently, a whole body of business structures and practices have grown up around the problem of pricing. There is some overlap between the four analytical approaches and between them and the rules of thumb of business practice, but also much in each that either is not taken account of in the others or is irrelevant. The Venn diagram in Figure 4-1 attempts to depict the nature of these relationships and their place in our discussion of developing business strategy.

As this diagram indicates, both legal and micro-economic theories contain much which gives little help in the formulation of competitive strategy. Whole libraries have been written on the legal aspects of pricing. But the law's approach is basically negative and covers a few limited aspects. It tells what cannot be done under a few formal aspects of pricing but gives no positive guidance at all. Even the negative side is very nebulous at points. Equilibrium economics contributes the two valuable concepts of elasticity of demand and of supply, and the principle of opportunity costs and losses. Beyond the bare bones of these concepts, however, the superstructure of traditional micro-economic theory is too exclusively concerned with equilibrium, whereas business must plan for dynamic innovative competition. In human behavior, just as in the physical world, the forces for equilibrium under static conditions are not the same as those for dynamic equilibrium. A bicycle cannot stand upright at rest but takes little skill to keep upright while in motion. The central part product differentiation must play in viable competition quite reverses the role of price and product in the strategy decision. Whereas the economist sees the product as a given and price as the variable, the businessman must see value perception (price offered) as the given and product as the only variable open to his choice. Additionally, the lengthy time lags between design and initial investment and later sales require product costs to be engineered to an estimated price.

The most important contribution of management science is a technique for optimizing returns in a competitive bidding situation--competitive bidding strategy.

By contrast, everything behavioral sciences can tell us relevant to price, value and product perception, and about approach and avoidance reactions in general, is of direct importance to business planning. Since business practice itself arises partly from a distillation of experience with human behavior and since accustomed business practices build expectations independently, we must take independent account of such practices and experience. While the negative aspects of legal limitations are far from unimportant to the planner, discussion of their intricacies would take more attention than is possible in a work like this, and is of no positive help.

By contrast, the correct economic formulation of the concepts of elasticity of demand and supply and the principle of cost measurement embedded in the concept of opportunity costs and losses are basic to all market planning.

THE ECONOMIC CONCEPT OF ELASTICITY AND THE PRINCIPLE OF COST MEASUREMENT

Probably the single most important unqualified contribution of economics to decision is a cost measurement principle--the concept of alternate opportunity cost and opportunity losses. Under this concept, decision costs must always be reckoned as the difference between the estimated cost of a proposed action and the cost if the next best alternative had been chosen instead. Similarly, opportunity losses are those profits that would have been made under the best alternative course but were foregone because the course was not taken.

In actuality, of course, many of us make personal decisions

on such a basis all of the time. When deciding whether to drive our automobile on a trip rather than fly, for example, we usually tend to compare only the extra money we will spend on gasoline with the cost of the air fare, and do not include other real costs of automobile ownership which remain the same whether we use the car for the trip or not: the license cost, tires, and the greatest cost of all--depreciation. These costs will be incurred regardless of whether we take the car along or not, whereas either the air ticket cost or the gasoline costs will result directly from the decision. If we have no choice but to make the trip in some manner, only the difference between the air fare and the fuel cost is attributable to opportunity cost, since that was the only cost we could avoid. It is the only cost relevant to the decision as to mode of travel, to the extent that money cost is the major consideration.

This principle of opportunity cost is central to all business decision and basic to management science tools. Obviously, the kinds of costs which result from this kind of calculation will be quite different from the kinds of costs shown on the accounting records. Opportunity costs may be either greater or less than the books of account would reveal, and opportunity losses seldom enter the accountant's journals. Planning on any other basis of cost measurement, however, will result in real losses which will show up on those books in some manner.

Similarly, rational price planning must take account of the exacting economic formulation of elasticity of supply and demand. Again, these concepts seem to resemble a common-sense observation that the higher the price, the more abundant the supply of a product is likely to be, given time to bring new production facilities into being, and the lower the price, the more of a product that will be purchased. However, the correct economic definition of elasticity goes beyond this almost uselessly vague popular formulation to clothe the concept with a necessary quantitative precision of extreme importance for decision guidance. To the economist, elasticity is a quantitative ratio--the ratio, at each point on the demand distribution, of the incremental quantity which will be sold because of an incremental change in price, and similarly for supply.

This quantitative aspect of the economic formulation is what makes it a useful tool of decision. Whereas the popular concept tends to indicate that a price cut is good under all circumstances, the economic quantification makes it clear that there are circumstances under which a price raise will be more profitable. These are the circumstances when the demand is relatively inelastic-- when conditions are such the gain in sales volume is less than proportionate to the size of a price cut. When the gain is more than proportionate, then a lower price would be more profitable.

Unfortunately, once we go beyond this basic formulation

of the concept to the refinements with which it is treated in equilibrium economics, we find that the theoretician is using too simplistic a set of assumptions as to the nature of competition and as to
the operation of value difference perception. One minor result of
this error is to focus on the wrong value figure--that of price instead of the apparent prospective profit margin. This could be
taken care of by using a derivative ratio: the profit margin/quantity
sold ratio instead of the price/quantity figure. More seriously, the
theory assumes a psychologically incorrect competitive situation:
that the items offered by two competitors can be actually and perceivably identical in a viable market, that demand is also homo-
geneous and unsegmented (that the offering everyone desires and
is purchasing is the same physical item), and that human perception
is a continuous function (that is, that buyers will respond to any
price change, however minute).

As already indicated in the discussion of product, markets
are inherently segmented and thus successive increments of buyers
will be searching for different products. Sellers who attempt to
compete by bringing perceivably identical offerings onto the market
will fail because the satisfaction drives of those attracted by the
initial offering are already appeased and later identical offerings
will fail to attract interest and attention. Success in market entry
therefore depends on adding a differentiated supply at a different
level of perceived value, not in simple price competition. For this
reason, a latecomer to the market, coming in with a lower price,
must offer also a product with different, not unusually less costly,
features. He must introduce a low-end product, not a low-priced
one. New entrants may, indeed, succeed with differentiations
which are more costly than that of the original entrant. When Detroit first started worrying about the foreign cars and brought out
its 1960 compacts, for example, the initial entry by General Motors--
its Corvair--did poorly until it introduced a deluxe version, at
higher prices and with sporty features. Thus the inescapable fact
of marked segmentation and the corollary of necessary product differentiation would alone vitiate the value of the kind of smooth supply and demand curves so popular in the classroom.

An even more important reason why sellers have never found
theoretical supply and demand curves useful lies in the observed
fact, thoroughly proved by psychological experimentation, that perception is a discontinuous function--or, in plain words, that perception of all kinds, including that of value, is subject to discrimi-
natory thresholds, to the phenomenon of the just noticeable difference, one which is far from minute. This means that some sizes
of price change result in no change whatever in demand, while
slightly larger ones trigger a major change.

For all of these reasons, the business strategist operating in the dynamic world of differentiated competition must leave the micro-economist to his games and pay close attention instead to what we know and can learn about actual consumer behavior. In so doing, the business strategist must use a much broader definition of price than does the economist--must go beyond the mere monetary quotation to take into account the totality of purchase-inhibiting attributes of every offering. Furthermore, he must recognize that most offerings involve a chain of offering assortments and of multiple transactions, and the pricing decision must take both the assortments and the multiplicity of transactions into account.

THE NATURE AND THE COMPLEXITIES OF THE PRICING DECISION

The class of phenomena sometimes oversimplified as a simple single pricing decision really comprises a squirming and quite divergent can of long range decisions, short range tactics, of service-buying decisions, market life cycle adjustments, of temporary tactical maneuvers, and of the poker of competitive bidding. Moreover, once an organization commits itself to development and production of a given merchandise mix and of a particular quality-level value, establishing its unique niche in the market, it can shift that position with only the utmost difficulty. The basic market niche and the price mix lock it into a specific segment of clientele, whether the seller be a manufacturer or a merchant. A change in basic pricing strategy can only succeed by changing the market segment served, and this must overcome habitual perceptions of the seller by buyers previously uninterested in his offerings.

Such a change in established expectations is an almost insuperable task, since it must overcome the barriers of both selective attention and mental habituation. Many merchants discovered this in the 1950's, when those who had built their merchandising mix to appeal to the working class found that the blue-collar worker was becoming a diminishing breed, being replaced by a rising lower middle class segment with quite different tastes and standards of consumption. Attempts to "upgrade" their offerings to meet the needs of these new segments were largely unsuccessful in attracting store traffic from the new target groups. In one instance, when the author moved to a new and unfamiliar city, he was told that his wife could find the best dress buys of the kinds she liked at the end of the month clearance sales of just such a store. This department store had begun to add middle-class dress design selections to their apparel lines, but the latter never came in to shop for them, and the blue-collar housewives did not find them attractive. Moreover, seldom is it easy or even possible to find a suitable niche in an

FIGURE 4-2. The Complex of Considerations Involved in the Pricing Decision

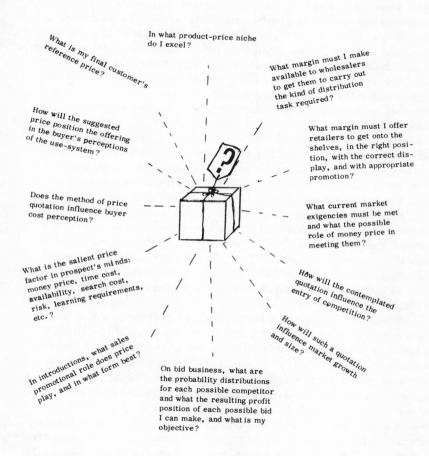

What is my final customer's reference price?

In what product-price niche do I excel?

What margin must I make available to wholesalers to get them to carry out the kind of distribution task required?

How will the suggested price position the offering in the buyer's perceptions of the use-system?

What margin must I offer retailers to get onto the shelves, in the right position, with the correct display, and with appropriate promotion?

Does the method of price quotation influence buyer cost perception?

What current market exigencies must be met and what the possible role of money price in meeting them?

What is the salient price factor in prospect's minds: money price, time cost, availability, search cost, risk, learning requirements, etc.?

How will the contemplated quotation influence the entry of competition?

How will such a quotation influence market growth and size?

In introductions, what sales promotional role does price play, and in what form best?

On bid business, what are the probability distributions for each possible competitor and what the resulting profit position of each possible bid I can make, and what is my objective?

already established market not already fairly well occupied by other sellers. If the latter are satisfying their customers fairly well, the newcomer starts out at a disadvantage on the experience curve, not only in the matter of costs, but also in relation to his feel of the market and what this means in terms of giving a good fit to the needs of his prospects.

The only merchants who proved able to upgrade in this manner were chains, and then primarily by opening new units in new areas where they were previously unknown. Since the prospective customers had no established habitual perceptions of their merchandise lines, they were free to develop a new niche in such locations, and the new units, since they were in new markets, suffered no experience disadvantage vis-a-vis competitors.

The price quoted by a manufacturer or other early element in the distribution chain also involves a decision as to distribution discounts or margins to be available to those sellers intermediate between the quotation maker and the final buyer, whose value perception must be the central focus of all pricing decisions. This distribution margin decision may be explicitly stated or may be implicit in a factory price, for example, based on an estimate of the probable final selling price. In either case, the margin provided for is a purchase price--an offer of money for necessary distribution services which complete the satisfaction bundle for the ultimate buyer. Both the final price envisioned and the margins allowed must be adjusted to market realities and changing perceptions of value as the product life cycle advances. As soon as an introduction meets competition, the seller will have to utilize many kinds of temporary pricing tactics to meet short-run competitive contingencies.

Whenever the seller faces a market situation in which his price offer is a competitive bid and the product specifications set by the buyer, and thus are undifferentiated, he has a strategic decision to make as to his objectives. These go well beyond the objective of profit on the particular transaction. The long-range effect of the quotation on market opportunities must always be a consideration.

Except in a competitive bidding situation, the seller is nearly always pricing an interdependent line or merchandise mix, and his concern is not with the margin on any one item, but with the overall result.

Manifestly, no single theory could cover all of these practical facets of pricing, even were the monetary price the only or even the major perceived purchase-inhibiting factor in the situation. However, no significant number of buyers reacts to money price alone. They consider the totality of several kinds of avoidance attributes-- of a combination of all the prices involved, of which monetary price

80

is only one element, and not always the controlling one. Moreover, all buyers relate price to product values as they perceive them, and discount them to the extent of the perceived risks of quality and dependability of future supply.

THE MULTIPLE DIMENSIONS OF PERCEIVED PRICE

Both economists and lawyers tend to recognize that a Chevrolet in Detroit is worth less to a New Orleans resident than the same car in New Orleans, to concede that a tire in the store, ready for immediate installation, is worth more than the same tire available only later through mail order. The economist also recognizes time and place utilities as product attributes. But since anything less than here and now is negative in value, they are really sales inhibitors, not positive utilities. The psychologist would label them as avoidance attributes in an offering.

Unfortunately, both economists and attorneys are loathe to recognize as different products the gasoline sold by an independent service station under its own label and the physically and chemically identical fuel sold out of pumps under the sign of Standard Oil of Indiana. Nevertheless, the customer undeniably treats the two as being two different offerings, making it necessary to sell the unrecognized brand for 2¢ to 3¢ less per gallon than the recognized brand, and even then only a minor segment of the market will purchase. The buyer perceives some risk that the unknown brand may not yield the performance he has come to expect from the recognized brand.

Time, place and risk are only three of the non-monetary inhibitors to the desire to purchase and possess an otherwise desired offering. There are at least four other kinds of avoidance attributes: time cost of use, search effort, learning costs, and design compromise costs. All cause the buyer to hold back from acquisition attempts to some degree. In determining price policy, business strategy planning must consider them as an interdependent totality.

Money cost is obviously one important avoidance characteristic of any offering. The buyer's supply of this useful commodity is always limited relative to his totality of desires and this limit forces him to choose which desires will be fulfilled, and to what extent. Time costs, however, are often more important than the monetary price. The buyer must allocate his available hours as carefully as his monetary resources.

In today's relative affluence, the time available to the buyer is more inelastic than monetary income. Many buyers can find ways to augment their monetary resources to some appreciable degree, if forced to. No one has yet found a way to add one milli-second to the 24 hours in the day. Consequently, many buyers place a stiff premium value on any offering perceived as costing less time than its substitute. One striking example has been the history of commuter traffic over the last two generations. When-ever and wherever the private automobile has promised a significant time advantage over public transit, even at a multiple of the cost, public transit has lost out. Whenever public transit has been able to deliver on a promise to substantially better the transit time of the private automobile, it has prospered, even when the fare was higher than incremental automobile cost. In such mixed transit situation cities as Chicago, bus lines which are caught in the same traffic jams as the private automobiles have continually lost traffic, while subway and commuter rail lines moving over privileged rights of way on convenient schedules have been able to hold or even gain business.

The importance of the time cost to the working housewife is well attested by the spectacular growth of sales of time-conserving convenience foods in recent decades. Frequently, their quality is not only not better than that of "scratch ingredient" dishes for which they substitute, but noticeably inferior, and their money cost is often very substantially higher. A parallel phenomenon has been the steady decline in the sale of fresh produce in the supermarkets, with the processed products displacing them even at the peak of their most delectable season.

Testimony to the price importance of search costs is the large number of goods we classify as "convenience goods"--goods for which a customer will freely substitute a different brand than his preferred one if the latter is not in stock at the place of purchase. Search effort is an unavoidable element of cost paid for any offering in our complex industrial society, and one which much advertising money is spent to offset. As with the money price, the only decision concerns how much search effort we can reasonably charge, not whether or not to do so. Search effort was not an important com-ponent of price for such offerings as were part of the normal con-sumption systems of buyers in earlier static rural societies. The buyer was usually thoroughly familiar with the identity and place of availability of the limited selections of goods and services he ex-pected to buy. Today, he often may not be sure which of the bun-dles of satisfactions he desires are available, or where. And as anybody who has ever changed localities can testify, even if he knows what it is, and that it is to be found, for instance, in the local supermarket in his new community, he may have to spend consider-able time and effort discovering the specific self-service counter on which the desired item rests.

Asking the customer to spend some search effort is unavoidable, but it can be minimized by making supplies available in as many and as diverse outlets and as close to the prospect as possible. Alternatively, search effort is minimized when intense promotional communications inform the customer of the availability of the satisfactions which he desires, and where they can be obtained. Information is thus a substitute for more numerous places of sale.

Any purchase situation involves some degree of risk that the desired satisfactions will not result even after the other prices are paid. The buyer looks for information clues which help him evaluate this risk, help him determine whether the promises of fulfillment the product makes are likely to be kept. From past experience, he knows that such promises are not completely certain of fulfillment. He will therefore discount the other prices by the degree of perceived risk in the purchase. To compare the money, time, place and search effort prices, we must know, in addition, what the perceived discount rate to be applied is. The experience of market furnishes many examples of such risk discounts: cut-rate gasoline, private brand retail items, the reluctance to substitute the new for the familiar, etc.

Another risk involved in many purchases is the risk of lack of future supply when desired. Most of our purchases either explicitly or implicitly are part of a desired series of similar purchases of indefinite duration. We all want "our daily bread", not just today's bread; a continuous supply of wholesome water, not just a safe drink and warm bath today. When we buy an automobile, we want assurance that when service is interrupted by a mechanical breakdown, it will be restored with the least possible interruption and cost.

The risk of continuity of supply is especially important to the industrial buyer. He does not wish to have to close down a multi-million-dollar assembly operation because a shipment of 10¢ screws got delayed or cut off. Indeed, dependability of the source of supply is fully as important to such a purchaser as is assurance that the supply itself meets a specific set of specifications. Such buyers will limit purchases to sources of supply which experience has proved do furnish offerings of known dependable content and assurance of steady adequate supply. New competitors seeking entrance into markets in which the perceived risk of supply interruption is rated as expensive must first find buyers to whom the risk is of less importance than to most buyers and must offer substantial compensating values. European sports cars and small sedans were first imported into the United States and sold in very small numbers to aficionados who put a very high premium on the sensitivity of their handling characteristics and were willing to pay a high price in probable out-of-service interruptions to get these attributes.

Acceptance of a specific design compromise is another price

83

the buyer regularly must pay. The composition and proportioning of the desire-sets of individual prospects vary so widely from one individual to another that only universal custom manufacture can even come close to giving each customer a bundle of satisfactions giving the best possible fit to the buyer's desire-set. Even a product made to order, however, involves some degree of compromise between incompatible desire elements in any given desire-set. Thus even the buyer of the made-to-order design has to sacrifice part of the fulfillment of some desires to attain satiation of other desire elements which, at the moment, are higher in the hierarchy of his desire-set.

Custom design is itself, of course, economically impractical for any large segment of the market, or even for much of the consumption total of the wealthy elite. Only some degree of standardized mass production can hope to deliver the optimum standard of living. But the greater the degree of standardization in the offerings, the larger the proportion of prospects who must forego substantial elements in their desire-sets and the larger the number of wished-for attributes they will not receive.

This is why the production economies of a single-model design must sooner or later give ground in the market to the consumption economies of a selection from a wide choice of models. In the early period of a developing automobile market, Henry Ford I could enforce an option of "any color as long as it is black". His grandson could start to build the market share lost through too-long adherence to this policy only by offering several distinct lines and any combination of 70 different options within the line. The more the enforced design compromise in the set of offerings, the less the money price which can be obtained for the same volume of production.

Learning-need price as an inhibitor of new offerings has already been discussed.

Correct market pricing strategy must take account of all of these multi-dimensional aspects of product avoidance (of price) in the offering. Not only are time, place, search effort, risk, loyalty, learning, and design compromise as much part of the perceived price as is the money asked for, but all eight aspects are viewed as a single whole by the customer and each is partly substitutable for others in the price-mix. One seller may reduce the place and search effort costs by developing an intensive distribution network, making the offering as widely available as the market system permits. Another may find it necessary to depend on the intense selling effort stimulated by selective distribution but compensate for the limited place availability through advertising which reduces the search effort otherwise imposed. The advertiser who lowers perceived risk through building a record for dependable brand quality

FIGURE 4-3.   The 8 Major Components of
             Buyer Perception of the Price
             of Acquisition

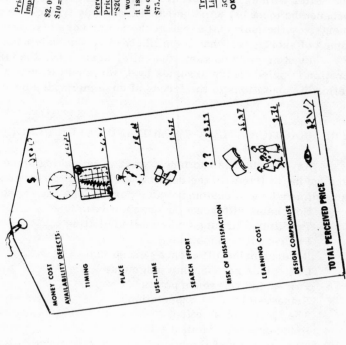

FIGURE 4-4.   The 8 Principal Parameters of Buyer
             Perception of Value

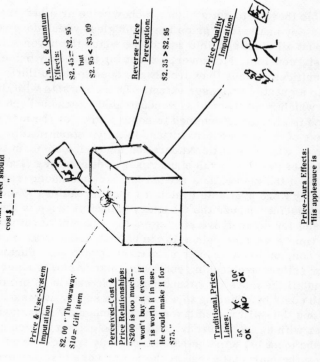

85

will be able thereby to get a higher money price or other preference of value. Any analysis of price is meaningless which does not take into account all eight possible sacrifices which the buyer will, indeed <u>must</u>, consider. Moreover, except for the money price, the other sacrifices he must pay are always open to the seller's discretion to a greater or lesser extent. This contrasts with the money price on which most theory has concentrated, because such monetary price is always determined to some degree by the market and in the case of standard commodities, is fully determined by market conditions. Exercise of this discretion must also conform to the way customers perceive value and react to differences of any kind.

Even if the kind of data needed for decision under traditional price theory were available (which it never is) sellers would still not find it useful because the monetary aspect of price is the one least useful for competitive strategy. Any attempt to cut price can offer no time advantage, since it can be matched almost immediately and thus can, by itself, confer no market advantage. Furthermore, all major sellers are seeking continuing markets over a period of time, and all the more important buyers are seeking a minimization of search costs by adhering to a continuous supply at reasonable prices and thus will not shift for some temporary advantage. Thus the seller with an intermittent supply is the primary price cutter, because he must be. And he can attract only fringe market segments, or the marginal needs of the major core markets except in times of shortages, when he is likely to be the high price seller.

Even more important, the seller seldom has the kind of discretion in price choice assumed by traditional theory. He must tailor his quotations to the forces of customer value perception.

THE PRACTICALITIES OF PRICE AND VALUE PERCEPTION

Anyone who has had much experience making price decisions, and having to live with the results, has learned to recognize at least nine dimensions of customer value perceptions and expectations:
Noticeable difference or quantum reactions
Traditional pricing or price-line slotting
Price-quality imputation
Reverse price-difference perception
Cost-price relationship judgments
Fair-price reference points
Price-use bracket expectations
The "price aura" effect
Price quotation method effects
The principle of the <u>just noticeable difference</u> reaction so familiar to the psychologist extends to the perception of price differ-

ences as well. The smoothly continuous supply and demand curves
we find useful for elementary classroom discussion do not exist in
the trade. The human reaction to continuously changing levels of
any stimulus is discontinuous. Only differences greater than some
specific percentage threshold value are perceived as different. The
subject of a psychological experiment who is asked to judge the difference between two piles of paper, one of 500 pages and one of 499
cannot do so without an actual count, nor can he tell the difference
between 500 and 490. Most subjects will require a difference of
nearly 10 percent before a difference becomes perceptible to the
subject. The reaction is the same whether the stimulus is visual,
tactile, or aural. Training in expert discrimination can lower the
threshold, but cannot abolish it. Similarly with price, the subject
may be able to count the difference between $4. 98 and $4. 95, but
most buyers will perceive no real difference, nor indeed between
$4. 75 and $4. 95.

In economic life, such noticeable difference effects seem to
revolve around round-number quantum points. Supermarket opera-
tors, for example, have found that a price just under $1. 00 will
move far more quantity than one just over the $1. 00 quotation, but
a price of 89¢ may sell no more than a quotation of 98¢. The author
himself has witnessed a number of real-life demonstrations of this
principle. In one case, successive price changes from $2. 45, $2.65,
$2. 85, and $2. 95 produced no visible effect on volume of sales of
the same item in the same stores, but a subsequent raise to $3. 09
(still a bargain in alternate opportunity terms) caused sales to cease
abruptly.

Even in the supposedly coldly rational procurement of industrial raw materials, research carried out by a colleague has disclosed that buyers of tinplate perceive a price difference of $ .50
per base box real, but a difference of 5¢ a box as a "chisel"--that
is, as not significant, or worth switching sources to profit by it.

This j. n. d. phenomenon is a proportional matter, both in the
psychological laboratory and in the marketplace. A difference of
50¢ is probably noticeable at the $5. 00 level, but only $5 might be
so at the $50. 00 level. When dealing with money values of the order
involved in the purchase of a $2500 automobile, the industry seems
to have found that a noticeable difference is of the approximate order
of $200.

Obviously, nearly all buyers can see, cognitively, that $2. 95
and $2. 98 are not the same figure, but they seldom act as though
they perceive a discriminable difference between the two. Likewise
with two leading brands of such a low-differential product as general
purpose household detergents, for example, many buyers may feel
that one is to be preferred to the other so long as they are not selling
at a different price. But experience has shown that so few buyers

perceive any sufficiently noticeable value difference that no one brand can sustain any persistent difference in price.

With products such as common detergents, in which the perceived differentiation is perceived as minimal, just as with true commodities, the price administrator has no real price discretion. He must attempt to sell at the same uniform price level as competing brands. Any success he has in developing any perception of quality difference must be reflected in a better market share, not in the price. Such a better market share can itself be profitable, of course, by minimizing his production or sales costs, or both. Uniformity of price quotations in these and other cases of standardized or near-standardized commodities is no evidence of collusion of any degree--merely a reflection of buyer perceptions of value.

Experience with the j.n.d. effect may underlie the tendency of merchants to carry goods in clearly defined, widely separated price lines. Whatever the origin of this practice, it has become such an integral part of buyer expectations as to constitute a special reaction of its own kind.

Traditional pricing and price lining involve the seller in the need to conform to a uniformity of a different kind--one related much more to habitual consumer expectations than to the actions of competitors. Consumers approach the purchase act expecting to pay a very specific price per unit of purchase and ignore offerings at any other specific price. The most extreme example is that of the standard 5-stick package of chewing gum. From well before the turn of the 20th century until 1970, the price held constant at 5¢. Neither the size of the package nor its contents changed except for a small volume of carton sales and of very large packages at lesser prices. When costs finally forced a price increase, the jump had to be to 10¢ for a 7 or 8 stick pack.

Other forms of popular confectionery have also had to adhere to traditional prices per purchase unit, and to specific price-line slots. A candy bar of whatever design has consistently had to sell at either 5¢, 10¢ or 15¢ and at no point in between. In this case, however, the actual size of the bar has been allowed to fluctuate with ingredient costs, and thus the price per unit of weight can fluctuate, but only in terms of bars conforming to traditional price slots.

Price lining is an omnipresent phenomenon in the merchandising of most if not all mass-produced consumer items in which a wide range of perceived quality is possible and desired. By price lining is meant the selling of somewhat similar products in the same category at widely separated, sharply defined specific price quotations, each price line point representing a sharply defined, perceivably different quality level. It is most obvious in such goods as clothing, but can be found in everything from fruit preserves on the supermarket shelf to automobiles. A corollary of this practice

FIGURE 4-5. Price-Demand Patterns: As Taught in the Traditional Economics Classroom, <u>versus</u> Experience
in the Actual Marketplace

A. THE PRICE-DEMAND PATTERN AS
TAUGHT IN THE ECONOMICS CLASSROOM
Quantity demanded and the elasticity of demand are presented as continuous functions
of price. That is, it is assumed that the
slightest shift in price will produce a corresponding shift in the quantity sold, and
always in reverse relationship, with no
definite limits on the relationship.

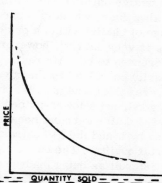

B, C & D. PRICE-DEMAND PATTERNS AS
THEY ARE FOUND IN THE MARKETPLACE

B. The Most Common: a Typical Result of the
j. n. d. and Reference Point Phenomena. (When
sales are confined to established use-systems)

Demand is a discontinuous quantum function of
price, and is characteristically lower both below
and above some reference point.

PRICE

QUANTITY SOLD

C. The Completely Inelastic Demand.

Up to some specific quantity limit,
whatever quantity is available can be
disposed of at a single specific price,
and none will sell above
that price. Above the limit,
none can be sold at any
price.

PRICE

QUANTITY

D. The Use-System Elasticity Pattern.
Within a single set of related use-
systems, demand is relatively
inelastic, but a price below
some specific critical
point uncovers
new and larger
markets, also
relatively in-
elastic.

PRICE

QUANTITY

89

is that it usually proves to be very difficult to find buyers for products priced in between the standard price line points, as one men's
suit maker discovered when he designed a suit to sell at a price
above the lower quality lines, but below the next level above. Although it was probably, objectively, the best buy in the store, few
buyers would consider it.

Generally speaking, quality differences between lines have a
substantive physical basis for the perception of difference, although
not always one which is immediately apparent to the untrained buyer.
Range of quality within a price line in the same outlet or in different
ones is very narrow, however. In any case, buyers perceive the
differences to be quite real. A man's suit priced at $85 is not nec-
essarily perceived by the buyer as the full equivalent of the $125
one, even though he may prefer the lower priced one. It is a lower-
end good, not a lower-priced one. He may nevertheless purchase
the $85 dollar garment because he feels his need is adequately ful-
filled by it and the $40 extra does not, for him, justify the incre-
mental quality. The buyer of the $125 suit, by contrast, perceives
the $85 suit as being inadequate to yield the full satisfaction bundle
he seeks, and the $40 difference as a bearable sacrifice relative to
the extra satisfactions of fit, tailoring and design he can get for
them. Both buyers, moreover, have become so habituated to finding
what they desire relative to price, that neither is likely to consider
even shopping at a different price level. Neither investigates clothes
prices at a level lower than he customarily buys because observation, experience or other basis for judgment has taught him that the
price sacrifice to which he is accustomed is needed to obtain a
corresponding level of desire fulfillment. Neither investigates a
line at a higher price because the habitual level has been satisfying.
During periods of generally upward-trending prices, of course, they
have to learn to shift the level of the price tag they associate with
the price line, but they can identify this level in terms of the brand
tag or the shop and its lines.

Price-line judgments probably tend to become somewhat cir-
cular, of course. Having learned to find the expected bundle of satisfactions at a given price level, the buyer perceives the price itself as a partial cue to expect a given level of quality. Economic
theoreticians have often noted a seeming anomaly in the prices of
such offerings as expensive perfumes--an upward-sloping demand
curve, with the demand increasing with price. A good perfume will
sell better at $50 per ounce than at a feasible $5.

The combined results of the j. n. d. effect and of habitual price
reference points lead to price-demand patterns at considerable variance from those typically taught in economics classrooms. (See
Figure 4-5.) The classroom chart leads the user to assume that
any price change, however small, will result in a corresponding

change in the quantity sold. By contrast, the j.n.d. phenomenon insures that only very substantial differences in price can result in any demand shift that such demand shifts will be by quite substantial increments.

Moreover, demand can be sacrificed by quoting lower prices as well as those higher than the buyer's reference point, so long as the market remains confined to established use-systems.

True elasticity results when the offering's reduced price taps either new markets or new use-systems, as in Figure 4-5D. An excellent historical example was the introduction of the Model T Ford in 1908. As Figure 5-4 in the next chapter shows, the market was beginning to level off at the time, due to the concentration of most makers on their higher priced lines. The introduction of a product equal in quality to most items selling for twice the Ford price tapped an entirely new market that set the automobile industry on the first of a series of pyramidal growth steps. Likewise, the aluminum industry was moved out of the pots and pans stage after World War II when prices were cut substantially to stimulate use of the war-expanded facilities. For the first time, volume structural markets which had been using only steel began to find aluminum a better value, as did also the electrical conductor market.

A less grandiose but equally pertinent example was the experience of the manufacturer of a minor fisherman's specialty product-- a trolling speedometer. A market test of dealers indicated a highly discontinuous demand curve remarkably similar to Figure 4-5D, with an extreme discontinuity at a retail price of about $5.00 (a typical round-number effect). A retail selling price of $4.95--just below this major break-point--did indeed prove to be the point of maximum profit. Any price higher than $5.00 apparently caused the offering to be viewed as needing too much consideration before purchase and restricted the market too severely. At just under $5.00, it was in the class with just another fishing lure, and the volume at $4.95 yielded a substantial profit margin, not available at a lower level.

The completely inelastic curve of Figure 4-5C may be true of a wide range of market specialty offerings which fit into a narrowly limited set of use-systems for a restricted number of buyers. One clear known example was that of a minor vegetable item purchased by a single ethnic group in a relatively localized market. Experience showed that a single price of about $3.00 per cwt. could be had for any daily quantity up to a very specific limit. Any quantity beyond that limit could find no market at any price.

This product, like many market specialties, was very profitable for those first in the market, but the restricted nature of that market inhibited the entrance of any important competition. This is one reason market specialties are, for their original introducers, often extremely valuable introductions, when handled with a clear understanding of the limited character of their reception. A great many industrial specialties with a derived demand probably fit this same price pattern. One company, for example, has continued prosperous year after year solely because it is the major producer of air-activated hand power tools. Although it has some peripheral competition, its long experience lead has maintained market dominance, and the narrow breadth of the market has had no attraction for possible large aggressive entrants. Outside this area, its performance has been mediocre or worse. Attempts to gain a market for their own brand of electrically-powered counter parts of their air tools have been largely unprofitable. This latter market is to large to escape the interest of better equipped and more experienced firms.

J. n. d. , price lining, and price reference points all clearly strait-jacket price decision, so that it is little wonder that businessmen find the pricing decision much less important than economist are wont to view it. Indeed, major discretion in pricing is largely concerned with introductory prices. At the moment of introduction, the initial quotation is open to some choice, and the initial price quoted can affect the perception of the offering itself.

IMPUTATION OF QUALITY FROM PRICE

The well-known perfume commands a premium price because of the tendency of buyers to impute quality from price when unable to judge relative performance directly. Such is, of course, the case for a substantial proportion of all the satisfaction bundles bought by almost any of us, and for a large proportion of the buyers of almost any complex product (including perfumes, whose smell is a necessary, but sometimes minor, part of a rather complicated bag of directly emotional satisfaction elements).

Experiments confirm the common observation that buyers really do tend to impute quality from price (Tull, et al. 1964; McDonnel, 1968). Indeed, it is clear that an ill-considered price cut can sometimes curtail demand rather than, as assumed in economic theory, promote it. A dramatic historical example was the damage done to the prestige of the now defunct Packard automobile, once a top-status brand, by the introduction in the 1930's of a lower-end model under the same nameplate. The brand lost its prestige market niche and never recovered.

The tendency to impute quality from price is an especially important consideration when introducing well-differentiated new items to the market. Too low an initial offering price can cause buyers to perceive the offering as being of inferior quality.

92

Undoubtedly, the buyer's tendency to impute quality from price comes partly from solid experience with the commonly inferior quality of low-end offerings. There may also be some inherent biological basis for it, if we may reason from the highly suggestive results of animal experimentation. It was found that rats chose food for which they had to work in preference to identical food when it was made freely available, even when first conditioned to receiving the handout. They returned to the free food only when the price became clearly exorbitant--ten presses of the lever for each pellet, instead of one or two (Carter and Berkowitz, 1970). Clearly, even rats have some kind of fair price reference point and are suspicious of goods which are perceived as too cheap, as well as those for which the price is perceived as too high! (We might speculate that the reaction has some survival value.)

Of course, it is not always true that all of the potential buyers for any product are unable to discriminate product quality from an objective standpoint. Since the knowledgeable and discriminating buyer tends also to be the tastemaker, the quality must really be there in some sense, and must, indeed be there in all aspects of the marketing mix. The Cadillac, Imperial, or Lincoln Continental has to be as fine a mechanism as the American mass-production line can build, and the service network must be flawless. The expensive perfume must be wrapped in an obviously well-designed package, with just the right muted shade of taste evident in all of the externals, and the perfume blend itself must be quality. Neither the odor nor the advertising can be blatant in tone, and the retail outlet in which it is sold must obviously cater to those with discriminating taste as well as lots of spending power. The best tailored mink coat would not be perceived as having adequate quality if sold in John's Bargain Store.

Thus the acceptability of price is obviously judged on the basis of associations, not solely on the basis of physical product and the monetary quotation. An important part of those associations is the other products in the assortment being offered by the same seller-- the price-aura effect.

The price-aura effect arises from the universal fact that the customer generally buys an assortment of satisfaction bundles at the same time and place, not a single item. He tends to judge the suitability of the price of one item by his judgment of the prices of other items important to him which are in the assortment purchased.

For every buyer, some of the items in the assortment sought are more salient than others--he pays more attention to their cost and relative quality. For any single customer, the items which are salient will normally be relatively constant, but will vary, even for similar desired assortments, between members of differing market segments. One group of housewives may be more sensitive to the price-quality relationship of the fresh meats in the supermarket, and these will seek out stores which do an especially good job with their meats. If the merchant also stocks reasonably good quality in his other departments at prices which are not completely out of line, they will consider his store the best. Other women are more concerned with the prices of canned goods and staples--they bulk larger in their meal planning. With still others, it may be specialty products and the possibility of a wide selection of cold meats needed for lunches. Each will pay closest attention to the prices and assortments available in that category of items of greatest importance to her. If the prices of the attention-attracting foods seem out of line, or the quality poor relative to the price she thinks appropriate, they will impute a similar out-of-lineness to all of the other prices, whatever the fact. This is why the merchant succeeds only when he tailors his merchandise mix and the accompanying price mix to the tastes and expectations of a specific set of market segments. Each segment buys a somewhat different assortment and discriminates price-quality relationships more finely for different items in that assortment. As the 1966 Food Commission discovered, the result is that there is no definable lowest-priced store, since a minor change in the proportioning and contents of the market basket can reverse relationships.

Other associations besides the assortments can affect buyer perceptions of a seller's pricing. A midwestern store which decided to run color newspaper advertisements discovered that people in their normal target market segment were beginning to feel that the ads were attractive, but the store "expensive". On the other hand, a prestige department store failed in a special bedding promotion because it utilized a blatant advertising format that its customers interpreted to mean that the product was of inferior quality (Martineau, 1957). Emotional expectation-sets can be decisive in the perceptions of value on which consumers judge prices. The figures are judged on the basis of what are considered clues to quality.

Moreover, when appraising the figures themselves, buyers bring to their judgment whole sets of expectations and interpretations which may, in some cases, cause them to perceive a different ordering of values than does the mathematician. Reverse-order perception is an undeniable fact of merchandising experience. As a result of this phenomenon, certain prices are viewed as more attractive by buyers than prices which are objectively lower. A $2.45 price often moves less goods than a $2.95 price, a 24¢ price tag less than a 29¢ tag. Some form of round-number interpretation may be involved. The widespread use of odd-number pricing ($2.98 instead of $3.00, for instance) may lead buyers to acquire some expectation set such that they perceive 29¢ as a 30¢ item, but 24¢ as essentially a 20¢ item. This same phenomenon may explain why a bin of packaged apples can be labelled "3 lbs. for 60¢" and another bin by its side, of identical loose apples, can be priced at 19¢ per pound, without hurting the sale of the packages appreciably, even though the loose apples give the buyer a chance to pick out his own. (In this case, however, we may also be dealing with the distaste many buyers have for simple arithmetic, and the perception-set that the multiple-unit package is generally a bargain.)

Of course, not all of such experiences are clearly due to poor arithmetic or to some kind of reverse-order expectation-set. Some are unquestionably due to a common "fair price" reference reaction (similar to that of the laboratory rats) which soon becomes familiar to any observant seller who works with pricing and its results. In many ways, it seems that the fair price doctrine of medieval economics philosophers had considerable validity in the way many buyers tend to judge prices. A great many buyers seem to approach price quotations with a single reference price in mind as being the correct level. Moreover, some form of social learning seems involved in determining the level of this reference point, since experience indicates that this tends to be the optimum-volume sales point when used. As a consequence, the actual demand-price curves encountered in practice are seldom if ever the smoothly sloping ones we used in the classroom, but often exhibit a very sharp "kink"--a point defining the price at which sales will be greater than at any quotation either above or below it.

This kink may be a specific monetary value, as it appeared to be in the case of a large chain merchandiser which was not satisfied with the volume on a relatively standard hardware item in its stores. A subsequent test in a number of stores indicated that the item appeared much more attractive to customers at $1.09 than at either 89¢ or $1.29. A very academic laboratory test simulation came up with a similar finding. When subjects were told to assume a specific price was the one they "usually paid" for the purchase of a familiar consumer item, they "bought" less at both greater and lesser prices (Tull, Boring and Gonsior, 1964).

At other times, the reference point seems to be, not a single specific monetary quotation, but the price of some item apparently associated with the item quoted, in some manner. Thus the sellers of a new soils texturizing agent found that the proper price seemed to be exactly that of a 50-pound sack of fertilizer, even though the function of the product was quite different, and the package much larger and much lighter in weight. It sold in the same store department.

This fair-price phenomenon seems to involve some imputation of quality from price in some cases. It could also be another reflection of price-line buying. On the other hand, it may at times reflect some kind of judgment as to proper cost-price relationships.

If buyers feel they know something about production costs for an item, they may react according to their judgment as to the propriety of the price in relationship to this cost. They will normally be willing to pay what they feel to be a reasonable mark-up over this cost but will resent any price they consider as exorbitant even though low relative to their own alternative sources of similar satisfactions. One example concerns a time when tractor-buying farmers were paying $200 for power steering options. One seller came out with a tractor design which enabled him to get the result with a simple device which competitors estimated would cost him about $12 to build. His sales department decided that the mechanically expert farmer would be unwilling to pay more for the power device as an option even though the same advantage cost $200 more on competing tractors. Accordingly, the firm decided to make the device standard equipment instead and include the price in the total.

In such matters, it really does not matter whether the judgment concerning the cost-price relationship is correct or not. A large aircraft builder, for example, ran into customer resistance on the cost of a simple-appearing spare part even though their own cost sheets fully justified the price.

The price paid by the buyer enters into the prospect's decision in a very interesting manner in goods purchased largely for gift-giving. No gift-giver likes to be judged as penurious, and there seems to be some kind of social standards as to the proper price to be paid for an acceptable gift. Thus, when a manufacturer of a new household novelty experimented with introductory prices, he found sales much better at $4.95 than at $2.95, even though the latter price would yield a comfortable profit. Some inquiry revealed that the item was most frequently bought as a gift, often from the wife to her husband. A similar situation, indeed, accounts for the height of perfume prices. The more expensive are far more often bought by men as gifts for women than by the women themselves.

Use-oriented price standards are not limited to gift items, of course. The price of a mere accessory item or of anything perceived as a disposable must carry what is currently considered as a modest price. Thus the actual cost of producing a hard-cover book justifies a difference of about $1.50 at retail, but the hard-cover text will almost invariably sell for a much greater differential over the soft-cover one because the soft-cover work is perceived as a disposable item, and if used as a textbook, as largely a supplementary item for which the price should be relatively modest.

At times, the price bracket itself may cause the product to be perceived in a different purchase and consumption system setting. Products selling for more than $5 seem to be viewed as requiring more consideration before purchase and more durability of construction than products priced below $5. Those priced below $5 seem to be perceived as more in the nature of impulse items and disposables, whatever their real satisfaction content. This is especially true if product clues or the product aura seems to coincide with the perception. A paper-cover text, for example, may be added to the course list as a supplement, even for use of just a couple of chapters, and thus may enjoy far broader sales than the same book in hard covers at $5.25. The latter would be adopted only if most of its contents were usable, and students would expect to be able to resell it when through, where they might throw away the soft-cover edition. By the same token, the instructor might hesitate to adopt a $3.25 or $4.95 paperback, however meaty from his point of view, as the backbone of his course because he would perceive it as "too thin", even in relation to a work with less real content.

Logically, all of the above rules of buyer behavior restrict the discretion of the seller rather drastically on the monetary quotation side of the coin. We would then expect that much of industry would thus start from quotation, and build the product (the value) to suit.

ENGINEERING TO A PRICE

Modern industrial production involves long lead times between product design and market release. Put in another way, industrial design builds in costs long before the customer is given a price quotation. Such a lead-time gap would lead to intolerable price chaos if the seller had no reasonably good basis for estimating the price he could expect to receive as much as three years later than he initiates his design.

In fact, of course, the existence of recognized price slots, of established price lines and of fair-price reference points permits just such an estimate. They furnish a target price toward which the product and its cost may be engineered.

Thus the traditional micro-economic approach to the price decision is necessarily reversed. The product is not built first, then a price decided upon. The price line (or price slot) of customer fair-price expectation is set as a target; then the product designed to meet customer value expectations at that level, as well as a cost structure which it is hoped will yield a customary profit. Successful products must be engineered to sell profitably at a target price, not built, then priced. The wise strategist first calculates what markets he can best serve, what satisfactions these markets desire and how salient each desire in the set, then builds the most appropriate design compromise he knows which should sell at the price these segments consider fair. He also must give attention to the expectations of every element in the chain which adds the distribution values to his offering.

Because of these tendencies to position an unfamiliar product value and quality in the light of price, the price-quality level to which new introductions are engineered and priced must be given thoughtful consideration. Until a set of value expectations is established, the price itself is more likely to serve as a cue to value and to the expected use-system than as a stimulus for purchase. No greater pricing mistake can be made than to introduce low-end models of a product requiring some value learning before premium-end models are introduced and established.

The introducers of the first plastic dinnerware made the mistake of engineering quality and price for the low-end market first, putting their offerings into the same price brackets with cheap crockery. They thus positioned their introduction as a cheap substitute for the low end of the market and barred forever the introduction of a quality product which might have appealed to a segment of the buyers of fine china, and certainly of the better qualities of crockery. In the process, they probably sacrificed some substantial share of even the cheap crockery market.

Whether or not the introduction should be engineered and priced initially for the extreme of the premium end will depend on the identity of the core market segment most likely to be waiting for the introduction of the particular kind of satisfaction bundle. If this segment has limited means to acquire the offering, as did the young families most valuing sporty automobiles, then the target price should permit purchase by these, as was done in the case of the pioneer mass sporty car--the Mustang. Note, however, the latter was introduced with options at the high-end price brackets simultaneously--options such as a more powerful engine which added to the sporty values for those who had the means for the purchase. The safe rule is to match the introductory price to a level which matches the value expectations of those seeing the highest value in the intended offering, and who would be early adopters. This is almost never the lowest-end price needed to get the less-interested market fringes later, and will always involve the inclusion of some degree of added value above the minimum basic functional ones in the bundle. Only after the value of the introduction has been positioned by the character and price of the initial offering will a price cut have any meaning.

EFFECT OF QUOTATION METHOD AND IMPACT OF PRICE
TIMING ON PERCEPTION OF COST

All of these perceptual phenomena are complicated further by the tendency to perceive the same price differently according to the method of its quotation and the impact of its timing.

Merchants long ago learned, for example, that considerable segments of the market practice "budgetism" with respect to credit purchases. That is, they regulate such purchases according to the level of the individual periodic payment rather than with regard to total expenditure. Neither interest cost nor possible premium price tag seems to have any significant effect on their purchase decisions. Thus a family which might balk at a straight loan cost of 10 percent per year will think little of the 1 1/2 percent monthly charge for a revolving charge account which they may carry for years. Television programs which require the purchase of a $500 receiver are perceived as "free". An extra fuel expense of possibly $150 or $200 per year due to lack of gasoline economy is painful to the automobile owner who never gives much thought to the much larger depreciation cost of as much as $1000 to $2000 per year. The persistent here-and-now fuel cost gets the attention, without much consideration of the time discount.

Quite clearly, the price side of the marketing strategy decision can never be left to a seat-of-the-pants decision at any stage of the product life cycle. The most careful consideration of the appropriate levels for each kind of price is an obvious prerequisite to good planning, from the moment of conception. Speed of adoption, or even success itself, may depend on the correct estimate.

SUMMARY

1. Since product is value, the pricing decision is an inextricable part of product and product life cycle management.

2. Pricing plays such an important part of the exchange on which civilization operates that price competition and price reaction are the independent concern of the law, of equilibrium economic theory, of management science and of the behavioral sciences. In addition, a complex body of business pricing practice has grown up independent of these disciplines.

3. The legal doctrines of competition restricting the pricing decision are quite intricate but largely negative in terms of guidance for decision and thus are left for separate study.

4. The important contributions of micro-economic theory are limited to the cost measurement principle of alternate opportunity gains and losses and the bare concepts of elasticity of demand and of supply. The quantitative formulations of the elasticity concepts are crucial for correct pricing decision.

5. The theoretical elaborations of micro-economic theory, however, have not proved to be of much help in making practical decisions because of their narrow focus on the single transaction

and on the money price only in that transaction, of a virtual ignoring of the universal necessity of competitive product differentiation, and by an incorrect model of the operation of human perception of value. The behavioral sciences are of especial help to practical decision in precisely these areas.

6. Both business experience and practice and what we know about human behavior indicate that the pricing decision is grossly oversimplified by economic theory and by any exclusive focus on the money price alone. Pricing is not a simple choice of a single figure but a complex of long-range product-mix and market niche decisions, of short-run tactical maneuvers, of allocation of what the consumer pays to a chain of intermediate providers of distribution values, and of the poker of competitive bidding on customer-specified offerings.

7. Money itself is just one, and often not the major, of eight purchase-inhibiting factors in the transaction, of the avoidance attributes in the offering design. Time and place availability can be a price more important in the movement of some kinds of goods. The product's time expenditure requirements for use place more rigid limits on the customer's range of choices than money at times. Search costs can be a major extinguisher of the desire to acquire and much of advertising cost is incurred to reduce this cost for the buyer. Perceived risk of inadequate satisfaction is a major element in creating price differentials between physically identical offerings. Dependability of supply is a price of major importance in industrial purchasing and for major durable consumer goods. The design compromise price is a major market segmenting factor. The character and extent of the learning price which must be paid to get the benefits shapes the speed and character of the initial growth stages of the product life cycle.

8. What we know about the character of perception and other fundamental behavior patterns plus the obvious effect of long-established business practices on buyer expectations reveals that at least a nine-dimensional structure of price and value expectations determines the effect of any price quotation or price change. The important dimensions include: noticeable difference or quantum reactions (the just noticeable difference effect), traditional pricing or price-line slotting, price-quality imputation, reverse price difference perception, cost-price relationship judgments, fair price reference points, price-use bracket expectations, the price aura effect, and price quotation method and timing impact effects.

9. The just noticeable difference (j.n.d.) phenomenon destroys the neat mathematical assumption about price response underlying most micro-economic (and legal) theorizing--the assumption that price response is at least approximately continuous.

10. The imputation of quality from price is a fact of high

importance at the time of the introduction of highly differentiated products. Introductory pricing can shape the product niche for the life of the product cycle, and the wrong kind of price reductions can obliterate the market for any product which has prestige as a major element in value.

11. The price aura effect is a major concern of all product and price mix planning.

12. The existence of expected price lines, of price-line slotting, and of fair-price reference points exactly reverses the relationship of product to price as viewed by the equilibrium economist. This combination of value perception patterns makes possible the setting of target prices at the time of design initiation and the engineering of product to sell at a specific price, for a profit. A dynamic industrial economy with inevitable long design lead times could probably function in no other way.

5

MARKET GROWTH: TRIAL, ACCEPTANCE, AND THE SOCIAL PROCESS OF DIFFUSION

Only in mythology do men or product markets spring instantly
to life with their full mature potential. Even the fad takes some
passage of time to reach its fatal zenith. However, the only time
period needed for low-learning products to reach their mature market share is that required by the communications process, that
needed to make prospects aware of the offering and apprise them of
the availability of the principal benefits interesting them. Adoption
of high-learning products involves more than awareness and understanding of the promise of the offering. Such acceptance requires
the prospect to perceive that the time and effort risked in a learning
process are more than offset by the value received.

Learning is a high-risk process. Whenever adoption requires
any substantial learning of any kind, research shows that logical
prospects are aware of the offering and its possible benefits long
before they adopt (Rogers, 1962). They rely on the advice of more
venturesome peers who have tried the new and validated the benefits. Thus the cumulative individual adoption which builds sales
growth depends on a process of social communication for diffusion
of use among the major portion of the market.

The product diffusion process thus depends on a series of
trials and social communication of the results through a chain of
social contacts. Analysts have come to classify the roles of those
adopting along this chain according to their relationship to the diffusion cycle, as innovators, early adopters, early majority, late
majority, and skeptics.

Innovators and early adopters come from those who value
highly the core benefits involved in an introduction and are thus actively seeking these attributes. Both are also distinguishable as
high mobiles, already inured to change and thus discounting risk
and learning costs. Innovators, however, are too far ahead of their

neighbors to be close associates and peers, whereas early adopters tend to be highly sociable and are consulted as experts by their associates. Each successive echelon of adopters depends on the advice of someone just a trifle more venturesome than himself, and each obviously perceives slightly less net value in the offering.

As the product grows in use and familiarity, new use-systems develop around it. At times, these call for a variation in design or new ingredient products which then come forth, catapulting the product into a new growth phase just as the market seems to be approaching saturation.

Because product diffusion is a social process, the existing culture sets the boundaries and the direction for the kinds of offerings capable of important success. Products which build on a favorable cultural trend fare best, those on a declining trend will have only a modest success at best. Declines in the culturally perceived value of major attributes are one important factor in the product life cycle decline.

THE CHARACTER OF SALES GROWTH RATES

Just as it is impossible for any physical object to pass immediately from a standing start to full speed, so no freshly introduced product can sell at full volume from the moment of introduction. From point zero, all successful products must undergo some period of accelerating growth in sales which finally slows down when it approaches the limits of the potential market. Since sales mean acceptance and purchase by people, the product life cycle is also an acceptance cycle, and the degree of sales acceleration is some measure of the growth in the number of people brought to at least the point of trial purchase. For many reasons, the initial trial purchases are made by a very small number of prospects, and the buyers tend to grow at a relatively steady rate, once these are convinced. It should thus be obvious that we are dealing with some kind of basic social phenomenon. We call that phenomenon the diffusion process.

The imperfections of the communications process plus the principle of selective attention are obvious reasons for the small size of the initial market. Making people aware of an offering and conveying a perception of the satisfactions it can render takes time under the most favorable circumstances. None of our communications tools is capable of reaching any very large fraction of the population at a given time, and of those reached, not all will pay attention at first. Thus even for offerings posing no acceptance risks, sales are a product of growth.

Even the most superficial of observation, however, reveals

that the communications lag is only part of the explanation for the sales acceleration process. Many fads and fashions pop up and reach flourishing proportions quickly, often prior to any commercialization and organized promotion. Dune buggies and the related sport of duning were a natural growth without commercial backing for at least two years before anyone developed even specialized vehicle bodies for sale. Outboard marathon racing boats were all homemade in the beginning. By contrast, other products with heavy promotional budgets have required years of learning before the market growth became obvious. Most people were fully aware of the availability of color television before the end of the first month of its introduction in 1954, but rapid sales growth waited a full decade, until 1964, to make its appearance.

The slope of the adoption curve up to the end of the period of rapid growth tends to approximate that of an exponential function. That is, the percentage rate of increase tends to be approximately constant up to the point of inflection on the growth curve. The difference between different kinds of product histories seems to be one of the size of this rate. High-learning requirement offerings seem to have characteristically low rates of acceleration. No-learning or low-learning requirement products have characteristically high rates of acceleration, have rapid growth from the start.

We are indebted to the rural sociologists for the original insights into the nature of the social process which accounts for this regularity of pattern and for identifying the different roles played by different types of personalities in the diffusion of new product use (Rogers, 1962). Others have supplemented the work sufficiently to outline the nature of the social process normally involved and the character of the marketing plans needed to take advantage of this knowledge.

PRODUCT ADOPTION AND THE DIFFUSION PROCESS

The rural sociologists were interested in a very practical marketing problem as a result of their close working relationship with the agricultural extension services: "How do new farm practices, ideas, and products get adopted and put into use?" They classified the people who adopted any new practice or product along a time continuum as innovators, early adopters, early majority, late majority, and skeptics. As we might expect, the cumulative acceptance by these groups looks just like the life cycle curve up to the point of market saturation. (See Figure 5-1). The innovators and early adopters are responsible for all sales during the market development phase. The rapid acquisition of people constituting the early majority is what builds up sales during the period of rapid

FIGURE 5-1. The Adoption Cycle, Adopter Characteristics, and Information Sources

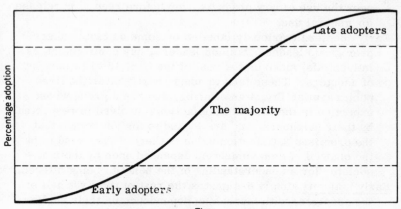

Early adopters	The majority	Late adopters
Distinctive Characteristics*		
Large farms	Average farms	Small farms
High income	Average income	Low income
Take risks		Security-minded
Usually under age 50	Age 50 to 60	Usually over age 60
Actively seeking new ideas	Receptive but not actively seeking	Complacent or skeptical
Participate in many nonlocal groups	Participate in some local groups	Seldom participate in formal groups
Sources of Information Used**		
College and other research sources	Adoption leaders and other farmers nearby	Other local farmers and adoption leaders
Agricultural agencies	Farm papers, magazines and radio	Farm papers, magazines and radio
Mass media sources	Commercial sources	Local dealers
Other highly competent farmers far and near	Agricultural agencies	Almanac
Commercial sources		

* In relation to characteristics of those in adjoining categories.
** Listed in estimated rank order of use.

SOURCE: Reproduced by permission from Herbert F. Lionberger, *Adoption of New Ideas and Practices*, © 1961 by The Iowa State University Press, Ames, Iowa, page 34.

growth. The late majority comes on the market during the slowdown of the maturation period, and the entry of the skeptics signals
the onset of the saturated market. The quantitative division of those
playing each of these five acceptance roles is about as follows:

Innovators comprise about the first 2 to 3 percent of those
who adopt. They are people inclined to seek out and pioneer the use of new products even before ready for release
for general use.

Early adopters (variously labelled by some as tastemakers,
peer group leaders, opinion leaders, key communicators,
influentials) make up the rest of the first 12 to 15 percent
of adopters. These tend to adopt shortly after the first
public availability of an offering, and are a group whose
expertise in the area of satisfactions involved is respected
by their neighbors, and are looked to for assurance that
the promised satisfaction value is there. They tend to be
the channel of communication depended upon by their associates for an understanding of the benefits being offered.

Early majority simply designates the rest of the first half of
the adopters, with increasing dependence on their earlier
adopting associates for trial and legitimation of the offering.

Late majority-- another third or so of the market which is
even slower to adopt the new, and accounts for the maturing
slowdown of the market.

Skeptics, the last 12 or 15 percent to adopt, as the market
reaches saturation.

The titles given each of these roles is obviously purely de-
scriptive, but a series of studies has shown that they are more than
empirical tautology. Innovators and early adopters have proved to
be quite identifiable personalities and to play sharply defined key
roles in the process of group acceptance. They have been shown
to be not only earlier in accepting, but to be those whose trials and
reports, to those with whom they are in social contact, determine
the willingness of their associates to buy.

Research by others, especially some published by Opinion
Research, Inc., has pinpointed more precisely the personality of
the early adopter group (Opinion Research Corporation, 1959). In
an intensive survey of sample families in one suburban community,
Opinion Research found that all of those who bought some 160 product introductions earliest during the preceding 10 years were
among the families in the highest one-fourth on a complex mobility
scale. The early adopters were thus families who had been exposed
to the most change in their lives and to the most new ideas. Mobility was scored on a multiple factor basis: geographical movement; job-to-job and generation-to-generation occupational movement; mobility across religious, ethnic, or social class lines in

FIGURE 5-2. Typical Adoption Pattern According to   FIGURE 5-3. Some Actual Adoption Patterns,
Mobility Theory   1945-1958

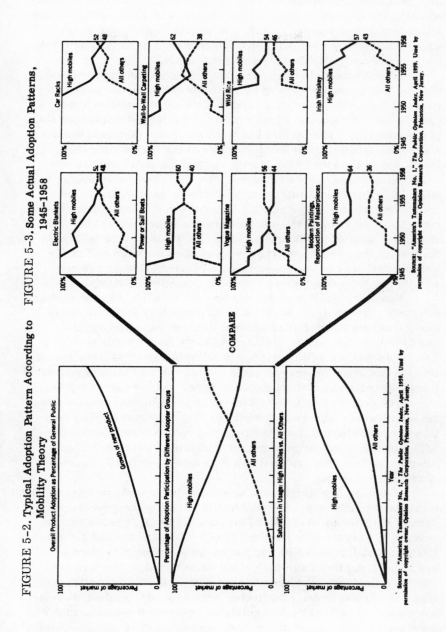

COMPARE

107

marriage; changes in income levels; educational exposure and
mobility; and intellectual mobility as indicated by an ever-widening
contact with various sources of new ideas. The high mobile is thus
a person who has learned to adjust to change in general and thus for
whom the avoidance potential of more change is perceived as a low
price for some highly desired new satisfaction.

Prior to the field work, Opinion Research had hypothesized
that the initial market for any new product would be composed entirely of high-mobile families and that the other families would
join the market later, gradually making up a larger and larger share
of the potential. The market share graph should thus tend toward
a scissors formation, as between sales to the high-mobile one-
fourth and to the rest of the families, until the latter became the
dominant group of buyers (Figure 5-2). The results generally
tended to approximate this scissors pattern, as Figure 5-3 indicates for a sample of the results. Moreover, an unpublished check
made by those running the study seemed to indicate that competition
reached a point of profit decline at the pivot point of the scissors
blades--at the point where the lower mobiles made up half of the
total market. This would accord with previous studies, since
adoption by the early majority would be complete at this point.

However, every high mobile was not an early adopter of every
offering. High mobiles were early adopters only for products in
classifications which had an unusual interest value for the given
family. The high mobile becomes an early adopter only when the
new product is one of importance to his value systems--one fitting
into the life style and use-systems of high value to him, particularly
those playing a simultaneous role in several of his use-systems.

The determining use-system could be inferred from the physical nature of the product sometimes, but not always. The adoption of exotic coffees, for example, was more closely correlated
with a high interest in politics than with a high interest in foods.
Adoption of boats was related to a high rating for family recreational use-systems.

The early adopter is thus a person who not only perceives less
learning cost in change, but who highly values a change in some
area of his special interest and his style of living. These two aspects of his personality may be closely related to income for some
kinds of satisfaction areas, as for example, among farmers in relation to farm practices which could be expected to improve production efficiency. But such is not necessarily the case with other
types of introductions. The young, with only very modest incomes,
were the early adopters of specialized recreation vehicles such as
dune buggies and dragsters because high interest in such mechanical
toys tends to be centered in the young. In industry, it is the outsider, and often a small one with no stake in current designs and

production processes and thus no re-learning to do, who is the best prospect for the really new advance. For instance, when transistors were first developed, the only segment of the established electronics industry which was interested was the hearing aid industry, where the sharp reduction in bulk and operating cost raised the perceivable value to buyers so high the industry could not ignore them. Otherwise, even the military had not incorporated transistors in a single major item seven years after release from the Bell Laboratories. Instead, entirely new enterprises, mostly those in Japan, carried the transistors forward into practical use. In discussing a development which may supersede some transistor use, <u>Fortune</u> magazine remarked that "the tendency is to choose the tried, evolutionary approach rather than the radically new" even among design engineers (<u>Fortune</u>, April, 1970).

Studies made of children, from shortly after birth to 14 years of age (Thomas, et al., 1970) would seem to indicate that the early adopters and innovators may also be so constituted congenitally. A substantial portion of their sample showed a stable pattern, from the first, of ready and even eager acceptance of new experience. If we allow for other kinds of differences in congenital and learned attitudes, we would get something like the proportions of early adapters we find in practice. Higher mobility may be as much a result of personal psychological make up as a cause of it.

Those who adopt early are clearly those to whom the product has a very high immediately perceivable value because of its fit into existing satisfaction objectives. For people already valuing highly the use system into which the offering fits, the satisfaction promised has a sufficiently high value to offset the avoidance risks involved in a purchase of the unknown and untried. Since these early adopters are recognized by their friends and associates as being especially interested and expert in the relevant satisfaction area, trial and approval by the early adopter serves to reduce the perceivable purchase risk for these others who are also aware of and desire the value promised by the introduction but question its complete validity until legitimated by the early adopter. Because being the first means being a person for whom the value counterbalances the risk, the early adopter would be one not only perceiving a high value in the new but who minimizes risk, generally because he has experienced great changes in his life and thus finds the strange less risky. He therefore hesitates less.

Each early adopter serves as risk-guarantor for more than one associate just because there are far more who hold back because of lesser general experience with the new, and also because they perceive less value in it. Considering that the level of the promised additional values and the degrees of risk cost associated with first purchase vary widely as between introductory offerings,

we would expect varying degrees of hesitation, or the reverse of
sales acceleration. The sales acceleration pattern thus tends to
be exponential because it must proceed by personal contact between
the earlier adopters and those adopting later, because of the dependence of later adopters on personal assurance from earlier
adopting friends. In other words, use tends to spread on a 2 x 2 x
2 x......2 basis, or some other multiple. The greater the learning
difficulty, the slower the speed of transmission. The exponential
curve tends to flatten out, then slow down as the number of actual
adopters approaches equality with the number of remaining potential users who have not yet accepted the offering. However, some
products do not level off to a saturated market plateau as they exhaust the initial growth potential, but develop into pyramided life
cycles.

PYRAMIDED LIFE CYCLES

Basic new inventions like the automobile and the radio often
take off on an accelerated burst of new life just as saturation appears imminent, just as a rocket can be propelled into a new orbit
by ignition of another stage. Bursts of new growth like these are
seldom pure accident but result from the emergence of new use-
systems and usually also of accessory new innovations, rendering
new bundles of satisfaction different from the core values which the
original bundle served. Such new desire-serving bundles can come
from either or both of two directions: from new technological modifications of the product or from external development creating the
possibility of new kinds of use systems.

The automobile has gone through at least three such secondary
growth cycles, and probably had entered a fourth in the late 1950's
and 1960's. (See Figure 5-4). Initially, the horseless carriage
was little more than a rich man's toy and an always ready emergency transportation device for those, such as city physicians,
needing quick transportation. Growing technological competence
enabled Ford to introduce a new era in 1908: a simplified vehicle
for a mass market needing cheap, relatively dependable transportation faster and more readily available than the horse and buggy.
The introduction permitted the development of a new use-system,--
an instrument of recreation permitting masses to escape densely
built-up cities to the open air of the nearby countryside on week-
ends.

The widened market created and captured by the Model T
awakened new desires for even wider mobility, and with it something
better than the clay tracks which then passed for roads. It was a
venturesome city resident who traveled many miles beyond the con-

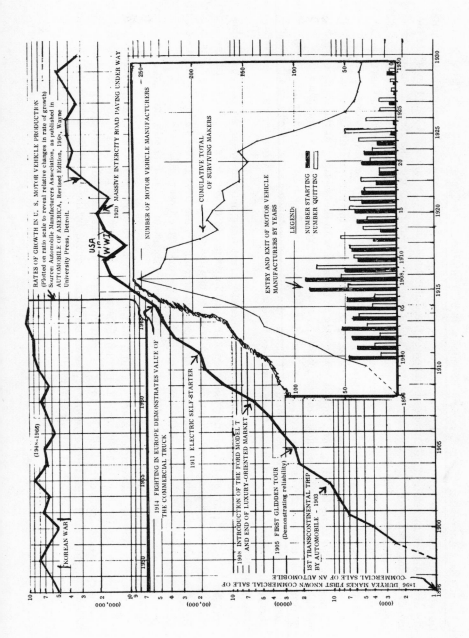

RATES OF GROWTH IN U. S. MOTOR VEHICLE PRODUCTION
(Plotted on ratio scale to reveal relative changes in rate of growth)
Source: Automobile Manufacturers Association, as published in
AUTOMOBILE OF AMERICA, Revised Edition, 1968, Wayne
University Press, Detroit.

1920 MASSIVE INTERCITY ROAD PAVING UNDER WAY

NUMBER OF MOTOR VEHICLE MANUFACTURERS

CUMULATIVE TOTAL
OF SURVIVING MAKERS

ENTRY AND EXIT OF MOTOR VEHICLE
MANUFACTURERS BY YEARS

LEGEND:
NUMBER STARTING
NUMBER QUITTING

USA
in
WWI

1914 FIGHTING IN EUROPE DEMONSTRATES VALUE OF
THE COMMERCIAL TRUCK

1911 ELECTRIC SELF-STARTER

1908 INTRODUCTION OF THE FORD MODEL T
AND END OF LUXURY-ORIENTED MARKET

1905 FIRST GLIDDEN TOUR
(Demonstrating reliability)

1ST TRANSCONTINENTAL TRIP
BY AUTOMOBILE - 1903

1896 DURYEA MAKES FIRST KNOWN COMMERCIAL SALE OF
COMMERCIAL SALE OF AN AUTOMOBILE

(1945-1966)

KOREAN WAR

111

FIGURE 5-4. The Automobile: A No-Learning Product with a Pyramided Life Cycle

1896: Duryea made the first commercial sales. The way for acceptance had already been prepared by the publicity attendant on the exhibit of European makes at the Columbian Exposition and by a long history of the
use of mechanical power in stationary engines and locomotives. Furthermore, the first horseless carriages were just that--familiar carriages which now needed no horse, with the attendant problems of stabling
and daily care and feeding. Within a year, other manufacturers followed suit. Entry was easy: dealers'
deposits alone almost financed a maker, and supplier credit furnished the rest of his working capital. Sales
were no problem. By 1900, 30 manufacturers were in business, and the number climbed to over 250 by 1908.

1903: Sales appeared to be levelling off but got a new shot in the arm with the publicity of the first transcontinental tour over the roadless landscape of that day, demonstrating the reliability of the auto.

1905: The start of the industry-sponsored Glidden tours furnished an annual publicity demonstration of reliability
just as the market seemed to be levelling off again. By 1908, acceptance was so strong, many manufacturers discontinued advertising of their lower-end models. As yet, all sales were for cash, and mostly for
luxury models.

1908: Growing symptoms of the saturation of the luxury-model market were masked by the spurt in unit sales
occasioned by the market-broadening tactics of the Ford introduction of the Model T, a car with features
found only in other makes twice its price. The renewed upward spurt of the market did not prevent a shakeout of competition. Exits from manufacturing exceeded entries for the first time in 1909, with those quitting making high-price cars, and the newer entrants competing at the lower end.

1911: Introduction of the electric self-starter improved the serviceability of the automobile and gave the sales
curve another upward boost.

1914: Trucks and commercial vehicles start to spurt, with the demonstration of their value on the war front.
1920-24: Saturation set in anew in 1920, only to pyramid upward by the paving of intercity roads, after which the
industry market again exhibited symptoms of maturity (and a Depression-induced decline) until after the
end of World War II and the beginning of the urban sprawl which, by the end of the 1950's, had virtually
enforced a two-car standard for many families, resulting in the last major pyramidal step.

112

venience and certainty of his paved city streets in the first dozen years after the Model T's introduction. In rainy weather, his country cousin usually left his vehicle behind in the barn and hitched Dobbin to get him to town through the rutted mud roads. Few roads were paved far beyond the city limits--the rest were a simple path over the natural soil, with the crudest of guideposts, when any existed at all. Relatively wide ownership of the auto soon made good roads politically popular, however, and both the Federal Congress and the states started cementing over the landscape and have not yet stopped. With the newly opened roads emerged the ubiquitous gasoline company maps and public road route numbering systems which took the mystery out of travel.

The new roads and the new levels of income which came with the end of World War I came close to putting a car in every home in the succeeding decade, and with it opened possibilities in new life styles. The country dweller could haul his produce to slightly more distant and larger markets, and he was no longer limited to the mail order catalog and the poorly merchandised crossroads general store. The city dweller did not have to confine his shopping list to the produce he could carry in a basket on his arm. When the mechanical refrigerator became a reality, the householder began to cut the frequency of his shopping trips and to drive to bigger stores for what he did get.

The wider potential shopping area soon made for ready acceptance of the one-stop supermarket with its parking lot. By 1930, the supper menu no longer needed to depend on the restricted inventory of the corner grocery, and the automobile was beginning to reshape the family's way of living in many ways. The job no longer had to be near either to home or to mass transit. Relatives, friends, and recreational facilities a couple of hundred miles away were a simple weekend jaunt, and the family could move to the countryside to live instead of just visiting it. Only the advent of the Great Depression delayed the explosive suburban sprawl which came with the end of World War II, creating with it the 2-car-plus family.

All of these earlier developments were duly capitalized on by the automobile industry, although the industry tended to tag along with customer needs rather than originate such design corollaries as trunk space in the car, for example. The lag was not nearly as profound, however, as the auto industry's slowness to develop designs for the purely recreational automobile--hot rods, drag racers, dune buggies, and campers--and the American industry virtually turned its back on the relatively large market for the lower-priced sports car the war veterans brought back from Europe in the late 1940's and the 1950's.

Likewise, the industry took much too long to recognize the latent demand for the handling qualities as well as the economics

113

of the small foreign sedan. The result was a strong beachhead
surrendered to foreign producers, and the first increase in the
number of major makers on the retail market since the 1920's.
Thus the pyramiding of the automobile growth curve has come largely through the gradual development of new use-systems by the
consumers, the concomitant development of external ingredients
such as roads and planned road systems because of consumer pressure, and the development of such other accessory innovations as
the supermarket and the weekend resort by other entrepreneurs.
Even such technological developments as the auto trunk came from
the outside and were years late in being made a standard part of
design. For the automobile industry, the renewed growth has developed largely without industry initiative, and without much reference to technology. The development of electronic communications,
by contrast, is a story of continual growth renewal largely facilitated by technological discoveries, although in this case, too, growing
consumer insight into possible new use-systems played a large part.

The origin of today's vast electronic industry was called wire-
less telegraphy. It was simply a system thought to be a supplementary form of code communication where wires could not be strung--
mainly at sea, and between ships and shore. But the nature of even
the early apparatus was sufficiently simple that the amateur could
build at least a crude receiver at home, and the more talented both
sending and receiving equipment, and many did. The invention of
the triode electron tube soon eliminated a major avoidance aspect
for the amateur by substituting the transmission of the human
voice instead of the telegraphic code, which had to be learned. Soon
the sophisticated amateurs were doing more than talking to each
other. Some started playing phonograph records on the air, to which
anyone within range could listen in with the simplest of receiving
equipment. This new benefit soon created a mass market capable
of supporting a retail system for electronic parts. This early mass
listenership was not long lost on local advertisers, and radio advertising was born, and also a market for commercially produced
receivers. Advertising, in turn, pumped in a profitable financial
lifeblood and made national networks both desirable and profitable.
The first national network show was a symphony, but the day-long
blaring radio soon became a cheap substitute for the comedy aspects
of vaudeville and for the cheap dramatics of melodrama, signalling
the decline of the live entertainment life cycle and furnishing a relief from housewife boredom. The invention of the television tube
completed the broadcast medium's ability to bring the stage into the
home.

Entertainment was never the only benefit of the broadcast industry. One of the earliest local broadcasts by the first receiving
station was the returns of the 1920 presidential election, and news

early became an important part of the satisfaction bundle desired. The musical programs never were completely superseded by the soap operas, either, and automobile drivers spending long hours behind the wheel began looking for ways to get the boredom-reducing set into their vehicles. One such was the chauffeur for Henry Ford, and his wish is said to have been the impetus for the development of the first of the personal radios--the auto radio. Some further personalization came with the miniaturization of components and the development of the small table radio after World War II, but these lacked real portability because of their dependence on an electric outlet. The development of the highly efficient transistor by Bell Laboratories was seized upon by a young Japanese firm seeking market entry who initiated the now ubiquitous pocket radio and led the way to a major Japanese invasion of the whole electronics market.

Meanwhile, the development of frequency modulation so necessary to television made possible also a much higher fidelity in the reproduction of music, and the development of the long-playing vinyl record enabled the growing middle class to satisfy its taste for quality music, both on FM radio and in the home, creating a newly specialized advertising medium on radio at the same time.

The growth of electronic knowledge spawned many industrial developments in addition, including the digital computer and a host of other kinds of business and industrial equipment, automating many previously tedious processes. The mass market for components created a financial base for strong research and development which improved electronic devices still further and contributed to improved mechanical equipment of all kinds, from toothbrushes in the bathroom to food mixers in the kitchen, to complex industrial process controls. The current culture has really become an electronic culture.

The automobile and electronic cycles differed in one major respect. In the auto industry, major producers covered developing needs so well that none of the pyramidal steps brought in lasting new entrants except one of the last--the economy sedan pyramid. But in the electronic industry, the cold shoulder major domestic producers gave to the transistor developments permitted new foreign enterprises to gain a major permanent foothold in the market and increased the number of entrenched suppliers.

From this it should be obvious that once the period of rapid growth is beginning to taper off, those producers who have established strong marketing niches can be relatively invulnerable to new competition, but only if and so long as they keep in touch with changing tastes in the market (well-made, easily handled, functional small sedans and sports cars for example) and incorporate new technology capable of creating substantial new utilities (the porta-

bility and economy of transistorized circuitry). Otherwise outsiders will slip in and grab off a major share of the unsatisfied
demand.

Whether the initial impetus for a new cycle comes from outside the industry or arises out of new technological developments
within, each new growth curve presents a new set of profit opportunities for those ready to seize them, because each such breakout
represents a new product and newly unsatisfied use-system in the
perception of the buyer, and usually a new set of buyers. Each
signals the onset of a new receptive cultural climate, bringing new
unsatisfied desire-sets to the fore. The culture climate change is
what creates the profit opportunity either in a simple product life
cycle or in a complex pyramided one. The receptivity of the current culture--the existence of large numbers of people with substantially unsatisfied desire-sets--is the major determinant of what
offerings can hope for adoption and when, and what offerings must
work hard for success or are bound to fail.

THE CULTURE CLIMATE AND PRODUCT RECEPTION

The general culture climate and the direction of cultural
trends, including fashion, are major limiting factors on the success of any offering. Market acceptance of any new product involves
some degree of culture change. Such changes can be induced only
when large numbers of people are at least potentially ready for some
degree of change, and only in those sectors of their culture which
they are ready to change--sectors in which they experience some
degree of tension due to desire-sets they feel are substantially unfulfilled.

Success of an offering is thus completely dependent on the
simultaneous working of three factors:

1. Existence of similar sets of substantially unsatisfied desire-sets among large segments of people in a given culture.
2. Development of offerings which would be able to substantially improve the fulfillment of these desires and are
   perceivable as promising this satisfaction in the context
   of a suitable and acceptable use-system.
3. Effective communications which can lead significant segments of the population to perceive the use-system benefits contained in the offering, to feel that these benefits
   have enough value to justify undertaking any change required in habitual patterns of action and thought, and to
   overcome fears of the risks they may perceive as involved.

Success hinges on fulfillment of all three conditions. Unless

116

a relatively noticeable set of desires is unsatisfied, prospects will
have no drive to even pay attention to the offering. Equally, they
will pay attention only when they can perceive the product as a promise of a noticeably greater degree of satisfaction. Finally, they
must somehow be persuaded to change their habitual perceptions
and expectations to some extent. Any new offering requires at
least a change in the perception of sources of possible satisfaction
and the acquisition of a feeling that the added value is there in sufficient amount to justify some degree of change in habits. Since
these habits and these perceptions are a cultural heritage, the acceptance of the new idea or offering of any kind is circumscribed
by the cultural setting.

How readily any of us will accept even a minor change in our
culture varies directly with the amount of change normally taking
place in that culture, and the direction in which that change has
been proceeding. Whenever the culture or subculture is relatively
static, nearly all members are afraid to risk change of any sort.
For people in such a situation, even those products which promise
the most obvious satisfaction for the gravest of their problems are
difficult to accept or try. Quaker Oats, for example, had extreme
difficulty gaining even a modest sales volume for an enriched cereal
product which could prevent much of the protein starvation which
kills a large part of the young in Central and South America, even
though the meal looked and could be used just like the corn meal on
which the prospects fed themselves. What sales they did succeed
in making were at some distance up the social scale, among families
used to at least some slight degree of change in their existence.
Similarly, the brilliant success of the United States Extension Service in revolutionizing American agriculture was accomplished only
among the more mobile upper half of the rural population. The Service found that the degree of socialization among the lower one-half
was too low and experience with success too rare among the lower
group to permit use of their ordinary voluntary educational methods.
Even with the upper group, initial success came extremely slow at
first, required a diligent search for some extremely vulnerable desire, and then largely through working with the young--a group who
had no established habits to unlearn and had to learn some system
in any event. The Service early learned the lesson which every
pioneer must take to heart: "Start where the people are." By this,
the Service means: find some high priority problem whose solution
is already being sought and which takes the minimum amount
of change to meet. Only then will those in a relatively static culture risk the attempt to change.

The job of promoting change in a dynamic culture is easier
simply because change itself has become a habit, because the risk
of the new is familiar and therefore not seen as great. But it does

not follow that everything new will be accepted if promoted. The acceptably new must even then swim with the currents of the cultural trend, must contain as its most valuable attributes those which are on the upslope of acceptance, not those which are in declining favor.

The product life cycle really depicts the broadening acceptance not of a physical offering, but of specific product attributes and attribute combinations. The upside of the curve signifies that increasing numbers of people are learning to perceive increasing satisfaction value in specific attributes and thus are seeking a validated source of satisfaction for desires well toward the top of hierarchy of those currently unsatisfied. New products incorporating these growingly popular attributes are readily welcomed. Introduction of products incorporating the advancing attributes is relatively easy and inexpensive in money and effort because they meet searching customers who value the attributes highly and have already accepted them.

The acceptance of such advancing attributes normally is the result of some other dynamic change in the culture. A good example has been the burgeoning of the demand for the convenience attribute in food items since the end of World War II. The reason is to be found in the introduction of housewives into the industrial workforce during the war and the steady increase in their labor force participation ever since. The eight-hour shift left little time for dawdling over the more tedious aspects of meal preparation, and products which shortened the time and simplified the task have met a ready reception. As this origin of the demand would indicate, the acceptance of the new convenience foods has been more marked in the cities, where industrial jobs for married women are more common, than in the rural areas. The lower time cost was more important to the urban working housewife than to her rural counterpart and she was more willing to forego some desired potential quality if need be.

Every kind of convenience food item has not shared equally in this growth, however--only those combined with dietary items and characteristics themselves in a growing group. Pie crust mix sold, and still does, but only in very modest volume. Pies, as a dessert, have come into increasing disfavor in an increasingly calorie conscious culture. Pie crust mixes and fillings, therefore, got an increasing share of a decreasing market, and thus captured very little of the supermarket shelf space. Similarly, the growing trend to a more diversified diet has benefitted the frozen vegetable market, not all vegetables. Fresh produce, which requires more preparation, has continued a long decline in sales importance because of the high preparation time cost.

Offerings whose core attributes are on the downgrade will

118

yield little profit for another reason: the perceived value itself is declining. Offerings containing major attributes of declining value are poor introductions because few people are seeking them, and even those have a decreasing incentive to seek them out.

Thus all cultural change is a two-way street. As some kinds of satisfactions increase in perceived value, others pass out of the picture and, with them, offerings containing them as a major appeal. The food industry, for instance, is relatively as big as ever and contains many as yet unrealized opportunities. But those foods perceived as mainly sources of cheap energy, such as bread and potatoes, face declining markets, at least in their traditional forms. Other products, perceived as incorporating primarily zest and flavor (such as lean meat products, frozen desserts, and sauces) are in increasing favor. In some cases, an energy food has been able to salvage some market by a change in form and use-system. Potatoes have lost ground as a main meal course, but as potato chips have had a rising market as a snack (or more usually, as an edible utensil for snacks, as a conveyor of sour cream and cheese dips, at parties).

Since such rises and declines originate with basic changes in cultural habits, procedures and attitudes, every new introduction should be appraised in terms of current cultural trends, as analyzed in terms of current use-system trends. Any aspect of any introduction draws its meaning in terms of cultural habits and expectations.

The culture defines for us what will look attractive and taste good, and it also dictates the use-systems within which products must be positioned. The Hindu will accept no meat product because to him the consumption of meat is a form of cannibalism. The Moslem shuns pork. While many tribes have found roast locust a delicacy, the American version of this insect (the grasshopper) has never been considered anything other than a very dangerous pest, and the periodic plagues have given rise to no food products.

These grosser social taboos are so well recognized that the illustration may seem almost contrived, but the food processor who tried to sell a frozen "fruit soup" made a mistake little different in nature. Although fruit soup is a well-liked chilled food in Mediterranean areas, it failed dismally in American supermarkets. To Americans, soup is not a chilled dish, but a hot one, and has a meat base, not a fruit one. It did not fit American cultural use-systems. (Yet if offered by the soup-maker as something other than a soup, it might well have succeeded in the context of a different use-system. Those who did try it claimed it made an excellent ice cream topping. But how many people would think of putting something labelled as a soup on ice cream?)

Current cultural use-systems also determine the limits of the

119

fluctuations of another phenomenon to which every product designer and market entrepreneur must constantly pay attention--the phenomenon of fashion. At one time, for instance, the length attribute of women's skirts could reach to the floor at the appropriate period in the cycle. Since the housewife became the family chauffeur, however, skirts of this length have never succeeded in house or street dresses--only in formals. Skirts going beyond midcalf are not compatible with driving automobiles. Within the limits permitted by cultural use-patterns, the fashion trend is one of the most decisive of cultural trends in regulating the acceptance of a design.

Culture trends themselves can be responsible for the decline of the life cycle curve as well as indirectly responsible, by creating a favorable climate for the acceptance of new sources of satisfaction of specific desires. The internal psychological reactions of consumers also play a part in that decline.

THE FICKLE PSYCHOLOGY OF THE CONSUMER

All product acceptance starts with the perception by some relatively large numbers of individuals that an introduction offers some kind of very substantial added satisfaction for some set of drives close to the top of their hierarchy of desires. As acquisition of the product satiates the desire, the drive which led to the initial interest subsides and some other less-well-satisfied drive comes to the fore. Part of the initial added value perceived in any introduction is the mere fact of its novelty. It seems well established that all sentient animals possess some kind of drive for new experience, some relief from the familiar and thus monotonous. As a product phases from the novel into the familiar, therefore, it loses some part of the initial added value, and some of the attention value can be shifted to something else which is now new. The decline of unit profitability and eventually of product usage is thus due to a combination of cultural dynamics, competitive development of better substitute sources of satisfaction, and something the layman might label as a form of boredom which accounts for the oscillations of fashion.

SUMMARY

1. The adoption of new products is the result of a social process in which various members of a group play one of five rather clearly defined roles: innovator, early adopter, early majority, late majority, or skeptics. The early adopter is the key to product success. His trial and approval of the product is a necessary con-

dition to acceptance by the others, who rely on his knowledge of the area to validate the product claims and reduce the risk they perceive in any trial.

2. Those playing each role are specifically identifiable types of personalities. The early adopter is a person who has experienced a high degree of mobility in his life and is therefore inured to change. He is an early adopter for those products, and only those products, which promise satisfactions high in his priority of values. He therefore possesses some kind of recognized expertise in the obtaining of some specific sets of satisfactions and is thus relied upon by his less expert social associates for validation of the claimed benefits. He is also a relatively sociable person, with numerous interpersonal contacts rendering possible the spread of knowledge of the product benefits. Once the initial trial period of the early adopters is over, growth in the acceptance of an offering tends to be geometric in character as the influence of each successive adopter is multiplied through his social contacts.

3. Each successive layer of adoption, however, represents people who see less value in the benefits, so that the perceived value of the introduction eventually begins to decrease with the acceptance by the late majority, signalling the approach of market maturity.

4. However, not all cycles reach maturity in a single step. Many basic new introductions take off on a new growth cycle just as saturation appears imminent. Increasing use develops new use-systems and new ingredients making these new use-systems possible. Continued product development also sometimes uncovers new technology creating possible new use-systems of high value. This pyramiding of the cycle may be initiated by industry developments, but is frequently partly a result of cultural trends set in motion by the acceptance of the original offering, and nearly always assisted by such developments outside industry control.

5. The culture within which the market operates, and the trend in that culture, defines what offerings can be successful and which are bound to fail. Some degree of dynamism in that culture is a necessary condition for success of any offering, and the direction of changes will ease the introduction of some kinds of offerings, render others relatively unprofitable.

6. The decline of the life cycle is due in part to the decline in the cultural value of major contained attributes, in part to the introduction of improved new sources of satisfaction by others, and in part to the increasingly lessened value of the familiar and the search for new experience.

6

FASHION: A COROLLARY OF DESIGN COMPROMISE

One particular kind of life cycle is of continuing importance to almost every seller: the fashion cycle. What is defined as attractive in any culture is partly a matter of the calendar, as can be seen by looking through any family album or periodical file. Moreover, any such review which spans a generation or so reveals obvious cyclical fluctuations. Fashion is always in a state of flux but forever seems to repeat itself in some manner. Clothes designers find their greatest inspiration in the museums. While we are most strongly aware of the fluctuations in the popularity of clothing styles, such popularity cycles can be found in every aspect of our lives, in the acceptance of ideas and products of every kind.

Any designer or introducer of products, services or ideas of any sort ignores such fashion fluctuations at his own peril. Designs or ideas out of step with the fashion trend die stillborn or lead an anemic existence. Efforts which catch a rising trend can be borne upward to success and profit even when poorly executed. Designers and promoters of every kind cannot avoid prophesying that most fickle of human attributes: what the near future taste trend will be. Fortunately, the fickleness of taste is not as whimsical as generally thought.

Fashion is neither a synthetic creation of designing designers and merchants nor a phenomenon limited to clothing or even to the commercial world. Such fluctuations in taste or what is approved are characteristic of the acceptance of products and ideas of every kind--of political themes, religious ideas and management practices, for example, as well as of dress, automobiles, architecture, and furniture styles. The fluctuations themselves involve the fringe attributes, not the core functions or the use-systems. They are an inevitable result of the compromises necessary in any design in-

FIGURE 6-1. The Swings in Fashion in Research Techniques.

No researcher, and no research customer can ever attain the kind of certainty which both hope to gain from the researcher's efforts, especially in the field of marketing. As a consequence, both the analyst and his customer are prone to bouts of enthusiasm over some magical new technique which seems to dispel some of the risks and uncertainties of predicting what the buyer will do next.

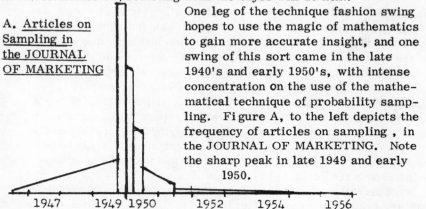

A. Articles on Sampling in the JOURNAL OF MARKETING

One leg of the technique fashion swing hopes to use the magic of mathematics to gain more accurate insight, and one swing of this sort came in the late 1940's and early 1950's, with intense concentration on the use of the mathematical technique of probability sampling. Figure A, to the left depicts the frequency of articles on sampling , in the JOURNAL OF MARKETING. Note the sharp peak in late 1949 and early 1950.

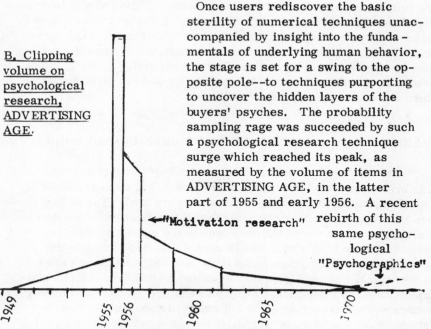

B. Clipping volume on psychological research, ADVERTISING AGE.

Once users rediscover the basic sterility of numerical techniques unaccompanied by insight into the fundamentals of underlying human behavior, the stage is set for a swing to the opposite pole--to techniques purporting to uncover the hidden layers of the buyers' psyches. The probability sampling rage was succeeded by such a psychological research technique surge which reached its peak, as measured by the volume of items in ADVERTISING AGE, in the latter part of 1955 and early 1956. A recent rebirth of this same psychological "Psychographics"

technique concentration, under the new label of "psychographics", was detectable in the rising volume of AD AGE articles and news items, by 1970. The interim had been occupied with the dazzling promise of the computer age. 123

tended to meet a desire-set with almost inevitable incompatibilities, of the dynamic changes of the normal hierarchy of needs, and of the social process of product diffusion. Most of us, for most of our purchases of anything new, lean on the experience and trials of others we consider slightly more expert than ourselves, and thus acceptance becomes cumulative. In the process, some of us tend to overadopt at times--to take on products ill-adapted to our personal needs and desires. Moreover, by satisfying the topmost desire in our hierarchy of desires, every fashion automatically extinguishes the drive which led to its adoption and activates a desire for the opposite kind of compromise. The classic--the style which is never completely out of fashion--is an integral part of the fashion phenomenon, apparently appealing to a self-assured market segment which values the core functions highly and is willing to settle for a relatively stable compromise which gives a balanced treatment to the fringe design attributes, satisfying none of them to the extreme. Something akin to the classic design would seem to be the best for initial high learning offerings and probably dominates the market in the decline phases.

Observation seems to indicate that fashion fluctuations seem most important after the product life cycle is approaching maturity and probably diminish in the declining phases of all products in which the cosmetic function is not central. Although fashion fluctuations are characteristic of wide ranges of offerings, some classes of products can be found which are unaffected by such fluctuations. These seem to be mainly offerings satisfying a single objective functional desire or such a narrowly limited set of such desires there can be no inherent incompatibilities.

FASHION: AN ALL-PERVASIVE, INEVITABLE PHENOMENON

Fashion is not simply a characteristic of the garment trade, hair styles, architecture, and automobiles. It is an unavoidable aspect of product and idea acceptance of every kind. The author's own review of the history of research techniques revealed repeated cycles around two recurrent emphases in the marketing field between the early 1950's and 1973 (Figure 6-1). A colleague's unpublished study of religious magazines demonstrated clear cycles in theological interests--an area unsullied by ordinary commercial exploitation and promotion. Any student of management techniques is aware of the recurring cycles of centralization and decentralization. Fashion, in other words, is not the synthetic creation of some powerful persuaders, but a normal aspect of every part of a dynamic culture. It is not the creation of those with something to sell, but a manifestation of swings in taste which those with some-

124

thing to sell or purvey in any manner disregard at their own risk.

Contrary to general opinion, Paris, Rome, and Hollywood do not dictate what milady will wear. Neither do the merchants (Figure 6-2). The designers merely attempt to guess the direction her taste will next take. The designer whose guess is correct is the year's current "design genius". When, as often happens, he guesses wrong the next time around, the genius title passes to someone else. At times, all of the experts guess wrong, yet the fashions change anyway, in an unanticipated direction. As the mini-skirt fashion of the 1960's reached its zenith, for example, designers in the 1967-68 period guessed that the flowing bell-shaped dress would succeed it in popularity. Some designers even thought that skirt lengths would go to the opposite extreme. They were correct for the trend in some formal dress, but women showed no enthusiasm for the trend. Instead, the pants-dress and the pants-suit came out of nowhere, with no famous designer's blessing, and even invaded the evening formal field. Women were, as the designers thought, ready to hide their legs and even ready for more of the feminine mystique, but not to give up freedom of leg movement.

Similarly, the fender fin craze in the automobile styling of the 1950's can hardly be traced to a designer's plot. The first fins to appear were rather modest ones on the Cadillac. Within months, auto owners were swarming to automobile accessory stores for auxiliary fins to bolt onto their own cars of other makes. The only trend started by the rather simple-appearing Chryslers (which came on the market at the same time) was away from Chrysler showrooms, and Chrysler rescued its later designs only by adopting the most extreme of fins. Lest it be thought that fins were adopted because of Cadillac's prestige, it should be noted that when another swing in car styling came, Cadillac had to follow the slab-sided style of a lesser competitor.

Designers can lead the fashion parade only when they hurry to get in front of the consumer in the direction he is taking, even in an area of consumption such as clothes, where the cycle is heavily commercialized. The superficial unanimity of designers is agreement forced on them by the market for their output, by the buyers, and the desire of designers to stay profitable. For this reason, every successful idea of any sort is soon copied, whether the idea be a dress design, an unusual advertising layout, or a winning political platform. Copying is easy because of the nature of the attributes which partake of fashion fluctuations--they are the more superficial attributes.

THE SUPERFICIAL NATURE OF FASHION ATTRIBUTES

The fluctuations of fashion revolve around the fringe attributes of an offering--around the less functional attributes which do not require much habit change--not the basic core attributes. This is easily perceived in the example of automobile design fashions. The surface elements of body line are clearly subject to such fluctuations. So are the power-weight ratios which determine "performance" and, conversely, economy. But the fundamental conformation of the transportation elements do not so oscillate: the engine position and basic type, and the seating arrangements. Changes in these fundamentals undergo a trend-type evolution and are accepted with caution, as is true of other fundamentals in the core transportation bundle: the distance capacity of the fuel tank, the degree of weather protection afforded, the softness of the suspension. Fashion, in other words, leaves the relative demand for the core attributes untouched but results in an oscillatory fluctuation among the fringe benefits of the offering. The amount of weather and climatic protection offered by a garment remains relatively constant, but the cosmetic attributes are in constant flux. The attempt to control and rationalize the management of organizations and make use of their human resources is a constant desire and aim of all managerial systems, but the superficial arrangement of interpersonal relationships oscillates between the highly structured and the highly delegated.

Since fashion is an ever-present aspect of the changes constantly taking place in any modern culture and is subject to similar oscillatory fluctuations wherever present, it seems reasonable to conclude that fashion is the result of some fundamental forces of human nature. We can, in fact, explain the observed fluctuations and their directions, and the corollary relative constancy of the classic styles also, by a combination of well-established psychological, sociological, and economic concepts already outlined.

THE FORCES WHICH ENERGIZE THE SWINGS OF FASHION

The oscillations of fashion can be fully explained in terms of three concepts: product as a bundle of utilities or satisfactions, demand as a set of internally incompatible desires, and motivation as existing in a hierarchy of desires. The most basic is probably the concept of any offering as an inseparable bundle of satisfactions. The drives for which we seek satisfaction are so numerous that we could not hope to search out and procure the means of satisfying each one separately. Thus every offering must simultaneously fulfill a rather large number of desires for each buyer--desires which the buyer perceives as being related in some manner. We purchase a steak dinner not only to allay hunger, but to yield a pleasurable appetite satisfaction. We desire its consumption,

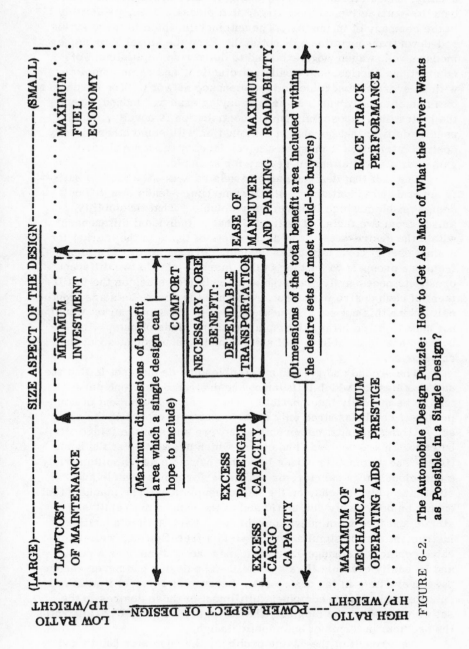

FIGURE 6-2. The Automobile Design Puzzle: How to Get As Much of What the Driver Wants as Possible in a Single Design?

127

usually, under circumstances yielding further aesthetic and social benefits--attractive table settings, in a pleasant area, preferably in the company of intimates. The automobile which is mere stripped-down transportation will not sell. Even the Model T or more modern Volkswagen were expected to deliver some minimum of comfort, aesthetics, and weather protection, and come complete with an everready service and maintenance network. The purchaser of a pencil usually wants an accompanying eraser. Indeed, even the hottest fad, whose only unique contribution is novelty, must usually deliver that novelty in combination with some other already desired attribute. It must be a novel dance step, a novel card game, or a novel attention-getter, for example.

The fact that desires come in related sets--the wish to satisfy several individual drives at the same time--leads to a difficult design problem which is never fully soluble. That insolubility arises from two facts. The first is that of individual differences within the desire-sets. The desire-sets of those in the market for a single set of core attributes seldom, perhaps never, are identical from one prospect to another in that market, nor do two different prospects necessarily place the same relative values on the fulfillment of each desire in that set, even when the desire-sets are identical. Were this not so, the meat counter in the supermarket would not need to be so large, to display so many kinds of cuts. And the butcher should be able to sell a steak and hamburger at about the same price.

The second and even more troublesome design fact is that the satisfactions for which fulfillment are desired by any one person tend to be mutually incompatible. The physical attainment of some in the set can be assured only at the expense of others in the same set. All design must compromise between some of the fringe attributes which are desired, and others which are wanted at the same time. The automobile cannot be highly parkable and simultaneously a capacious cargo carrier, or a high-performance vehicle and simultaneously one easy on the fuel consumption. The machine tool cannot be both highly automatic and at the same time relatively simple and free from service problems. Even a simple writing instrument cannot simultaneously yield a free-flowing, well-lubricated contact, a smudge-free permanent record (as does a pen), and be easily erasible (like a pencil). The design can never encompass every item in the desire-set. Because of physical limitations, an acceptable design combines fulfillment of those desires in the set which are, at the moment, the strongest. Figure 6-2 illustrates the problem in terms of automobile design.

As a result of the design problem, the customer has to and does make choices with which he is bound to be unhappy in some degree. To understand how he makes these choices, and which

128

ones, we are indebted to psychology for the concept of the hierarchy of motives.

None of us can hope to fulfill even a substantial fraction of all our drives, or even of a substantial proportion of our desire-sets, at any one moment of time. Fortunately, nature has provided us with a choice mechanism: the drives we experience at any one moment are not equal in intensity but exist in some kind of hierarchy of intensities, with some in top position. These latter dominate our actions for the time being, are perceived as most important. Part of this feeling of greatest importance arises from the fact that the topmost drive is for the least-well-satisfied desire-set, and for the least-well-satisfied item in that set.

Satiation of the topmost drive in the hierarchy automatically extinguishes its intensity. The drive to satisfy our hunger diminishes as the steak is consumed, and some other drive begins to take precedence. This newly dominant drive will be the one next least-well-satisfied, and the least-well-satisfied drive in its set. From the designer's point of view, this tends to be just that drive whose satisfaction was promised by the physical attributes most highly sacrificed to achieve the originally attractive design. The customer, in other words, has lost interest in the very fringe attributes which gave popularity to the first design conformation and now wants an offering which requires emphasis on the very fringe attributes he was willing to forego before. Having obtained the compromise he truly sought, he now wants the opposite compromise. The automobile designer whose high-performance designs gained a major market share is now asked for fuel economy. The politician who held taxes down finds himself with a strong demand for costly public services in spite of their cost. The dress designer whose curve-revealing models have captured the feminine fancy is now forsaken for garb which requires less confining undergarments. Both politician and designer have long ago learned to live with the plaint, "What have you done for me lately?"

We can thus explain the fluctuations in individual taste in terms of three concepts:

1. The concept of an offering as a compromise design fulfilling many desires inseparably and simultaneously.
2. The concept of demand as for fulfillment of a desire-set, as simultaneous satisfaction of many wants, some of which are incompatible and thus force design compromises which leave some of the desires in the set partly or wholly sacrificed in order to deliver other more wanted desire-satisfactions.
3. The concept of the hierarchy of motivations, or desires, in which the fulfillment of certain desires takes precedence over the satisfaction of others until the desire for

the dominant ones is extinguished by fulfillment.

By themselves, however, these concepts would lead to a simple statistical form of fashion, since there is nothing in this explanation so far which accounts for the social character of fashion--for the fact that there is obviously some generally acknowledged standard as to what is acceptable at a given instant. The explanation for fashion as an element in culture must look to the nature of the product acceptance process and to the place of group standards in the learning process which product acceptance involves.

PRODUCT ACCEPTANCE, EMULATION, AND OVER ADOPTION

Fashion can occur in clearly defined cycles because product adoption is, like most of our other learning, a socially structured process. Even the initial trial by an innovator requires that he first learn to perceive an offering as a possible cue to satisfaction of a felt desire. Adoption itself signifies that the adopter has actually learned to perceive the product as a superior source of satisfaction. Few of us go through a personal investigatory process for any of the products we adopt, none of us can for any large proportion of the products we accept. We have to and do rely on the testimony of associates for our initial perception of possible satisfaction, on the expert knowledge of someone we feel has tastes similar to ours, and whose expertise in what is acceptable can be trusted. We trust the judgment of such associates because we recognize that they concentrate more attention and interest in the area of consumption involved. The innovator and earlier adopter is followed because he is known to be an expert in his particular sphere of interests. He tries out new offerings and is more willing to accept an occasional disappointment as the price of ferreting out better sources of a group of satisfactions he values especially highly. We emulate him only in such areas of consumption, however. In other areas, we know he does as the rest of us do--he saves time and risk by depending on the advice of other friends and other associates whose interests in these other satisfaction categories are recognized as much greater than his.

Thus those people most interested in a major satisfaction attribute of an offering will be the first to try and adopt. Those a little less expert will look to the reports of these others before trying the new themselves, and in turn will pass on advice to those just a little less expert than they are. Adoption thus proceeds by multiple stages, from those with the greatest expertise to those associates with enough knowledge to recognize the greater competence of these others, and so on. The build-up to a saturated mar-

130

ket takes time because of the need to move through these successive waves of personal advice. The earlier adopters accept the offering early because they are the people to whom the new in the offering presents the greatest perceivable value. As the cycle reaches the rest of the prospects, each new wave is a group which perceives less net added value in the offering. Those who adopt last may indeed perceive little or no added value for themselves other than the fact that the offering is "in style", and thus has both some novelty attributes and attributes of social approval. They may even buy simply because it is the only style on the market, and consider it a relatively unattractive offering. The needs and desires of individuals vary widely both in intensity and kind. Consequently, some emulative or even forced adoption (because of lack of alternatives) occurs which does not fit the needs of the people adopting late.

Every new cycle and every new product inevitably results in some over adoption, then, because some adopt solely on the authority of others, or even because there may be little choice. The successful offering thus tends to gain a wider following than the valued attributes would alone justify. The overly plump girl stuffs herself into the currently popular sheath dress which accentuates the worst aspects of her build because svelte fashion-conscious associates have certified it as the currently most acceptable. The business firm buys the computer lease with expensive capacity far beyond its need because other firms known to be "progressive" have one such. The family who has a son with high manipulative mechanical skills but no feeling for books, sends him on to college and a career as a mediocre clerical worker because college work, not mechanics, has prestige. The voter who has few vulnerable areas to be taxed in, but a real need for expanded public services, votes for the "economy in government" candidate because his property-owning neighbors are upset over their tax bills. Since such over-adoptions cannot lead to permanent satisfaction, they create early dissatisfaction and some decline in the general valuation of the offering. Sooner or later, the over-adopters become aware that the promise of satisfaction they perceived was, for them, a false promise, and they become receptive to some other offering promising a better fit for their particular desire-sets. Such disaffection is one force leading to the decline of the cycle.

FASHION REVERSAL AND ITS TIMING

It would thus seem that the impetus for the decline of a fashion cycle comes both from those it satisfied originally and from those for whom it never did a good job. The first becomes restless because of the compromise price he pays for desired attributes, the other because he has learned he never received what was promised. The decline of product acceptability is thus also a learning process.

The unlearning process takes time for both segments. The current fashion yields a glow of desire appeasement for a while for both those who really do gain noticeable value and those who gain only social approval. The growth of dissatisfaction takes time to crystallize and create a substantial receptive audience for some one new direction of style. Furthermore, whatever new offering takes over must go through the same multistage acceptance process. Those who are expert enough to trust their own judgment are few in number, and the associates of the true innovators are not large in number either. Thus the market for the displacing fashion overlaps that for the old for a considerable period, and the numerical weight of acceptance will be on the old. There may ensue a period during which the trend to the new appears ambiguous. It is probable that a true graphic representation of the fashion cycle is not a pure sine wave, but a series of partially over-lapping product life cycles. In any event, the fashion cycle is no simple one-dimensional movement in any complex urban culture made up of many semi-independent sub-cultures. In fact, an analysis of what is acceptable in any fashion series will always reveal a set of designs which have a steady following of some size without undergoing major alteration during any of the swings. These are the "classic" styles, worthy of far more attention than they usually receive. They, too, are part of the fashion cycle phenomenon.

CLASSICS: DESIGNS WHICH IGNORE THE FASHION SWINGS

The cognoscenti in any area of consumption can point out a set of styles which they all agree can be termed classics, but probably cannot define just what makes them so. Operationally, a classic is any design which is always considered acceptable. While it may or may not have been the ruling style at some one time, it normally does not become a phase of the repetitive cycle. The term can be applied either to whole product bundles or to single product attributes.

Whatever the year and whatever the current fashion, the woman in a tailored suit can always feel confidence in the appropriateness of her grooming. The current version may vary slightly in details from year to year, but one several years old need not look out of date. In a simple black pump with medium heel, she can always feel suitably shod. In dress attributes, a length just below the knee will never look dated. Automobile styles similar to the 1947-49 Studebaker are always considered good-looking--so much so in fact that the French-built Peugeot found it wise to retain the similar 403 model when it introduced the succeeding 404. An off-white automobile will sell well whatever the year. Such deathless designs and design attributes could be cited in every kind of product area: the Cape Cod home design, Federal style furniture, etc. Because little or no research has been directed to this ever-present corollary of the fashion cycle, we must look to observation to formulate a behavioral definition of the forces which create the classic.

Such observation seems to indicate that the term "classic" applies to items which are never at the extremes of the range of fluctuation, are generally close to the midpoint. In general, also, they could be termed "conservative" designs--always pleasing, but never exciting. Further consideration seems to reveal a tendency toward a high degree of simple functionality in such designs, without sacrifice of good aesthetics. They seem to be aimed more at serving to the fullest the core functions of a product and to have sacrificed the extremes of most fringe characteristics to gain a moderate amount of each.

Such functionality of the classic is most easily perceived in the case of the classic single attribute, such as off-white color in automobiles and the just-below-the-knee dress length. Artistically and psychologically, white is a "neutral". As a color, it has none of the excitement of either the warm red of the optical and fashion spectrums or of the cool bright greens and blues at the other extreme. Functionally, a white or off-white car has high visibility on any highway, under any light conditions, and thus is somewhat safer to drive. With the inclusion of just a hint of tan pigment, the off-white car is made to order for the driver who wants minimum maintenance attention--it can go for weeks without washing, yet not look dingy.

Similarly, the below-the-knees length in a dress exhibits the most attractive portion of a woman's underpinnings without calling open attention to them, yet deemphasizes any tendency toward knock-knees or bandy-legs which many seem to have. From the standpoint of the clothing function, such a skirt permits an optimum amount of leg movement freedom, yet serves a high degree of temperature protection. It is, in fact, close to the typical length of that typically functional herder's garb--the kilt.

Such observations suggest an insight into the behavioral set of the market segment to which the classic appeals. Quite clearly, this substantial segment of the market places a much higher value on the central functional aspects of the offering than on the fringe attributes. It is not unmindful of the cosmetic values in clothing but is willing to settle for an adequate minimum of the cosmetic effect in order to gain a maximum of core-value utilities. Manifestly, this is the attitude of a person who is emotionally independent and self-assured--who feels little need for the reinforcement of mass emulation. Although the purchase of a classic design contains some element of economy, such buyers generally are not in the market for low-end goods. Indeed, they often tend to buy well toward the top of the price lines. They are clearly people who do not need strong stimuli, since they shun the extremes. This is a characteristic of the well informed and well educated. All of these characteristics parallel closely the description of people who are likely to be innovators in the case of functionally new offerings.

Design for and sale to the classic-seeking segment can be a profitable business for the firm which knows how to serve it. The market desires functional quality and is willing to pay for it. It can discriminate between the genuine quality and the not-quite-so-good, and thus tends to shun the product which has been cheapened in order to give the appearance of a price advantage. It probably also tends to be relatively loyal to a source which serves it well, and thus makes entry of competition doubly difficult. Once its patronage is gained, the moderate size of the market becomes relatively unattractive to others. On the other hand, since this segment values core function so highly, it must be given constant real product improvements--the seller cannot rest on his product development oars.

The classic is plainly a corollary of the fashion cycle--not a separate phenomenon. Classics are sought by a market segment which places a positive value on stability of design, dislikes the early obsolescence of mere superficial change. Service of this segment is one policy alternative which must be considered as seriously as must the service of those riding the swings of fashion. Classics arise from the same forces which create the fashion fluctuations, but from a different kind of personality. Classics are relatively stable design compromises which gain that stability by minimizing the dissatisfaction which comes from either extreme of the swing and maximizing the core functional attributes a specific market segment seeks. They probably assume greater importance only after the market has approached full maturity.

RELATIONSHIP OF FASHION TO THE FUNDAMENTAL LIFE CYCLE

Fashion is manifestly not a separate classification of life cycle, since it does not involve the core function or the use system, but only the fringe or superficial aspects of the offering. It can only be a second order or superimposed element on that life cycle at certain phases. Lacking any known research on this relationship, we must rely on observation and logic. The logic of our behavioral model of fashion acceptance would seem to indicate fashion as becoming important only during those life cycle phases in which the objective core function of the offering is being taken for granted and the fringe elements become the main focus of attention. Additionally, we might expect classic models to become dominant and design fluctuations to subside or even cease once the initial high interest level in the product group recedes in favor of interest in other aspects of consumption or is replaced by a growth of interest in replacement offerings.

This reasoning would seem to accord with the known history of such major life cycles as those of the automobile, the radio and major home appliances such as mechanical refrigerators.

Although the annual automobile model originated in the early 1920's, automobile styling was subordinate to physical performance characteristics in popular interest and did not become a major market factor until the automobile life cycle was well past its first growth period in the 1930's. For a period of about 3 decades, the glass-and-metal wrapping became the dominant element in value and a mistaken prediction of public style acceptance could be disastrous, as Chrysler learned in 1934, 1950 and 1962, (and Ford learned with the 1958 Edsel). While it would be difficult to detect signs of cycle decline in the 1960's, it is clear that the automobile was losing its dominant position in the family ambitions by the end of this decade and the social status attributes beginning to pass on to other kinds of consumption--swimming pools, a college education for the young, etc. The cue to this downgrading was the growing popularity of imported models whose styling was extremely stable.

During the heyday of the mature radio broadcast cycle of the 1930's and 1940's, the cabinet became the principal element of value. When television took over the entertainment function, the highly styled radio cabinetry gave way to various functional designs which needed no annual face-lifting. Furthermore, styling got no new lease on interest when the radio cycle was revived with the transistor radio and with high fidelity FM. Indeed, the very highest quality FM receivers were almost starkly functional component assemblies.

Similarly, when the home appliance life cycle attained a stable maturity, annual models of refrigerators and ranges lost any clear sales appeal.

Such observations would seem to indicate that fashion values become dominant after the first rush of rapid growth and decrease in importance or disappear whenever the desire-sets leading to purchase narrow to objective function and to a single or few functional use systems. This would also explain why some types of products are not involved in any significant fashion fluctuations.

FOR WHAT KINDS OF PRODUCTS ARE FASHION VALUES IMPORTANT?

Widespread as fashion fluctuations are, it is also possible to find examples of products and use systems which show no such fluctuations. Systems of fastening industrial materials--nailing, bolting, riveting, etc. --have undergone only such changes as would be expected from developments in materials and technology. The wooden peg ancestor of today's common nail gave way in smooth progression to the more easily driven cut iron nail, and the latter in smooth progression to the cheap steel wire nail of today. The riveted skyscraper skeleton whose deafening construction was familiar before World War II has been replaced with the bolted skeleton and prestressed concrete construction. Such products and systems, of course, perform single or limited objective physical functions and thus do not involve incompatible competing desires. They are not subject to the winds of taste of either engineers or consumers. (Other industrial products do involve matters of conflicting design aims. The author discovered one such case in the matter of temperature control devices for a heater flame. Some designers preferred snap, or positive action because it permitted a different burner design. Others preferred the closer control of throttling action.)

It would thus appear that styling values and fluctuations are important only when the desire-set to be satisfied is relatively broad and includes either incompatible physical performance attributes (such as high acceleration and fuel economy in a vehicle) or psychological associations which conflict with other elements in the desire set (status, for example, with low cost and durability). Whenever the latter is the case, we would expect fluctuations in styling to lose their value as the market matures. Whenever the incompatibilities involve some inherent element in the offering (as the decoration element in architecture, clothing, greeting cards, or other offerings by which we perceive ourselves as judged by our peers), we would expect fashion fluctuations to be a permanent part of the life cycle.

Whether passing or permanent, if fashion is an element, the designer must be able to predict the trends as far in advance as the lead time between drawing table and the first purchases.

SUMMARY

1. Fashion connotes a cyclical fluctuation in design popularity which is an inevitable component in every area of product acceptance. Acceptable designs must be in step with the trend at the time

of their introduction.

2. Fashion swings are not a synthetic creation of the designers but are due to fundamental swings in consumer taste which the designer must foresee somewhat in advance.

3. The fashion swings are limited largely to the superficial aspects of the design--to the fringe attributes, not the core functions.

4. The swings of acceptance can be explained as the combined effect of forces covered by three concepts: the concepts of the offering as an inseparable compromise bundle of potential satisfactions; demand as a set of desires for simultaneous satisfaction of several drives, some of which are mutually incompatible in physical terms; and the concept of a dynamic hierarchy of drives.

5. The cultural aspect of fashion--the tendency for there to exist an approved style trend at any given moment in time--is due to the social structure of diffusion of innovations, to the tendency of people to emulate those they consider more expert than they in judging what gives the greatest amount of satisfaction in some area of consumption.

6. This emulation tendency saves time and effort for the adopter but can lead to acceptance of products which are ill-fitted to his desire-sets, and thus deprive him of the satisfactions he thought the product was promising, leading to early dissatisfaction. Even the person whose desire-set is relatively well-fulfilled develops an increasing dissatisfaction over time because of the need to accept a compromise.

7. The decline is just as inevitable as the rise of the fashion, therefore, because of accumulating dissatisfactions with the compromise inherent in physical design.

8. Classics are designs with a relatively stable but moderate demand because they are, for a given market segment, a continuously acceptable compromise. They seem to be designs which place a high emphasis on the core functional values and give a substantial measure of all important fringe attributes without fully sacrificing any of them. The market segment desiring the classic would seem to be the emotionally independent sort of person, and the market can be profitable for those knowing how to serve it.

9. Fashion is really not a separate kind of life cycle, but a second order cycle superimposed on the regular life cycle at certain phases in its existence. For most cycles, these phases seem to be during the upper part of the growth phase and the earlier part of the mature phase. Fashion seems to become a major element in perceived value when the objective core function starts to be taken for granted and the interest shifts to the fringe attributes. It seems to decline in interest as the offering shifts from stage center to make way for some other major interest. In products by which

137

people tend to perceive themselves as being judged, however, like religion, management practices, dress, architecture, etc., fashion tends to be a permanent part of the cycle.

Part Two. Managing the Product over the Length of the Cycle

Since the product life cycle is also a profit life cycle, maintenance of comfortable profit margins requires the organization to deliberately develop a continuing stream of new products of those kinds best adopted to its experience skills and interests, and to continuously review the status of its product line with respect to that cycle, changing the structure of product management and the nature of the marketing mix to harmonize with the status of each item in the line. Such a new product focus implies some kind of guidelines for new product search and an understanding of the process of product gestation and development. Comprehension is also needed of the manner in which product design, communications methods and objectives, pricing strategies and tactics, and distribution policies must shift with the cycle. A thorough understanding is needed of the complex nature of the pricing tool, of the extent to which most price strategy decisions are actually product, not money-oriented, and the many forms of pricing which are useful as short-term tactics. Finally, the constant flux of the competitive structure necessitates the proper organization of marketing intelligence and management control in order to guide the product profitably through the cycle.

7

DEVELOPING THE FRAMEWORK
FOR A SUCCESSFUL PRODUCT
AND DIVERSIFICATION POLICY

The need to maintain profit margins by means of frequent introduction of new products of some kind connotes a twin need for clear policy guidelines for product development. No firm can safely attempt the introduction of every possible kind of new product, so it must decide ahead of development which types of new products fit its resources, experienced-developed skills, and interests and in what manner it is best fitted to diversify.

New product introductions are of four types:

(1) Deeper market penetration--seeking to serve a broader group of market segments.

(2) Continued product improvement.

(3) Wider market development--penetrating new use-systems and new geographical areas.

(4) Product diversification.

The first two of these are a necessary part of any comprehensive new product policy. By contrast, the type and amounts of wider market development and of product diversification to be undertaken will depend on the resources and the capabilities of the particular organization to handle each specific possibility.

Product diversification may be purely of an investment nature, or it may proceed in one or more of five possible operational directions: focus on internal or external acquisition, with a production or a marketing orientation; consist of pioneering or be limited to emulation of the successful introductions of others; be lateral or vertical with respect to marketing channels; emphasize one or another type of management skill. External acquisition is simpler than internal development, leads to earlier returns, and requires less skill in managing development, but is costlier and less safe legally. A purely production-oriented policy can be unprofitable and a purely market-oriented one pass up legitimate opportunities, so that most successful firms compromise with some mixture of both.

140

Pioneering typically requires massive resources and patience but can lead to enduring payoffs, whereas emulative introduction is the opposite in nearly every regard and requires a high degree of promotional skill and fast footwork. Lateral and horizontal diversification are not in necessary opposition to each other, and the wisdom of any specific opportunity must be weighed in terms of the amount of resources, experience and executive attention required and available.

Within the direction chosen, the range of choice open to the individual organization is limited by the markets to which the seller can gain access, by the kind of competitive effort he is best fitted by experience and inclination to handle, by his physical and financial resources, and by the interests of major executives.

Any new product opportunity is a chance to provide some important market segment with a set of values perceivably higher than any available. Such can be sought by analyzing: satisfaction gaps on the structure of competitive offerings, missing links needed to complete use systems of offerings already growing in popularity, new needs and desires growing out of marked changes in the living patterns of buyers, emergent technology capable of producing new desire satisfactions, internal gaps in the line offered by the seller and the filling of which would improve his assortment values, and the development of new markets for established satisfaction packages.

THE NEED FOR POLICY GUIDELINES

The inevitability of the product life cycle makes continued innovation the main source of profit. The organization must have a stream of improved models and new offerings to replace the older lines with declining profit margins if it is to maintain life and growth. No matter how securely entrenched, the company which rests on its laurels is headed for declining profits. This is especially true of one-product firms, as Tektronix and Polaroid found out, but also true of wide-line firms.

Successful innovation usually means product innovation of some degree: either product improvement or product development or, preferably, both, either through internal effort or by acquisition of businesses and product offering developed by others. The only new product policy choice is "how?", not "whether?"

Determining the "how" and "what" of the organization's product policy is a matter to be conducted with the greatest of analytical consideration. The wrong kind of product policy can ruin the profit structure more quickly than does the slow erosion of a status quo policy. Not every kind of innovation, not even every kind of consumer-desired innovation, is automatically successful. The

141

innovation must be one within the limits of what the organization is equipped to develop and must represent an opportunity at which it can excel and to which it can and will devote a major effort.

Only those firms with strong financial resources and great executive patience can afford to attempt to pioneer a high-learning requirement product, for example. Even the financial muscle itself will avail little if the skills and interests of the firm are in a different type of product, requiring unfamiliar kinds of marketing approaches.

Furthermore, no organization can scatter its attention and efforts in very many directions without wasting the effort of its executives. A coherent, directional product policy is required by the limitations on human attention and energies. Even the right product is wrong if it does not somehow build on the going interests, experience and resources of the organization.

Continued success thus requires development of a set of product policy guidelines which give a clear focus to all research and development as well as acquisition efforts. Such a policy provides understood limits to the search for product concepts and keeps development plans within the constraints imposed by the unique resources, skills, and interests of the organization and its executives, guiding both to the kinds of opportunities likely to be most profitable to the particular firm. The first and probably most basic element in formulating such a policy is an appraisal of the type of product introductions most appropriate for the particular firm.

THE POSSIBLE TYPES OF PRODUCT LINE INTRODUCTIONS

Profit-bolstering introductions are of four different basic kinds:

Improved market penetration usually involves getting more business from current customers as well as serving more customers whose desire-sets are similar to those being served, thus may not be thought of as a form of product introduction. Such increased market penetration, however, inevitably requires opening new forms of sales communications with both old and new customers to change their perceptions of the organization's offerings. Consequently, although there may be little or no physical change in the product, the result is a degree of new product introduction from the customer's viewpoint. Attention to the possibility of increased market penetration should normally be part of any rational product policy.

Product improvement and development is really an extension of any form of market penetration policy, for it aims to give large segments of the market a better fit to its desire-sets. An example might be the development of self-contained, lightweight power source in power tools, increasing the portability and convenience attributes. Generally speaking, continued product development efforts are a key element of any successful policy at every stage of the cycle except the decline.

Wider market development may appear to be similar to the last two types, since it involves a form of product improvement, but it does so with a slightly different perspective. Wider market development is usually accomplished by planned modification of the attributes of an offering to give it a special fit to the desire-sets of new and different market segments, without necessarily abandoning the unmodified design which fits the needs of segments already well served. For instance, auto manufacturers were able to better serve the camper market when they introduced specially equipped pick-up truck models whose springing, steering and other attributes were designed for the special stresses of camper use. Farm equipment manufacturers were following a wider market development policy when they modified their farm tractor designs for construction and lift-truck use. Such a policy of wider market development is not necessarily profitable, since the new markets sought may require quite different sales channels and a divergent type of promotional effort, thus leading to a possible scattering and dilution of the firm's marketing energies. Any product policy must therefore set some guidelines as to the limits of sales-energy diversion which is thought consonant with the organization's resources.

Product diversification: the addition of new and substantially different offerings, serving new and noticeably different desire-sets, either by means of internal product development or through acquisition of other organizations or their products. Any such product diversification of any substantial degree is a major effort and will fail if that effort is not planned for and put forth. Thus when Tektronix decided to introduce an advanced machine-tool controller, it failed to anticipate the need for and to make an all-out marketing commitment, and lost an opportunity (Business Week, August 4, 1973, p. 85).

Some executive attention and major resources are bound to be diverted if the move is to have any chance of success. Hence every such introduction should be taken only within the confines of guidelines so planned that the gains estimated will more than offset the cost of such diversion of physical and human resources.

The same product strategy policy will inevitably encompass both wider market development and product development. Any wider market development move requires some form of innovation, some kind of new service-bundle offering to the customers. Similarly, all product diversification moves imply some significant potential development of wider markets.

143

The first decision to be made concerns the type of strategy best adapted to the firm's special resources, experience, skills, and interests and the kinds of profit opportunities these make possible or rule out.

THE BASIC TYPES OF PRODUCT STRATEGY GUIDELINES

A workable product diversification strategy must develop satisfactory answers to at least six fundamental questions:

Shall the diversification be essentially operational or investment oriented?

If operational, shall diversification be internal or mainly by acquisition?

Shall it be production oriented, market-structure oriented, or attempt both simultaneously?

To what extent should the organization attempt to pioneer?

Should the diversification be mainly vertical or lateral?

What kinds of management skills and experience should be the central theme?

Investment-Based or Operational Diversification?

The diversification moves of some organizations are little more than the investment of available funds in autonomous going enterprises to get a higher return than would be available through internal expansion. Such moves are essentially financial in character, although some economies of financial integration and overall management services may be implied. The contrasting policy extreme is an operational diversification aimed at development of a broader set of offerings under a fully integrated management. Investment-oriented diversification is really the sale of funds and may involve little more corporate integration than some supervision of finances. Sometimes, however, the diversifying investor is seeking out situations with a poor profit record which can be strengthened by management reorganization, but still left relatively autonomous afterward. In such a case, the diversifier is really conceiving his skills as those of a seller of management reorganization services. Such a diversification is really not a marketing one in the normally used meaning of the term marketing.

Operational Diversification: Internal or External?

Although operational diversification of any kind is also an investment decision, its primary orientation is the firm's marketing operations--operational diversification seeks to gain some kind of

144

market advantage by broadening the firm's offerings. That advantage may be conceived of as a cost advantage through fuller or steadier use of production facilities, through a wider use of its technical know-how, or through the economies of marketing a longer line. Or the advantage may be a better market position made possible by improvement of the product assortment offered to current customers, or through a broadening of the customer list. Any of these forms of operational diversification may be achieved through internal research and development or by means of external acquisition of other firms or parts of their product lines.

Internal diversification requires skill in the management of research and development and quite often in the pioneering of market development. One usual side benefit is a relative freedom from attacks by the anti-trust lawyers. By contrast, external diversification by acquisition requires less development of management skills and reduces (at a price) the time lag between initial investment and profits, but can arouse the suspicions of the Justice Department in the United States.

Production-oriented diversification is guided by a focus on the organization's technological skills. Offerings are sought which utilize technical know-how, the current physical plant, or both. One aspect of the Carborundum Company's expansion of the early 1960's is a prime example. Originally a producer of ceramic abrasives in the form of grinding stones and wheels, the firm early broadened out internally into the production of refractory furnace linings and electric furnace electrodes, then acquired the Spode chinaware business by purchase. Such product-oriented diversification is sometimes labelled as a policy of congruent production diversification.

The contrasting extreme of policy is to orient expansion entirely around the firm's existing market structure--its know-how in serving a specific segment of demand. Thus the mergers, acquisitions, and internal product development of SCM (formerly Smith-Corona-Marchant) have centered on the office equipment market. Such a policy may avoid investment in production facilities as much as possible, in order to concentrate all energies and other resources on the skills at which the firm considers itself most adept--the provision of marketing service. SCM, for example, early shed the production of carbon paper and other related office supplies while retaining the sales rights.

Generally speaking, firms tend to some degree of compromise between the two extremes of production-centered policies and the completely market-centered focus. Although some of the Carborundum Company's diversifications have, as noted above, been carried out to take advantage of its ceramic know-how, much of its line expansion has been to offer its industrial customers a more

145

complete assortment of "metal removal services": sand blasting machines and belt sanders as well as grinding wheels. Expansion of its metal removal line has stayed within the limits of its knowledge of abrasives, however, and not crossed over into metal cutting tool production, in which none of its experience was on a par with that of those already in the market.

To What Degree Should We Pioneer?

All product introductions carry some degree of risk and all involve some modicum of patience in the wait for profit eventualities. The range in the degree of possible risk and in the amount of patience needed is extremely variable, however, from the minimal to the very high. When both risk and the profit time-lag are high, the financial strength required to carry through to success is obviously very substantial, but so can be the profits if the organization possesses skills in pioneering. Every firm must therefore decide what financial resources and degree of fortitude it both can and is willing to commit. It must make a thoroughly objective analysis of just where on the scale of pioneering it is both able and willing to work--at what point between the extreme of minor product differentiation, of the introduction of purely emulative products, and the opposite one of pioneering very high-learning introductions.

Success in introduction of emulative and adaptive products, of really attractive new differentiations of well-established existing service bundles, can itself require quite a bit of skill--largely in imaginative sales promotion--and the pay-off is not always minor in any sense, as the fortunes built by those in the toiletries and cosmetics industries well testify. But as the histories of these industires also indicate, product profit life tends to be brief. In the health and beauty aid fields where such "new" emulative and adoptive products are the way of life, the A. C. Nielsen firm (1973) finds the average brand life span to be about three years, and in food products, where a similar emulative policy is also rampant, about two years. Furthermore, the initial extra perceived value of the most successful introductions seldom are large enough to command significant price margin premiums over existing compeition. The lack of substantial added value is an inevitable corollary of the learning curve phenomenon. The longer a use-system is in existence, the smaller the value of the refinements and improvements which can be made in it. Similarly, the brevity of the product life of minor improvements is an inevitable corollary of the quick profitability which flows from the ready acceptance which renders the launching risk so small, so cheap and easy. The limitations on product profit life and on price premiums constitute no argument against a "no-pioneering" policy, as the profits of such firms as Procter and

146

Gamble and General Motors show. But they do mean that the firm
which adopts such a policy must be quick on its marketing feet,
sound in its judgment of customer psychology, and possessed of a
reasonably high level of both promotional skills and promotional
resources.

Success in launching emulative products is not automatic. The
introduction must first ferret out a possible market niche, and this
will never be obvious. Other sellers will normally be serving most
potential buyers in some degree, and thus what is offered must have
some kind of very substantial perceived added value if it is to get
through the selective attention barrier of even the fringe segments.
Differentiation of some kind that will take full advantage of experi-
ence-developed skills is also important. Unless the potential emulative introduction can capitalize on some kind of special production,
design, or marketing skill of the firm, the firm starts out at a substantial experience disadvantage relative to those already established and must depend on the latter going to sleep and thus not
taking advantage of that experience. The tendency of emulators to
introduce low-end products is often well founded on this need. Economy motel chains sprang up in the 1970's because their builders
had special experience in construction, and thus could keep investment low and penetrate segments not previously well-served by
higher-service offerings of those with motel experience.

The opposite extreme of developing and promoting new high-
learning products can also be quite profitable, but demands a different set of skills and resources. One important essential resource is financial. The firm must be able to finance the development of a new technology up to the point of an adequate buyer service bundle, then on through the prolonged period of deficits characteristic of a market development phase. Normally, also, pioneering high-learning products requires a very special skill in choosing
technologies on the verge of new product development and in managing the ensuing development process. The firm needs either insight or luck in recognizing emergent technologies which could lead
to profitable market offerings and the ability to coordinate the efforts of the research scientists, the development technologists, and
of marketing management. That such a product-pioneering policy
can also pay well those with such insight or luck is well attested by
the record of such firms as duPont, Polaroid, and Xerox.

Vertical or Lateral Diversification?

Careful consideration needs also be given to the directions
and their degree when diversifying. Diversification can be <u>vertical</u>
--up and down the same channel of sale--or <u>lateral</u>-- adding a
broader line of offerings at the same level in the sales chain. The

147

Carborundum moves discussed earlier have been both. Adding a line of furnace electrodes made the firm a supplier of production goods it had been purchasing, and thus was a vertical move. The addition of sandblast equipment was a horizontal broadening of its offerings to the metal-working trade. Similarly, some food chains have diversified vertically by the establishment of henneries to supply the eggs they sell and horizontally by the creation or acquisition of drug outlets and even discount department stores to supply a wider assortment of goods to their customers. Tire and shoe manufacturers have diversified vertically into retail distribution of their products and related lines.

Diversification in any direction tends to spread executive attention over a wider area of activity, and care must be exercised that such attention does not become spread too thin. A horizontal move which merely broadens the assortment available to the same group of customers may do little more than add personnel at the junior executive level. But when, as in the Carborundum expansion into china, the move is into a line using a different sales channel, reaching a different kind of customer, the firm is adding a whole new business. A food chain which builds a hennery capable of supplying its minimal egg requirements may need to add only a minor middle management level of supervision for the producing unit, but the forward integration of a tire producer may be successful only if the firm gets into the merchandising of a much broader line of goods than it makes--garden equipment, fertilizers, kitchen appliances, and wheel toys, for example.

Thus the organization needs to think beforehand about the amount of diversification it is able to undertake in each possible direction. These, and all preceding considerations will enter into the formulation of the basic theme of all diversification planning.

What Basic Theme for Diversification Is Appropriate?

Since product diversification is of many degrees and can proceed in a multitude of directions, each requiring a different mixture of talent and resources, it should be clear that some careful choices must be made beforehand. Since every choice must be made well in advance of known specific alternatives, every firm needs a specific guideline summed up in a specific theme which will govern the kinds of opportunities to which it will give serious consideration. Otherwise, the organization risks galloping simultaneously to the four winds of the market, straight toward disaster, as Scripto, Inc. found out. A leader in the $300 million writing instrument field in the 1950's, the firm turned its main attention to totally different markets--markets it did not know: carpets, ceramics and copying machines. All proved such losers that there was a real

148

question of the company's viability. It finally got in the black only after shedding the new lines. (Business Week, February 17, 1973, p. 46).

That product theme should define in very specific form the kinds of marketing innovation the firm is best structured to develop at an advantage over possible competition, those markets in which its own special forms of accumulated experience gave it an advantage over possible competition, or at least equal initial footing. Scott Paper Company, for example, defines its efforts as the development of "food store products" (clearly of an inedible sort, currently). Although the firm's production technology is founded on paper, it has no compunctions about using plastics which fill related needs and, conversely, has not entered some of the larger volume paper production lines such as newsprint. Even the industrial items it develops were closely related to the specific segment of the ultimate consumer mix it sells, up to recently. Similarly, Pillsbury views itself as primarily a food service firm, not as a grain miller, and thus has diversified into poultry production and the operation of hamburger stands. The Coleman Company concentrates on camping and outdoor activity equipment. Litton Industries concentrates on translating new technologies into commercially saleable products, a policy which has led it into such seemingly diverse fields as office equipment, shipbuilding, and education of the underprivileged, but caused management to shun a merger which included a brewery. A Litton move into the food industry through acquisition of Stouffer proved unsatisfactory (Wall Street Journal, December 21, 1972, p. 26). None of its experience was much value in this case.

Diversification moves often can involve some sideline opportunities which do not seem to fit the chosen theme. These may be taken on when they can be made profitable without major top executive attention. Coleman's sheetmetal working skills and experience led it into subcontracting parts for bombers, but the firm did not pursue this into aircraft engineering and design which would have diverted top executive attention from its main markets and gone beyond its experience base in both marketing and production. Pillsbury's poultry production efforts resulted partly from the fact that it could not avoid producing feed by-products in its milling operations, partly from the possession of well-developed skills in development of feed formulation and market timing, permitting it to obtain more profit from feeding the grain than from selling it.

Such sideline diversification, in other words, is best when governed by the same rules as those which accord with the chosen product theme:

> Take advantage of the firm's position on a particular experience curve, in markets in which this experience is a basic

149

factor.

Take advantage of special talents and special physical and
financial resources possessed by the firm, skills and resources which grant it a special competitive advantage.

Operate within the limits set by available resources.

Take on opportunities which accord with the interests of the
controlling personnel in the organization.

Go where the major profit opportunities are relative to the
resources and time involved.

Discovering just what kinds of products fit an organization's
experience, skills, and interests requires the most careful of analysis of every aspect of producing and marketing to learn what factors in the firm's operation are critical in granting it the market
advantage responsible for its existence and health. Too often, executives look at some single factor, and often one that is not really
relevant. Thus Ryan Aircraft, a maker of airframe and airframe
components, plunged into the manufacture of aluminum coffins after
World War II cut back the aircraft market simply because they had
production experience in bending aluminum (which led company
workers to quip, "Fly'em and die'em with Ryan"). They neglected
to perceive that no casket manufacturer built his profits on the basis
of production know-how. Marketing and distribution skills and contacts are responsible for the market niche for coffins, not production cost.

Every diversification decision should be a rational balancing
of the best estimates possible of the known restraints on what the
organization can attempt wisely and the various profit opportunities
open in view of the restraints, capabilities and interests of the
members of the organization.

No organization of any sort, commercial or otherwise, has a
completely free choice of product or market strategy. The choice
is limited by the markets to which the organization has access, by
the aspects of competitive endeavor in which it has the personnel
talents and experience to excel, by the kinds of skills it possesses,
and by the kinds of risks it knows best how to estimate and take.
Physical and financial resources comprise a further set of restraints. Finally, every market introduction and subsequent sales
management requires a sustained high level of attention to its own
specific kind of administrative detail and its own form of imaginative invention. Consequently, the kinds of activities which develop
the high level of interest needed to sustain this attention and develop
imaginative tactics will determine what types and degrees of innovation an organization can wisely undertake.

The most obvious restraints on choice of opportunities are
the physical and financial, particularly the latter. The introduction

150

of color television demanded the extra finances to support the broadcasting of color programs which could have no adequate audience for some considerable period, and the manufacture of an initial inventory of sets sufficient to supply a national network of dealers. Obviously, even though the 10-year-long market development lag was wholly unforeseen at the time, it took no special prescience to realize that only a major firm with both the broadcast and manufacturing interests and also the financial strength of RCA or CBS could afford to pioneer such an undertaking. While launching a new line of toiletries involves rather modest manufacturing facilities and materials costs, and even the physical production can be farmed out, finances for a very substantial initial advertising budget are required. Likewise, a new line of cosmetics implies a strong distributive foothold in department and specialty stores and carefully trained salespeople. On the other hand, many missing-link products succeed so quickly that they require only modest financial strength, and almost any individual can publish a book which meets the need of a waiting market with only a handful of dollars for the initial printing and mail promotion.

On the other hand, once the market development phase is completed, the market entry fee is relatively modest for any new competitor who introduces some emulative variant well designed to attract a specific segment of the now proven market. Indeed the relative resources required is a major reason the market development period is relatively free from competition and why competition burgeons once the period of rapid growth is clearly evident.

Of course, whatever the stage of the product cycle, some kinds of enterprises require much more extensive resources than others. There really is no inexpensive form of steel mill. But soap, other toiletries, and cosmetics can and sometimes are produced from easily obtained ingredients on equipment little more elaborate than that found in any housewife's kitchen.

The restraints imposed by personal skills, capabilities, and interests are somewhat less obvious than those imposed by limitations on physical resources, but they frequently are much more restrictive than the lack of physical and financial sinews. All organizations are composed primarily of people, and all people are, by the very nature of the experience and skills acquisition process, limited in what they do best. The principal asset of any organized group is the reservoir of physical and intellectual skills residing in its membership and its accumulated experiences of various kinds, relative to others in the field.

The allies could and did virtually demolish the physical structure of German and Japanese industry during World War II. Once the fighting and occupation ceased, however, the reservoir of accumulated industrial experience in both nations permitted quick recovery as major industrial powers, stronger than ever. On the other hand, Russia has clearly shown that more is required to cross the gap between a subsistence, peasant agriculture and a modern agricultural industry than equipment and other physical appurtenances similar to those in agriculturally more advanced nations. A long process of revolutionary change in the work habits, skills, and thinking of everybody concerned--the gradual accumulation of experience by government as well as farmer, must be undergone, and after more than 50 years, Russia has not yet accomplished its goal in this.

Skills are inherently unbalanced. To do one type of task well requires an habitual way of working and thinking which can be completely inimical to the performance of a different type of task. A really good proofreader, for instance, almost never is capable of quickly grasping the overall significance of the whole presentation, and the person who is good at the latter has acquired a degree of perceptual closure which causes him to gloss over and miss real errors in detail. Likewise, a precision craftsman finds himself outclassed in the rapid assembly of low-tolerance work. The habits of thought needed to excel in the frantic pace of toiletries promotion are contrary to the patient development of a high-learning product introduction. Even very similar-appearing marketing operations can take incompatible skills and experience. The Toni Company, for example, discovered that its demonstrated expertise in selling toiletries did not fit it for success in cosmetics. Toni's skills in advertising promotion did not carry over to give success in the personal-sales-oriented promotion of cosmetics. Others were too far ahead of it on the experience curve.

For this reason, the first and most important element in the development of a sound product strategy must be a thorough and a thoroughly objective analysis of the personal skill and experience requirements of each product strategy under consideration. The second need is just as honest and just as penetrating an analysis of the skills the organization either possesses or can develop to the point of superiority relative to competition. This latter depends partly on experience, but since skills are learned, not a gift of the genes, they depend also, like all learning, on the direction and intensity of management interest. Given a high enough level of interest and willingness to change, a firm can even break completely with its past experience. Such instances are rare, of course, because change is distasteful to most of us, but it can happen, as the Peerless Motor Company demonstrated. Faced with the collapse of the luxury market for their prestige automobiles during the Great Depression, and imbued with a driving desire for some kind of profitable business, the firm switched to brewing, and as Carling's Beer, had a succeeding profitable career. But it should be noted

152

that this was done at a time (1933) when all competitors were, in effect, at the start of a new experience curve.

Obviously, an unbiased, objective appraisal of its own resources, skills, and interests will reveal to the firm the limits on the kinds of markets in which it can hope to succeed. But such an analysis is only the first step--it does not of itself point out the specific policy which will produce success. Indeed, the superficial application of such an analysis is likely to lead to the very dangerous no-change no-innovation policy. The incentive to innovate and the indication of the best direction and degree of innovation come partly from an analysis of the opportunities that are open.

THE POSITIVE SIDE OF POLICY FORMULATION--OPPORTUNITY ANALYSIS

Some kind of new product introduction policy is needed simply because old products inevitably represent declining profit opportunities and must be replaced in the interest of merely sustaining the profit structure. New and better profit margins can come only from offerings which are new, in some sense, to the market--offerings which promise the customer perceivable satisfactions previously unavailable or available in substantially lesser degree. Even when such introductions are mainly emulative copies of competing items, they must promise some kind of additional value. Generally speaking, if they are to yield the desired wider profit margins, they need to be offerings in the growth phase of their cycle. Those in charge of product planning need thus to be on the alert for new opportunities for customer satisfactions and for new customers to serve in ways the organization is equipped to serve them.

The systematic search for such opportunities takes a blend of skilled analysis of market and technological intelligence and of imaginative insight into possible customer satisfactions. Such opportunities can develop from one or more of six possible directions:

Gaps in the structure of competitive offerings in relation to the totality of satisfactions sought by various market segments interested in the specific product category.

Missing links needed to make already growing offerings readily available and widely usable.

Unfulfilled newly emerging desires and needs arising from changes in the market, in the life styles of buyers.

Emergent technology, capable of producing new desire satisfactions or of substantially improving on the satisfaction of desires now partly appeased.

Gaps in the line of existing offerings which, if filled, would make the organization a more satisfactory source for some

153

substantial market segment.

The emergence of new markets or market segments for existing offerings.

Almost any product category is bound to contain possibilities of market coverage gaps. Feasible satisfaction desire-sets are extremely diverse and complex, and the general tendency of those serving a given market is to concentrate on the larger and more obviously popular desire-sets, hoping either to gain a dominant position or expecting that even a minor share of a big pie is the most profitable opportunity. The very intense competition for the large-user market, however, means that gaining a large share of it is possible only at the expense of profit margins. Moreover, the dynamics of the acceptance cycle are such that what is most popular at the moment has already lost much of its high early-market value in the prospect's eyes. The buyer, by now, is already seeking possible new and as yet unfulfilled satisfactions. Not only the unit margin, but often the total profit is greater for the organization which seeks out and develops specialized satisfaction bundles matching fringe desire-sets in the product category. U. S. Steel, for instance, dominated the industry volume from the moment of its founding, but the profit margin of some of the small specialty steel producers has long been better than the margins of "Big Steel".

Generally, of course, desire-set coverage gaps indicate opportunities for minor evolutionary product improvements, good for quick early profits but not long-lasting ones. The one exception is the missing-link product.

The missing-link product may be defined as an offering which completes a consumption system already gaining acceptance and thus makes this system truly available on a wide scale and easily adopted. In the early days of radio, the broadcasting network was such a missing-link product, giving the already growing audience of listeners high-value live shows instead of mere phonograph recordings, and delivering a mass nationwide audience to the mass advertiser. In the development of the computer market, it was the program library and the programming program, without which few firms could have afforded to use the new machines. Similarly, the development of rubber tires for tractors changed the long-time slow increase in tractor usage into an overnight mechanization revolution, and the political invention of Rural Electrification abolished the barriers to urban amenities in rural areas.

Alfred Sloan's introduction of systemized installment selling and the trade-in was one of the main elements in General Motor's climb to dominance. In any teaching field in the United States, widespread adoption of any developing instructional approach is dependent on publication of a suitable textbook or other supporting instructional materials, and the first well-designed production will gain an immediately large adoption if the approach is already in use.

Such missing-link introductions, when properly developed before introduction, are inevitably very profitable because of the limited need for investment in market development and the speedy growth in acceptance, enabling the innovator to leap frog the deficit period of market development most revolutionary products face. Imaginative foresight will often reveal such profitable missing links to full use of most revolutionary introductions.

A very similar type of opportunity, and often just as profitable, is that for innovative offerings which take cognizance of changes in the structure of markets and consumption patterns arising from natural social and economic evolution--changes in such matters, for instance, as the place and form of residence, in the age and sex composition of the population, trends in employment patterns, and trends in mobility. Every such change creates new potential needs and desires, changes the habitual use-systems which make up our pattern of living.

The five-day, 40-hour week, for instance, opened the way to a family recreation boom which created major industries around golfing, boating and many other activities formerly confined to a select few. The growth in the trend to lifelong careers for married women opened the supermarket shelves to volumes of quality convenience foods. The modern tendency for large numbers of young adults to take jobs hundreds of miles from familiar home territory created a market for specially designed "singles" apartment projects which offer a meeting place and special recreation facilities as well as attractive shelter to high-paid middle-class professionals and technicians. The first such projects built in California quickly developed waiting lists at a time when ordinary apartments had high vacancy ratios.

Such opportunities will be revealed by analysis of the multiple changes taking place in population and industrial trends, and of the implications of these changes for living and for production. They are missing links in newly arisen use-systems.

Of quite a different character, and requiring far greater resources, are opportunities to develop offerings which require learning of new use-systems. The immediate profit in such introduction is usually nil, and deficits must usually be expected for extended periods of market development. But such learning requirement introductions can yield the best-intrenched market opportunities to organizations capable of supporting the market development expenses and wise enough to continue product development after introduction, to keep one step ahead of potential competition when profits do become clearly visible. Many organizations which deliberately avoid such pioneering introductions are highly profitable, but the profits they reap are far more vulnerable than those which accrued to such introductions as Frigidaire, as DuPont's nylon, and Xerox. Perceiving the opportunities to develop such high-learning introductions requires insight into the directions the advancing state of scientific art seem to be leading, combined with perception of the possible consumer desires such developments could satisfy. But it gives the initial firm a strong lead on the experience curve.

The potential offerings represented by the types of opportunities discussed above all contain added value which is self-contained in some manner. They are all products which would be perceived by buyers as "new" in some sense. Not all opportunities necessarily come from products the buyer perceives as new, however.

A product which is new only to the firm's own line may nevertheless be perceived by the buyer as having substantial added value because it lowers his search or procurement cost, by completing an assortment he already has found attractive.

Gaps in the product line can thus represent true product opportunities. The physical product itself need be no more than equal in quality to what is available from other sources (although being better helps, of course), so long as it rounds out an assortment desired by customers and thus decreases their necessary number of sources and shrinks the search cost necessary to obtain a desired assortment. When food markets added pet supplies and health and beauty aids to their merchandise lines they were not adding items unfamiliar to their customers, but the addition was profitable because the simplification of shopping was a real value for the buyer. Valuable opportunities for new introductions can thus be revealed by a consideration of the assortments the customer desires and matching the product line against these to find gaps in the assortments offered.

One final set of opportunities may involve no change whatsoever in the physical offering, merely a communicational change--a change in the promotional story which causes a new market segment to perceive the offering as a possible fulfillment of a previously unfulfilled desire. When American Tobacco Company started advertising cigarettes to women in the early 1920's with the theme, "Reach for a Lucky instead of a sweet", it rode a coming trend in female emancipation by giving the ladies an acceptable excuse to take on one of the symbols of masculinity. Honda greatly broadened the market for motorcycles by promoting its light-weight models with middle-class coed types as riders, not the power-hungry young males generally associated with the older powerful models. The fragrance industry penetrated the male market by discreet appeals to masculinity, first through "after-shave lotions", then through

FIGURE 7-1. One Product Policy Appraisal Check List

ABOUT OURSELVES:

1. What is the position of each of our product groups in the Product Life Cycle?
2. What is our position in each industry in which we are involved? What is our market position, at what price level(s), and what our types of products?
3. At what aspects of each phase of our business are we clearly better than our competitors?
4. At what aspects are we in less than a top position, and what is the chance for gaining the requisite experience to improve this?
5. What market segments do we have the experience to serve best?
6. What are the relative importance for success of each kind of skill and experience, for each product group in our line:

Research and development
Design skills
Styling skills
Production skills
Cost control expertise
In distributive strength and
dealer cooperation

Promotional adroitness:
In mass media--selling over the dealers'
heads
In personal sales, and working through the
dealers
Service network
Other_____

ABOUT THE OPPORTUNITIES:

1. What profitable opportunities are open to us?
2. What is the position of each in the PLC?
3. What is the probable learning requirement of any introduction we could make?
4. What noticeable difference could we offer the buyers?
5. What kinds of skills are needed to gain a strong market niche in each?

Design skills & feel of the market?
R & D management?
Production skills?
Cost control expertise?
Distribution: What channels would
be used and how well do they co-
incide with the ones we know how
to work with?
How important is channel coopera-
tion?

Service network: How important is after-
sales service to the buyer, and do we
have or could we create an adequate
network?
Promotional knack?
In mass media? (and how much experience or knowledge do we have of this
kind of buyer?)
In personal sales: is this the same kind
of customer our men deal with now,
and does it take the same kind of sales
effort?

6. Executive experience and commitment:
At what executive level will this require concentrated attention and experience
Is this the kind of business at which our executives at that level have experience and a deep interest? If not, can experienced staff be hired easily?
7. How much of a commitment of executive interest and finances are we prepared
to make for this, and is this clearly adequate to open up a major niche in the
market?

other toiletries.

All forms of product opportunities reduce to a single principle: all new product search is a hunt for substantially unfulfilled
buyer desires which the firm's resources, experience, skills,
and interests are best suited to satisfy. Without the potential desire, no offering is possible. Without some special advantage in
introduction, the organization is likely to see someone else profit
from the opportunity. It is a search for a chance to offer the customer added value substantially greater than the cost involved.
Once found, the next step is to develop a concrete saleable form of
the idea.

The difference between those firms highly successful, year
after year, and those which stumble sooner or later is really a
difference in the clarity of their product policy framework. Consciously or unconsciously, the successful have followed a well-
planned, consistent product policy based on their individual skills
and interests. Although it would be claiming too much to insist
that such success cannot come unconsciously, a carefully conscious
appraisal similar to the check list in Figure 7-1 would be a good
periodical step for any firm.

SUMMARY

1. The fact of the product life cycle makes continuing innovation a continuing necessity for continued profitability. Innovation
itself is not automatically profitable, however. It needs to be guided
by a policy which directs attempts in directions which harmonize
with the interests, resources, and potential or actual skills of the
seller. No group of people has an unlimited ability to scatter its
attention and interests in a multitude of unrelated directions.

2. Of the four basic forms of new product introductions, improved market penetration and continued offering improvement are
necessary parts of any sound new product policy. Wider market
development involves some degree of innovation and will be limited
by the extent of promotional and channel diversification the seller's
resources and abilities will support. Any substantial product diversification is bound to involve some diversion of executive attention and energies and must, therefore, be confined within pre-
considered guidelines.

3. Product guidelines need to be set with regard to at least
six different possible sets of diversification directions;
    --an operational or an investment orientation
    --mainly internal development or mainly external acquisition
    --a production orientation or a market orientation, or both
     simultaneously

--pioneering or attempts to capture parts of markets pioneered by others

--vertical or lateral moves, relative to marketing channels

--one or another kind of management skill emphasis

4. The choice of an investment orientation is not really a
marketing decision in the usual sense, but an attempt to sell some
form of managerial or financial services. Only operational diversification enforces choices in the other five directions.

5. An exclusively production oriented policy is not likely to
continue successful for long, whereas an exclusively market oriented one may neglect opportunities to capitalize on well-developed
special production abilities. Most firms strike a balance somewhere between these two extremes.

6. The choice of a pioneering policy normally means possession of considerable patience in the wait for profits and of rather
hefty resources needed to tide over a long period of market development deficits. The degree of pioneering attempted must obviously
be matched with the resources and executive skills. The payoff
for pioneering, however, can be quite attractive and long-lasting,
provided management knows how to manage pioneering introduction
and how to stay ahead of burgeoning competition during the period
of rapid growth. The innovation-follower policy usually results in
less enduring gains but can also be profitable when executed with
skill and in full understanding of the need for innovative differentiation even in imitative offerings.

7. Lateral and vertical diversification are not necessarily
mutually exclusive, and the decision in each case rests on an evaluation of how much diversion of energy and executive attention is
necessary.

8. The choice of product diversification policy is far from
being a free one. The opportunities for success are limited by the
markets to which the seller can gain access, by the kinds of competitive effort best suited to the available skills and talents and the
kinds of risks a seller can judge well and will take, by his physical
and financial resources, and by the kinds of innovation which will sustain his administrative attention and his imaginative invention. Different kinds of markets and offerings pose quite divergent requirements in each of these directions.

9. The choice of diversification policy is also restrained by
the types of opportunities available and visible to the seller. Finding the best requires a systematic search effort.

10. Any opportunity is basically a chance to reward some
market segment with a noticeably higher sought-for satisfaction
value not otherwise currently available.

11. Most new product opportunities are to be found in one or
more of six possible directions:

- --satisfaction gaps in the structure of competitive offerings
- --missing links needed to complete use-systems of offerings already growing in popularity
- --new needs and desires arising from changes in the living patterns of buyers
- --emergent technology capable of producing new desire satisfactions
- --internal gaps in the line offered by the seller, the filling of which would improve his assortment from the buyer's point of view
- --the development of possible new markets or new market segments for an established core satisfaction.

8

PRODUCT DEVELOPMENT: CONCEPTION AND GESTATION OF NEW PRODUCTS

Growth and even maintenance of organizational vitality and profits depend on regular introduction of new products. This constant renewal of the profit lifestream depends in turn on maintenance of some kind of organizational device for systematic new product idea search, screening, and development. The most common forms of formal organizational new product search and screening are new product committees and full-time new product executives or departments. Committees can do a fairly good job when properly constituted and the inevitably conflicting viewpoints of different departments well balanced. Historically, however, they have tended to restrict attention too narrowly to minor innovations rather than to true diversification. Companies with extended histories of successful innovation have tended toward establishment of some kind of full-time new product department.

Any kind of new product effort involves much more than finding and identifying suitable new product concepts. Good ideas often fail of development and success for lack of some kind of executive champion--some person or group with adequate authority committed to the idea's development and success, who will follow it through the product development stage and preferably see it well launched on the market development phase. Task forces, product managers, and venture teams have all proved of value in this connection.

The first step in the process is a dedicated search for new product ideas of any and all kinds, from any and all of the multitude of possible sources. The first task of the new product group or department is to screen these ideas to identify those which could fit the firm's resources, capabilities, position on the experience curves, and interests and which seem technically feasible and also offer a substantial added value for customers. The group thus must start with some well-developed criteria for acceptance, based on established new product guidelines. Ideas which pass this screening

161

should be recommended for development with definitely spelled out product performance and, preferably, costing goals. The specificity of each will depend on the degree of innovation being attempted. One crucial aspect of the development process is the creation of a substantial degree of differentiation.

Physical product development must be paralleled with market plan development from the beginning, preferably based on a critical path or PERT analysis working back from the most desirable point of time for successful introduction. As the moment for that planned introduction approaches, the seller must make as certain as possible that the product as developed is really ready for the market, that the assembly line version contains no serious flaws in design or production which could spoil market acceptance before value is established.

THE NEED FOR A SYSTEMATIC NEW PRODUCT SEARCH

The obvious inevitability of the product life cycle and the profit implications of this fact should make manifest the need for formal provision for a constant search for new product ideas and for their vigorous development into innovative market offerings.

The greatest profit contributions of any offering are harvested in its youth, during the period of rapid growth of acceptance. Buyers' perceptions of the offering's value to them is highest during this phase of the life cycle, and they are then least critical of costs, least inclined to search out competitive offerings and scrutinize relative values. This is why the greatest profits accrue to organizations oriented to production of a continuing stream of new products appropriate to their skills and resources.

Maintenance of the continuity of this stream of new products requires minimum dependence on the accidental and maximum attention to the purposive cultivation of new product concepts and their nurture to viable market birth. Such breeding and gestation of new product concepts is so important that it is never wise to permit it to be a secondary consideration of executives whose main job is close attention to serving today's markets. For this reason, an increasing number of firms have made new product search, screening, and development the primary formal responsibility of a separate part of the management structure.

NEW PRODUCT ORGANIZATION WITHIN THE ENTERPRISE

An adequate new product operation must make provision for both the broadest possible search organization and for adequate follow-through of products approved for development.

Formal permanent new product organizational forms have generally been either committees drawn from some relatively high level of management or, increasingly, a person or group whose sole responsibility is the search for new product opportunities.

The committee form was devised because new product search and development requires a creative compromise of basically conflicting viewpoints between those responsible for the functions of sales, of research and development, and of production. Those in charge of production are accustomed to definitive, carefully scheduled plans in their areas, based on definitive data. They dislike change of direction and are used to fulfilling mainly short-range goals. Sales personnel tend also to focus largely on the short range, but are enured to a high degree of change and instability in their planning, causing them to think in terms of less structured operations. R & D personnel, by contrast to both, tend toward a long-range interest horizon and an even less structured form of organizational relationship. Even more importantly, their sole aim in life tends to be change. All three functions are intimately involved in any new product planning, and the needs of all three must somehow be harmonized.

Some committee-type new product operations seem to have done well at both compromising these conflicting viewpoints and at producing a stream of successful new products. On the basis of a study of two similar plastic firms, Lorsch and Laurence (1965) indicate that such committees may work best when staffed with somewhat lower-level management in close operational touch with the working problems in their own areas, provided that they are about equally strong in committee influence and committed to development of new product ideas. On the basis of their analysis of the experience of these two companies, Lorsch and Laurence seemed to feel that higher-level executives, when in such a committee, were more likely to attempt to avoid conflicts in ideas and viewpoint than to attempt to compromise them, and thus stultify the search for the disturbingly new. In any event, such higher-level executives are bound to be engrossed in their own day-to-day problems and find it difficult to concentrate on a longer-range focus.

New product committee systems share the weakness of all committee systems in any case. The attention and judgment of each individual member is certain to be restricted by the focus of his everyday and more dominant responsibilities. The sales representative is concerned mostly with the kind of change which will improve his short-term operations because he is held responsible for that short-term. The production representative is naturally concerned with minimizing the interruptions to the continuity of his operations, interruptions which lower the output efficiency on which he tends to be rated. The research man's whole orientation is to change and the future, and he may find considerations of even the time range relatively unimportant, disruptions caused by constant change of little interest. Achieving an even balance between such divergent viewpoints is a difficult task and one not certain of accomplishment. Yet the dominance of any one will certainly doom either the search or the profit picture. The production viewpoint will doom any really worthwhile innovation; dominance of the sales viewpoint eventuate in product improvements whose short lives offer limited long-range profit potential. On the other hand, R & D's focus on the distant future may so drastically divert energies needed to maintain the momentum of current profits as to bankrupt the whole operation.

The lower-level committee which Lorsch and Laurence prefer poses another difficulty--that of maintaining top management contact and backing. Those in command of the new product function must have the authority and stature to secure contributions from various departments of the organization and must be privy to the long-range policy of the firm. They also must be in a position to suggest modifications in that policy, if opportunities can be improved in this manner.

Whatever the level of the committee, past experience with such systems seems to indicate that they have a strong bias toward a narrowly restricted point of view, toward products most like those currently sold and thus toward products least likely to tap the real profits of major innovation.

Committee system weaknesses have caused many of the larger and more successful organizations to turn full responsibility for new product development over to some form of new product department whose sole responsibility is innovation. At duPont, Central Research has long had the task of screening new ideas and conducting the preliminary research needed to define the likely product. At this stage, Central Research must then sell some operating division on sponsoring the idea for applied research development and eventual marketing.

The duPont system seems to be an obviously technically centered one, well suited to a firm whose innovational strengths have been largely technical. Other organizations, such as General Mills, have developed new product operations completely independent of any of the other internal operations. After long experience with a new product committee, the company abandoned the committees for a specially appointed team aimed exclusively at developing ideas for new product diversification, reporting directly to the president. S. C. Johnson and Company was one of the early developers of a formal new products department and has given considerable publicity to its organizational structure (Johnson and Jones, 1957).

164

FIGURE 8-1. The S. C. Johnson Classification of New Products
by Product Objective

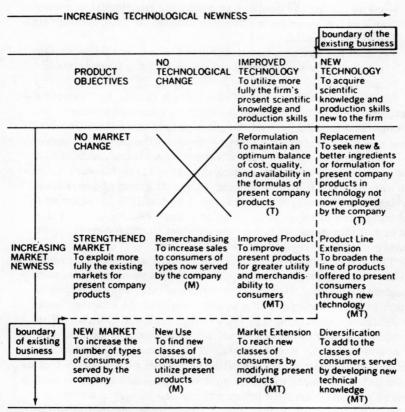

INCREASING TECHNOLOGICAL NEWNESS ⟶

PRODUCT OBJECTIVES	NO TECHNOLOGICAL CHANGE	IMPROVED TECHNOLOGY To utilize more fully the firm's present scientific knowledge and production skills	NEW TECHNOLOGY To acquire scientific knowledge and production skills new to the firm
NO MARKET CHANGE		Reformulation To maintain an optimum balance of cost, quality, and availability in the formulas of present company products (T)	Replacement To seek new & better ingredients or formulation for present company products in technology not now employed by the company (T)
STRENGTHENED MARKET To exploit more fully the existing markets for present company products	Remerchandising To increase sales to consumers of types now served by the company (M)	Improved Product To improve present products for greater utility and merchandis-ability to consumers (MT)	Product Line Extension To broaden the line of products offered to present consumers through new technology (MT)
NEW MARKET To increase the number of types of consumers served by the company	New Use To find new classes of consumers to utilize present products (M)	Market Extension To reach new classes of consumers by modifying present products (MT)	Diversification To add to the classes of consumers served by developing new technical knowledge (MT)

INCREASING MARKET NEWNESS

boundary of the existing business

boundary of existing business

PRIMARY RESPONSIBILITY LIES WITH:
(T) Research and Development
(M) Marketing Department
(MT) Marketing and Research and Development jointly

Source: Adapted from S. C. Johnson and Conrad Jones, "How to Organize for New Products," *Harvard Business Review* (May-June, 1957), pp. 49-62. Reprinted by permission.

165

The Johnson New Products Department was given the responsibility for:

- --reviewing each suggested new product idea, classifying the problems involved in its development, and determining its possible place in company plans. The classification scheme used is illustrated in Figure 8-1.
- --coordinating the people and activities implicated at every one of the steps from idea formulation to final commercialization and sale.
- --gathering any new knowledge needed to make decisions on products for which prior experience of the firm is inadequate.

The search and screening organization is not, by itself, sufficient, however. Because new products are bound to meet some resistance and inertia in even the most progressive firm, successful new product development usually requires the persistent advocacy of someone connected with it--it needs a strong champion. Johnson provides for this by setting up a task force for each idea which survives the initial screening--a small group of representatives drawn from every major function which will be implicated in the planning and development. The primary responsibility of the members of this group is to see the product through development and make sure it is ready for market success.

The Johnson task force taps some of the energies of entrepreneurship which often give the small new business an advantage in product introduction. However, in organizations less oriented to constant product turnover, this system may cut the offering loose from dedicated management at the critical moment of birth. The first market year is just as crucial for new products as the first year of life is for the human infant. Turned over to a marketing organization already engrossed with the familiar day-to-day tactics of established products may expose it to inadequate attention and to resource malnutrition. Reluctance to devote adequate attention to tomorrow's probable breadwinner is likely to be intensified if the introduction seems to threaten to nibble off some of the market of the organization's other established products. When Chrysler turned its newly acquired Simca automobile import over to its Dodge dealers in 1959, the import effort languished and all but perished because Chrysler officials and dealers apparently feared that Simca acceptance might diminish the market potential for the newly introduced Valiant (completely ignoring the probability that it would gain far more from the markets for other makes). They neither promoted it strongly nor developed the necessary repair parts and repair service capability that were a necessary part of any purchaser's desire-set when buying an automobile.

166

Much of the success of Procter and Gamble's long-established product manager system must be ascribed to the autonomy given the product manager to develop the sales volume in competition with other P & G products as well as with the products of other toiletry manufacturers. Indeed, given the nature of toiletry manufacture and marketing, the P & G product manager system contains some of the relevant elements of what is otherwise a relatively new form of product development and introduction organization--the venture team, brought into being in the 1960's by such firms as duPont, Minnesota Mining and Manufacturing, and General Mills.

Under the venture team plan, some interested corporate manager is granted permission to explore a possible satisfaction area or a product or service concept thought to present a major profit opportunity for the firm, either as an offering new to the market or as an acquisition of some going enterprise. If adequate anticipation of success really develops, the manager gradually adds assistants--research, marketing and finance personnel and, if needed, production personnel. If potential sales and profits develop to the organization's standards, the operation may assume the status of a company division, or of an independent operation within an established division. General Mills officials reporting on their experience (Advertising Age, Dec. 29, 1969) have indicated they found that some central concept screening is first necessary before appointing a venture manager. Originally, any member of management could volunteer to investigate a venture he thought interesting without prior corporate evaluation of the idea. When some such ventures proved barren, the General Mills corporate growth department was given the responsibility of first screening suggested diversifications for areas that would be interesting to General Mills, challenging, promising of growth opportunities, and fitting the corporation's specific strengths. General Mills has also applied the concept to technical personnel and technical projects, permitting technical personnel with an entrepreneurial outlook to become venture managers for product developments in which they were interested. An interesting sidelight of venture team experience has been disclosed by Albert J. Melberg of Minnesota Mining and Manufacturing: it works best if the venture team works in a "poor-boy" atmosphere, with the teams housed in "old garages around St. Paul" rather than in "shining tiled laboratories or carpeted offices" and forced to work with restricted resources (Melberg, 1969).

The General Mills corporate growth department does not limit its oversight to merely screening suggested ventures and coordinating their management, minimizing overlap. The department actively searches out and investigates opportunities on its own, to turn over to volunteer project managers.

However the new product function is organized, whoever is in

167

charge must have innovation as the priority responsibility. Quite clearly, one of the most important tasks is the sympathetic but careful screening of suggested new product concepts. Then these ideas are reviewed at appropriate milestones in their development to drop those not likely to achieve the objectives set, and the rest are pushed through to success. The entire process might be conceptualized as in Figure 8-2.

COLLECTING NEW PRODUCT IDEAS AND SCREENING THEM

Any new product search must begin with completely open-minded receptivity to all possible ideas from every conceivable source. These initial concepts then need to be thoughtfully screened to eliminate those which cannot be expected to fit the seller's skills, resources and interests. Only those passing the first test (usually about half) should be sent on for further investigation which can cause some commitment of funds. As investigation and development work proceeds, most of the remaining will also fall by the wayside. In general, something like 40 ideas may have to be considered to get one successful product. Such a low ratio of output to idea input manifestly emphasizes the need for the largest possible volume of idea inputs and the urgency of seeking for such ideas in every possible nook and cranny.

Useful new product concepts are initially of two general types. They are either someone's concept of some new object or service which could be produced if it could sell, or someone's idea of something which would sell if it could be produced economically. Both producibility and marketability are necessary components of any worthwhile product concept, and the screening group must satisfy itself that both "if it can's" translate into "probably so" before committing further energy and funds into development. This screening, however, is the second step. The first is to assure a plentiful harvest of ideas to be sorted over, then submit them to analytical attention.

Anyone can be the source of a new product idea, from the customer, to the janitor, to the chairman of the board. Lewyt got its initial profitable start as a home vacuum manufacturer because an assembly line worker saw the possibilities in one of their industrial products. The first rule of product search is to develop a super-sensitive receptivity to product concepts from any and all sources and to stimulate constant awareness that the organization is constantly seeking advice in this matter from anyone: workers, officials, suppliers, customers, own sales force, service personnel, distributors and dealers, as well as R & D personnel and the marketing department. The most productive sources should normally be the relatively informal intelligence from the sales organization

168

FIGURE 8-2. Basic Steps in Management of an Efficient Product
Development Effort

Aggressively search every possible source for and collect ideas
or concepts about objects or services which:
   a.   might sell if produced
   b.   could be produced if a market exists

Screen all concepts collected to discover those which:
   1.   appear likely to be both producible and saleable
   2.   pose product and market development requirements
        within the limits of the seller's physical, human, and
        market resources and also of the interests of executives
   3.   Seem likely to fit into the organization's product and
        profit objectives

Research each remaining product concept to determine, if
possible, the likely market acceptability and to define an
appropriate set of target performance and price goals for
development.

Develop a PERT Program for the process of developing both
the product and the plan for marketing it, with predetermined
milestone review points and standards for approval of further
development, market release, or rejection.

Turn product development over to R&D under the supervision
of a task force which also has the responsibility for parallel
development of marketing plans as product development
crystalizes.

Before release for any kind of market exposure, review to:
        a. determine if adequate differential value is incorporated
        b. if marketing plans accord with estimated learning
           requirements
If no to either, return for further development of product or
marketing plans, or both

| Produce some product under ordinary production conditions and check in ordinary use to check for defects. | If possible, market test to reveal defects in marketing and distribution plans |

Correct any defects in either product or marketing plans and
if product looks viable, market with all possible vigor

169

FIGURE 8-3. The Possible Sources for New Product Ideas

FOR PRODUCTS WHICH COULD SELL IF THEY COULD BE DEVELOPED OR CUS-TOMER NEEDS AND DESIRE-SETS IN NEED OF SOME FULFILLING PRODUCT OR SERVICE	FOR PRODUCTS WE COULD OFFER IF A MARKET FOR THEM COULD BE DEVELOPED

Principal Sources:

Salesforce:
  Felt needs of customers
  (unfulfilled desire-sets)
  Weaknesses in currently available
    offerings
  Weaknesses in competitors' lines
  Needs for improving flexibility of
    product design

Repair and service Personnel:
  Remediable defects in own lines
  Remediable defects in competing lines
  Product attributes desired but not
    available
  Product simplifications which might
    attract some new market segments

Marketing research:
  Product-in use studies: How could
    current offerings best fit the
    customer use-systems?
    What avoidance aspects are present
    in current designs which might be
    worth eliminating?
  Analysis of irritations produced by
    present design compromises

  Trends in taste and new life-styles
    which could be creating new un-
    fulfilled desire-sets

Other employees
Free-lance inventors, stylists, and
  designers
Competitors: opportunities revealed
  by both their mistakes and their
  successes

Research and Develop-
ment:
  New process which
    open up possibilities
    for less design com-
    promise or even ful-
    fillment of new de-
    sire-sets
  New materials, mech-
    anisms or services
    which might have
    value for some kind
    of desire-set ful-
    fillment
  Product possibilities
    which could meet
    known unfulfilled
    desire-sets

and distribution channels, the repair and service personnel and technical representatives, the systematic efforts which can be contributed by marketing research, and of course the insights of the R & D personnel. (See Figure 8-3.)

Intelligence feedback of many sorts should normally be a substantial part of any salesforce activity, and market need concepts should be a significant part of this feedback. In complex systems selling, such as is common in major aerospace industries, product concept feedback is the major responsibility of the salesman, as it also is in such detail sales activity as that conducted by textbook publishers. The purpose of such feedback is the definition of satisfaction-sets desired by major market segments. Salesmen as well as service personnel are also in key positions to discover weaknesses in the firm's own product or in the products of competitors, as well as other needs for product improvement or for product flexibility. They are also often in an advantageous position to discover ways in which a product can be made more valuable to distributors and dealers, as well as to final customers.

Repair and service personnel and distributors in contact with buyers and users are in an excellent position to learn of defects in the seller's product and also in those of competitors, as well as product attributes being sought but not available in any of the competitive offerings. Most such ideas will not reach management unless formal and informal efforts are made to open communications channels tapping them.

The main purpose of marketing research directed to uncovering new products should be to define high-priority unsatisfied needs among specific market segments, discover trends in tastes and needs which are creating new market segments for new satisfaction packages, and reveal consumer irritations with current designs which could be met by major product improvements. The latter is often best carried out by careful studies of the product-in-use: analyses of the use-systems surrounding the product and the avoidance aspects of these use-systems. Long after the fountain pen had reached the saturation plateau, and before the ballpoint had taken over and downgraded the market economically, such a product-in-study revealed to the Sheaffer Co. that the filling of the pen was a major source of irritation to users--requiring the wetting and cleaning of the nib. Knowing this much, the engineers came up with the "snorkel pen"--a design with a retractable tube which could be dipped into the ink for filling, avoiding any wetting of the nib with ink.

Wholly new designs may also be revealed by careful study of the irritations caused by design compromises. In the process of researching what rug patterns people preferred, a research firm discovered that most women really preferred best those carpets made by the velvet weave process, but avoided them because such

171

rugs showed footmarks. After considerable prodding, rugmakers came up with the sculptured wilton weave, which showed no such footmarks and quickly became the dominant design.

The research of taste trends is especially important to makers of any item in which fashion is an important component of value. It was a long-continuing project on small-car design, started when small foreign imports began to develop sales significance in 1954, which enabled Ford to capture a major share of the compact market in 1960 with the Falcon, then go on later to the triumphant introduction of the Mustang and the later Maverick, in 1969. Likewise, it was the failure of management to heed research findings into the contents of the sought-for satisfaction-set which resulted in inadequate options on the first Falcon and caused the shortening of its life cycle. This mistake was not repeated with the Mustang, which became the most successful new model introduction in over three decades.

Other sources of ideas concerning unfulfilled desire-sets sometimes come from suppliers. Free-lance inventors, stylists and designers often contribute valuable input to the new product grist mill. The mistakes as well as the successes of competitors can be a useful source of suggestions.

Research and development personnel are more likely to come up with fundamental new product ideas than product improvements. They would normally be the source of ideas concerning technical developments which make possible new physical products whose marketability is worth considering. The development of nylon and the succeeding synthetic fibers arose from a knowledge that polymer chemistry had reached the point where some kind of manufacturable products might be possible. duPont was not looking for a substitute for silk stockings when it put Carothers to work in 1932--simply felt that something useful could result. When a textile fiber seemed possible, its characteristics suggested a replacement for silk in what was then its most important use--ladies hosiery.

The first task of the new products group is to sift through as large an accumulation of such ideas as can be garnered, picking out those which can probably be both produced and sold economically, which fit the skills and experience of the firm, and which accord with the long-range goals of the seller as determined by its previously decided-upon guidelines.

Careful attention should be fastened on:
--the seller's basic marketing goals, interests, and skills
--relative position of the firm on the relevant experience curves
--the probable competition and the degree of competitive advantages with major market segments--what the product offers which is not otherwise available to these segments

172

--possible suppliers and supply sources for the raw materials
  and components, their adequacy and dependability, and the
  ease of working with the suppliers
--internal resources of facilities and personnel needed to develop and produce
--capital outlay needed to develop, produce, and develop the
  market to the growth point
--ability of the seller to develop and service the market
--the expected sales stability, or otherwise, once introduced
--estimated profitability, near term and long range
--risks involved
--probable shape of the product life cycle and the time and
  resources needed to preempt a substantial market position
  or establish acceptance.
--legal clearance problems--design patents, trademarks,
  copyrights, regulatory restraints (FDA, for example)
--uniqueness and degree of vulnerability to early competitive
  imitation, competitive improvement and/or marketing at
  other price levels, above or below
--fit to the current product line.

Ideas surviving the initial screening must then be converted
into a set of concrete recommendations for development. Performance and cost goals must be spelled out to whatever degree permitted by the level of innovation being attempted, and milestone review points planned for.

SETTING GOALS FOR A SPECIFIC DEVELOPMENT PROJECT

Ideas recommended for development must be translated into
a set of performance specification goals. Such performance specification goals should never be left vaguely to chance, and they should
aim at little greater precision than the market demands. They
must blend both the production and the marketing viewpoint. If left
to the R & D personnel, the result can be a product with greater
perfection than the customer is interested in, at a higher price than
he considers fair. A good example was that of a refrigerator which
held every zone close to the point of ideal appropriate temperature,
but resulted in a box whose external size was the same as competitors but contained substantially less storage space, at a price
$75 higher (need we say it did not sell?).

On the other hand, if the marketing viewpoint over-rides the
production too far, the result can be a cost disaster such as almost
hit Volkswagen, when models were proliferated without adequate
component commonality.

The possible precision and specificity of such goals will vary according to the degree and type of development which is foreseen as necessary to bring the product to marketing stage. In general, what is new and innovative can vary from mere promotional innovation which uncovers new market segments and uses for a known physical product to the discovery of new scientific relationships or processes which could lead to radically new satisfaction sets.

Product concepts which involve little more than innovatory promotional approaches or means or novel distributory arrangements are normally an understood part of sales management responsibilities and thus are not likely to be channeled through the new product setup. Even such concepts, however, may require some product modification, if only in packaging, and thus may need the cooperation of R & D personnel with an appropriate set of performance specifications.

Whenever real physical product development is clearly involved, it can be perceived as occupying some point on a continuum from a mere package change to basic scientific research, with at least five possible degrees of perceivable innovative effort:

- --peripheral product improvement: changes in packaging or other elements not important to the core service function
- --product improvement and perfection: elimination of defects and creation of added utilities
- --product development: creation of specific satisfaction-sets not previously available to buyers, utilizing known scientific relationships
- --pre-development research innovation: finding extensions of existing knowledge which could result in products offering possible new buyer satisfactions
- --basic scientific research: searching for new knowledge in areas of ignorance so great that the end consequences of possible discoveries are completely unforeseeable.

The first three of these are best designated as marketing innovation, the last as true research innovation. Very specific goals as to product and market targets can normally be set for any of the forms of marketing innovation in advance of any effort other than the assessment of the intelligence needed to define the goals and their feasibility. On the other hand, the purest extreme of basic research has traditionally been avoided by industry because any end result is too distant and the possibility of setting any meaningful goal too vague to justify as a prudent use of stockholder funds. Such really basic research is generally left to be funded by society, through academic and governmental funds.

Some relatively fundamental types of research, just short of basic in nature, have, however, proven amenable to justifiable corporate objectives and have, in fact, paid off well for those firms, such as duPont, who are skilled at research management. As we ascend the technical scale, we extend the foreseeability and the immediacy of possible results to a level within the means of even relatively small sellers. Indeed, those sellers are likely to be left behind in the competitive race who avoid continuous consideration of the simpler forms of product development: product improvement and product evolution.

SETTING GOALS FOR PRODUCT IMPROVEMENT

The obvious primary goal for product improvement is to enhance the value of current lines for the market being served, and to broaden this segment. The perfect product does not exist, if for no other reason than the fact of design compromise. The very fact that the offering involves some tangible form as a rule, can only be obtained at some price, and gives up the desired benefits through some kind of use-system are inherent defects, the form and extent of which should be under constant scrutiny to see if they can be minimized.

Constant attention to product improvement possibilities is the price of maintaining market position at any point in the cycle, particularly improvements resulting from new technology. When all-solid-state TV receivers became possible, Magnavox decided to move gradually and wait for a brighter picture tube also. The result was a decline in sales during an industry boom.

At least five constant goals for product improvement can be cited:

--simplification of the use-system by which the customer obtains his desire-set. (Good examples have been the wide use of aerosol packaging and of pre measured portions.)

--rendering the delivery of the satisfactions more dependable (minimizing service or adjustment requirements, for example)

--building more flexibility into the offering package, so that the buyer may tailor it more closely to his own special desire-set (modular construction, permitting a wide variety of optional designs, was one factor which accounted for Ford's success in the introduction of the Mustang)

--eliminating or minimizing as many as possible of those tangible characteristics which have no positive value--such items as weight, size, odor, thickness, awkwardness of handling, difficulty of service access, etc. (Thus the gauge of steel for metal containers was taken for granted by the steel industry too long, until the freight savings made possible by competing materials cost the industry sizable markets and forced it to develop thinner tinplate, for example,

175

which could earlier have warded off the competition.)
Care must be exercised, however, to make sure that such
attributes are not really positive in the perceptions of the
users. Aladdin's lamp may come close to being the ideal
transportation system from the standpoint of some market
segments, but other buyers would miss the solidity and
even the flash they seek--the visible evidence of prideful
ownership.
--improving the handling, storing or selling qualities of the
product for the benefit and profit of the intermediate buyers
through whose hands the product must move to reach the
time and place desired by the ultimate buyer. Such changes
may involve symbolic coding of the packages, for instance,
to simplify picking it out of stock quickly, packaging for
easy display, or other provisions which simplify the distributor's task, such as packing canned goods top-to-top to
make splitting the case and price-marking easier. All such
improvements make the product more valuable to the intermediate customers and thus more available to the final buyer.

Defining the goals for mere product improvements requires
only some clear knowledge of customer irritations and of weaknesses in the use-systems.

Of course there is no clear line between mere product improvement and true product evolution, yet there is clearly a discernible difference between the development of an automatic transmission for the automobile and the creation of television out of radio. We might define mere product improvement as the elimination
of avoidance characteristics in an offering which would have been
viewed as a substantially negative value at the moment of introduction. Even the earliest automobile drivers must have looked upon
gear shifting as a positive nuisance. On the other hand, Marconi's
first successful commercial radio had such substantial added value
over other means of conveying signals that there is no record that
anyone complained of the lack of an accompanying picture or even
of the necessity to use telegraphic code in the transmission.

The ability to use direct voice transmission would certainly
have been welcomed when the first radio stations were set up, but
many evolutionary developments in other products would have had
only minor perceivable value at the time of the introduction of the
core product. Most of the added value of the evolutionary improvements become perceivable only after the original offering satisfies
a desire-set higher in the hierarchy of needs and thus extinguishes
much of the drive to get it, elevating to first place a second stratum
of desire. When the first buyers of push-power lawn mowers turned
in their sickles in trade, it is doubtful that many of them would have

176

taken keen interest in powered riding mowers, or paid much more for the power. The perceivable gain in cutting ease of the new reel-type machines was so great that anything additional could have seemed trivial at the time. Once the hand-powered machine became the usual tool, however, the back labor required became an irritant providing high perceivable value in its elimination, and the market was ready to pay for power. Established usage of the push-type power mower, in turn, paved the way for the riding mower even on relatively small suburban lawns. Similarly, the best machinery to introduce to the industries of developing economies is often small-capacity batch process types long discarded by the more advanced nations.

The goal of evolutionary product development should thus be to perfect that which should become the next step of high perceivable value when the product approaches wide acceptance. Code radio could have been expected to give way to voice radio, as it did. Voice radio opened up the possibility of adding other audible values, such as music. The broadcasting of this led to the desire for quality programming which only a national audience would justify, making network broadcasting the logical next step. This permitted a wider variety of programming and formed the financial base for broadcast of drama, widening the audience. The latter, in turn, is deficient without a picture. Etc. Similarly, the development of knowledge of the etiology of a disease and a therapy for it leads to the desire for a preventive vaccine. Perfection of an injectable vaccine leads to a desire for an oral type. The latter leads, in turn, to a desire for something which requires less individual effort and initiative--perhaps something harmless added to the water supply or baked in the bread.

Every major product introduction thus paves the way to a foreseeable higher evolutionary step. The purpose of evolutionary product development is clearly to prepare to make the next step in the pyramided product life cycle when the time is ripe--when the period of growth slows down. Just what that next logical step is, however, depends on two different factors--on the structure of user desire-sets and also on the current state of the art, on what is most nearly possible.

Experimental work on television, for example, was already under way as early as 1920, just when the first feeble local radio broadcasting efforts were emerging. Neither the state of electronics nor the willingness to spend for receivers was adequate as yet, however. Twenty years of broadcast and set development had to pass before television was possible, just on the eve of World War II. Similarly, within electronics, the first receivers most homeowners used were "crystal" sets--receiving instruments which used a crude solid state device--usually a crystal of natural galena--to

177

rectify the incoming wave. Today's transistor is the lineal descendant of these early crystals, but radio took a by-pass through the use of the triode vacuum tube for nearly three decades, until the state of the art of producing ultra-pure materials was perfected.

The highest and least predictable form of product development consists of applying a known state of the art to develop a hitherto non-existent product. This itself may grade from a more or less foreseeable application of well-worked-out scientific and engineering principles to something like the atom bomb in the Manhattan Project--the development of some kind of engineering research needed to make use of already-known scientific principles. Even the goal of such engineering research is clearly definable: it is simply aimed at finding the best means of solving a particular buyer's problem, using known scientific relationships. The problems chosen for solution are those which fit best into the set of desires a firm is accustomed to meeting or into those desires toward which its future marketing efforts are aimed.

RESEARCH INNOVATION GOALS

The boundary between development and research is no sharper than that between the different degrees of product improvement. Any form of development always involves some extension of knowledge-- the use and even the creation of new materials, for example, or insight into new configurations of services and mechanisms. So long, however, as satisfaction of a particular user desire-set can be aimed at and reasonably well predicted in advance, we tend to recognize such extensions of new knowledge as a minor part of the effort and label the design work as developmental in character.

When, on the other hand, the research is likely to come up with something which raises the question, "What consumer needs can we satisfy with this?", then we are entering the area of research innovation, where the focus is on finding applications for some new state of the art, for some developing technology. The end results of such research break-throughs are notoriously unpredictable, even when the research has developed something tangible. The earlier experimenters with television were not dreaming of a radar system. The scientists who worked on the laser seemed to have been seeking a better communications carrier, but as late as a half dozen years after its introduction, the communications equipment seemed as far away as ever, and although many uses had been developed, scientists were still not sure what the major uses would come to be. Meanwhile, the early predictions of their use as "death rays" seemed too destined to remain in the realm of phantasy and some of their principle values--such as holography and line-of-sight survey in-

178

struments--mere by-products of some basic characteristics of the laser beam not originally thought to be important when work on lazer development was initiated.

Since the end result is unpredictable, it is certainly a legitimate question whether a seller should underwrite and try to give direction to research innovation. Certainly not every organization can afford to undertake such an effort. Only enterprises with strong resources of patient capital can afford the extended effort and the long time span between initiation of the effort and a profitable payoff. As immediately acceptable as nylon proved to be in hosiery, it took 9 years of waiting from Carothers' hiring by duPont in 1932 and the sale of the first stockings in 1941. Five years elapsed between the first laboratory productions of the polyamide resins and the production of a saleable pair of hose. Fortunately, nylon hose looked like silk hose except that they could be knitted in somewhat sheerer weights and were almost free from runs when manufactured in the gauges then common for silk stockings. Thus they were a superior product in a familiar pattern, requiring no learning for adoption. Had the early nylon uses required more learning, the payoff would have taken much longer, taken a full 15 or more years from the beginning of the research. Such lengthy time lags between research initiation and market payoff clearly imply heavy resources of both funds and patience. Many firms have too little of either to justify attempts at research innovation.

Nevertheless, the history of nylon also indicates the attractiveness of the profit opportunities such research can generate when correctly chosen and well managed. Nylon has been a long run profit winner, with successive waves of market penetration and pyramided growth for three decades, a mainstay for duPont and other firms long after the original patent protection expired. No mere product improvement would have had a profit life cycle of more than a small fraction of this length.

The history of nylon also illustrates both the kinds of guidelines necessary to the correct choice of research innovation and the limitations on that choice. The limitations may perhaps be the most obvious. The original project did not foresee a new fiber nor any other specific outcome. Neither did it aim at changing the hosiery sources for the women of the world.

But the choice was not a random one either. The firm was investigating an area of knowledge--chemistry--which fit in with duPont's production and marketing experience and which could be expected to yield some kind of product which would serve some kind of needs of its normal types of customers--industrial buyers of some kind. It focussed on an area of chemistry--the development of synthetic giant molecules, or polymers--in which the basic knowledge appeared to be approaching an applications break-through point. The possibilities of developing many kinds of products had been trumpeted in an American Chemical Society book (Slosson's <u>Creative Chemistry</u>) over a decade before duPont hired the leading American worker in polymer chemistry, Carothers, and gave him the assignment. Given duPont's wide coverage of the chemical field, the chance of developing something of value to duPont was excellent. And had the resulting product been too far afield, duPont could license others operating in the proper market.

The correct goal for research innovation might accordingly be defined as the choice of an area of knowledge well enough developed to give a high probability of yielding a usable practical application and in which the kind of product likely to result parallels established production or marketing experience, or preferably both. Once the kinds of applications possible are clearly visible, the effort should then be concentrated on developing first those specific offerings which will give the most immediately perceivable added value to the buyers and require the least amount of learning.

Whatever the level of innovation, a major aim of the development period must always be to develop an offering which promises a substantial degree of added value of some kind to the buyer. It must be more than just as good as something already available. It must be substantially better in some way, for some market segment, or it will get no market attention and will fail.

DIFFERENTIATION AS A NECESSARY ELEMENT OF DEVELOPMENT

A viable product is one which meets or can be perceived as meeting an existing and substantially unmet desire for some important segment of the market. Differences perceivable by the buyer are of one or more of three general types:
   --differences perceived as inherent in the physical product
      itself or in the associations it cues
   --differences in location or other aspects of ready availability
   --differences in the terms of sale, in the services accompanying the sale, or in the risk attached to the source of
      purchase.
The boundaries between all of these possible forms of differentiation are far from clearcut. Physical differences can be perceived even by professionals and industrial purchasers where none, in fact, exist. Women will often swear to a perceived difference in odor, for example, between their favorite perfume in a familiar container and the same essence in a strange bottle. Beer drinkers taste differences between the same beer in a brown bottle and in a clear bottle. Physicians trust the medications from an ethical house

much more than its chemical twin identified with makers of well-known proprietary drugs sold over the counter to the general public.

That most buyers see much difference in gasolines is doubtful, but the brand which is most convenient to the driver's route of travel will get preference. Avon's toiletries and cosmetics are undoubtedly of good quality, but what won first place for the firm was the fact of the greater ease of buying in the home, for the relatively heavy-using young housewife with children.

Availability is always a major consideration among buyers of standard specification industrial products, of course, and purchasers are sophisticated enough to recognize the lack of physical difference in the offerings. Nevertheless even when the availability is comparable, buyers usually have strong preferences based on the tie-in benefits which go with the sale, or the friendship and trust developed through a long association with the sales personnel. Sideline benefits accompanying the sale can include many kinds of related services, such as engineering and technical advice, high quality repair and maintenance service, training arrangements, programming (in the sale of computer services), etc. Tie-ins may also be in the form of coupons or other types of merchandise premiums. If everyone else is loading their offerings with some kind of tie-in, the lack of any, and a corresponding price concession, may differentiate the product favorably. Thus when most food stores were giving trading stamps, supermarkets which dropped them in favor of a discount policy were able to capture a substantial market segment.

One of the most important differentiating services is that of the accompanying offering assortment. A product that is as good as but no better than the same individual item from some other source may be seen as better simply because it has become part of a broad assorted line of products regularly purchased from the same source, and thus more convenient to get.

Physical differences imparting a noticeable degree of attractive differentiation can take many forms: differences in performance, in aesthetics, in uniformity and dependability, or in packaging, for example. Industrial users particularly prize uniformity of quality, whatever its level, because of the aid such uniformity gives to the smooth flow of production, often making the difference between handicraft methods and production line operations. One of the great attractions of the new leather substitutes is the fact that, unlike cattle hides, the product comes in regular dimensions, in rolls, of entirely uniform quality. Hides, by contrast, have widely different qualities in the same animal, and are quite irregular in shape. Packaging may impart a quality expectation through its own quality of design, or may make the offering more acceptable to distributors by making it easier to handle, store, ship, or display.

Differentiation is thus part a matter of engineering, part one of market planning, and neither side should be overlooked. Product development clearly involves more than the R & D laboratory personnel and needs the oversight of someone or a group to make sure that all elements are proceeding in parallel.

COORDINATING THE DEVELOPMENT EFFORT AND PUSHING IT THROUGH TO CONCLUSION

Any new product needs a champion. The very fact that it is new means that it threatens the even round of corporate existence. New products call for disruption of the accustomed procedures of production, for planning for new kinds of market reactions, interject new elements of uncertainty into all corporate decision. Furthermore, the crises they pose are postponable, are largely in the future, the problems with managing current offerings are here and now, and must be met. New product development can easily be shunted aside, postponed, even blocked, unless every aspect of physical and market development is made the primary accountable responsibility of some special section of management. All firms in the forefront of continued successful innovation have found it wise to appoint some person or group with centralized responsibility to coordinate physical product development, marketing plan development, and capital planning. One method used is to set up a task force for each approved product, made up of junior executives from R & D, marketing, production, and sometimes from finance or other likely interested divisions of management. It is this group's task to see that the idea succeeds and that everything is kept on schedule.

Even when well sponsored, most ideas will fail. The engineering problems of meeting the right desire-set may prove impossible--there may be no way of improving on currently available offerings and thus producing a saleable product. Costs may prove excessive in relation to the reference prices target market segment customers seem willing to pay.

Consequently, every project must establish review mileposts at which progress toward established goals will be weighed and a go-no-go decision made. Since development gets increasingly expensive with each succeeding stage, it is important to pinpoint early those projects with a low probability of success. Obvious mileposts are such natural points as the completion of consumer concept tests, completion of the initial laboratory design, completion of consumer use panel tests, and completion of semi-works plant and market tests, when competitive conditions permit.

Product and market development involve such a myriad of

independently pursued efforts that every such project should start
out with a carefully worked-out critical path or PERT analysis to
make sure that all phases of both engineering and market plans
will be thoroughly coordinated and will function at the optimum
point in time for profitable market introduction. Many a product
loses out to competitive introductions or misses the market entirely because foreseeable and preventable delays were not recognized in advance and forestalled. Needless to say, the critical
path analysis must encompass every aspect of the market plan as
well as those of physical product development--all phases of advance development of labelling, promotional literature, advertising
production and placement, and sales and distributional planning,
all tagged with realistic estimates of the time required and the
necessary sequences involved.

GETTING READY FOR THE INTRODUCTION--PRODUCTION
RUN AND MARKET TESTS

Products need to be checked for both production readiness
and market readiness before they are launched. There should be
pilot commercial production runs and if possible market tests.
Minor, remediable flaws in the production or promotion, or
both, have wrecked many potentially successful introductions because the birth was premature--because the infant introduction was
launched before these flaws were spotted. Minor production weaknesses and the resulting irritations have given many a product a
bad reputation before it had a chance to gain a good one. Minor design weaknesses not visible before introduction have killed or stun-
ted the potential for many other products.
Waterjet boat propulsion, for example, got an early bad name
which permitted the inboard-outboard design to take over a major
share of what might have been the waterjet's market before the
sloppy maneuvering mechanism and improperly sealed bearings in
the original waterjets was revealed and finally corrected. Similarly, seemingly attractive promotional themes have caused consumers to position products in their use-systems in such a way as
to sharply restrict potential or even kill it. When General Foods
introduced its first dehydrated, storable dog food, Gainesburgers,
the market test promotion caused buyers to perceive it as a treat
or supplement, rather than as a dietary mainstay, sharply cur-
tailing the initial potential. Fortunately, General Foods had chosen
to market test first and was able to correct this flaw in its promotional approach.
Promotional, sales, and distribution plans thus need as careful testing as does the physical product, within the confines per-

mitted by market circumstances and the degree of innovational effort attempted. Flaws in the physical product cause buyer resistance and leave the innovator open to loss of the fruits of his pioneering to a more perceptive innovator who spots and corrects the
defect. Even if this does not happen, market growth may be ham-
pered or even threatened by the passing on of the experiences of
the key early buyers, and thus every precaution should be taken to
insure that such experiences will be as satisfactory as possible.
The initial success of the Volkswagen was built partly on an initial
market entry policy of never opening distribution in a territory before strong, well-stocked service facilities were available. When
General Motors introduced the Vega as its first truly small-car entry in 1970, officials planned in advance to make sure of the tight-
est possible quality control on the first 100,000 units, staffing the
production line with the most experienced, highest skilled assem-
blers available. Avoidance of flaws in the promotional, sales and
distributive mixes are equally important. Such marketing mix
flaws can cause the correct target buyers to fail to notice the product altogether or to fail to perceive as present the real benefit that
is there.

The degree of advance physical product testing necessary and
the degree which may also be advisable will vary with the degree of
technical innovation in the introduction. If the product is basically
a variant of known products made according to familiar production
processes, market testing should probably be avoided altogether
and certainly stopped as soon as a feel for the success of both product design and promotional plan are visible. Such products have
a very short time lag between initial success and competitor entry,
and there is no point in making a gift of the introducer's market
insight to well-equipped competitors.

At the other extreme, products of radically new technical
design, with major construction innovations and using unfamiliar
processes, should always be thoroughly use tested by sampling
final consumers under actual use conditions whenever possible. The
laboratory or proving ground technician can almost never uncover
all the flaws that the less careful final user will create. Such testing almost always should involve simultaneous production tests in
the form of a semi-works process, where production quantities
will be similar to those of the final plant, using workers no more
knowledgeable than final assembly line personnel. Skipping of this
step has caused many a product to fail on initial introduction. For
instance, when Dewey and Almy developed a new two-piece offset
printing blanket to replace a poorer one-piece blanket in lithography
shops, it went to market immediately after the apparent success of
a mere two-month's use by a small panel under close technical
supervision, involving the production of less than 100 pieces. The

required production process at this stage put too few of the strains on success of a multi-layered product design, and the supervision of use was too close to reveal possible consumer problems. The result was a product which developed structural flaws after 6 months, and which had superficial characteristics unattractive to many buyers. This resulted in a costly return to research and development, delaying market success for a long time.

A very important caution before market introduction is to make certain that the initial design minimizes learning requirements as much as possible. Initial waterjet boat designs, for example, steered by using deflectors on the water stream used for propulsion. This design element was so inefficient that the tighter the turn, the more the engine had to be speeded up--a maneuver the exact opposite to that which was necessary and habitual with current inboard or outboard propeller propulsion, requiring a complete reversal of the motor habits of the very kind of experienced boatmen who would be the market for an improved propulsion system. Only after the initial market interest died back did the industry do what it should have done first--used a gimballed exhaust jet to improve steering.

DuPont's leather substitute, Corfam, foundered because it could not be worked like leather in the shoe factory. The later Scott Chatham Tannera substitute got ready acceptance because it caused no production adjustments. General Foods first freeze-dried coffee, Maxim, was very attractive to those who measured it out carefully, but the average buyer was less accustomed to precise measurement and got a bitter cup. So Nestles' less critical Taster's Choice took over twice as large a market share. (General Foods made the same error with Max-Pax.)

Not all learning requirements can be avoided, but any not an essential and completely inescapable aspect of developing the most highly desired innovative attributes should be avoided as much as is technically possible, and as few learning requirements as are feasible introduced into the design at one time. Seldom does the optimum introductory design prove to be the ultimate design.

Just as important as the design of the physical product itself is the provision of necessary elements in the use-system, as well as the correct design of the marketing system. The errors which have delayed growth of the microwave oven are a good case in point.

The microwave oven was inherently, under the best of conditions, an extremely high learning product, when first introduced to consumers in the middle 1950's. It required a completely different approach to the timing of meal preparation because it was a single speed, single energy level input device. The only variable was time. To cook a large quantity on her usual stove, the house-

wife generally uses a bigger pan and turns up the heat. If she uses
an ordinary oven, 3 items at one time take no more time then one
does. In a microwave oven, she took twice the time for twice as
much, and 3 items took as long as the sum of the individual cooking
times. Planning her starting time was a matter of some very complicated arithmetic.

Furthermore, the way it cooked and the appearance of the
end product were quite unfamiliar and required a great deal of perceptual learning. Ordinary cooking acts by conduction: the surface
of the item is heated, and this heat then conducted to the center.
Thus the surface gets more heat than the center. The beef roast,
for example, can have a brown crust on the thoroughly cooked surface, yet be the pink of lightly cooked beef at the center. But microwaves penetrate the surface for some distance (about 2 inches in
the usual model) and cook about equally fast as far as they penetrate. Thus the meat gets equally well cooked all the way through,
and is the same gray at the surface as at the center.

One particular perceptual problem is the cooking of pork.
All of the housewife's training is summed up in "cook until done,
then cook it that much longer again." But pork that is done is still
gray in a microwave oven, and if heavily overcooked is dried leather. She can, of course, if she wishes, for aesthetic reasons,
brown it in her pan or oven afterward, but she need not do this for
flavor and safety, and she cannot use browning as a test of doneness.

In addition, she cannot use most of her current cooking utensils. Nothing with any metal can be used--it causes sparking and
destruction of the key magnetron tube.

Pyrex and Corning Ware are usable, but few people have
full sets of these (and getting open-stock pieces of covered Pyrex
utensils is not always easy). Paper plates are acceptable since the
utensil is not itself heated by the oven, but this takes some getting
used to. Even the plates and bowls used for table service will work
(but not if they have metallic decoration such as a gold, silver, or
platinum band!). Melamine plastic ware could be very useful--but
nobody designed such until 1973 and then only for campers.

Furthermore, she has to do most of her learning without
much help from the manufacturer or others. None of her cook book
directions are in microwave terms. The directions on the frozen
and other packaged convenience foods are for ordinary cooking
methods--not microwaves. Moreover it costs as much or more
than a good range.

Despite all these avoidance barriers to adoption, the microwave oven was bought by some people, enough to stay on the market. It had some very attractive features for certain market segments. First, its energy requirements were low. The ordinary

186

"portable" (a countertop model weighing better than 50 pounds) could be plugged into any ordinary 110-volt socket because it took the same input as an ordinary electric toaster or hand iron (1200 watts).

Next, the oven produced no appreciable heat in the kitchen. The energy output was in the form of heatless radio waves. They were transformed into heat energy only inside the food, when they hit its water content.

Since it cooked as fast on the inside as on the surface, it was fast (provided the quantity was limited). It was especially valuable in preparing frozen foods straight from the freezer, thawing them quickly, and all the way through at once.

For a similar reason, the microwave oven is ideal for re-warming, fast, completely, and well, food set aside for someone late to dinner.

Not every family would find these attributes important. But some families might value them highly, and the marketing plans needed to pinpoint these segments, direct their copy to them in terms important to them. And the sellers needed to limit the learning content to the inescapable minimum. None of this was done.

With the middle 1970's marking two decades of promotion, the major sellers were promoting the oven in terms of the greater speed of doing large roasts and similar bulky items which were not well handled by a microwave. (They need frequent turning, and do not save all that time, and also need browning.) The instruction books were not more extensive than those which come with an electric skillet and gave little help in the complex arithmetic of handling several small items simultaneously in the oven. The problem of cookware was left up to the housewife to improvise and solve.

Was it any wonder that sales attained only 100,000 by 1970 and about 325,000 by 1973, nearly 20 years after introduction? Or perhaps may it not be a wonder that it survived to gain even that much sales?

For the market was not one that any of the promotion was aimed at. People did not cook "a 15 lb. turkey" in it frequently, or even once a year (to quote a common advertising claim). They did use the oven every day --to prepare frozen convenience foods quickly, to solve the evening rush for the 2-worker small family, to solve the conflicting time schedules of the large family with teen members, and to solve the problems of the travelling motor camper and his limited energy sources.

Indeed, the importance of the latter was recognized, finally, in 1973 when one plastics manufacturer put the first set of melamine plastic microwave cookware on the market--but only through camper outlets!

Certainly, a rational marketing plan design could have eased some of the learning by designing and furnishing appropriate plastic cookware with the oven. Some careful panel research could have pinpointed the use-systems and the segments, and, with the help of some home economists, produced some cook books and instruction translation formulas for those outstanding. And some follow-up of purchasers would have revealed the actual use-systems and the appropriate promotional approaches.

Even with this, introduction would have been slow, but a well-tested, properly targetted promotion could have shortened that market development time by half, by attracting the attention of the right buyers, with the right themes and minimizing the learning requirement.

PROMOTION AND MARKET TESTS

The most efficient types of promotional appeal and promotional plan tests are small-scale psychological, portfolio, and theater tests which can be produced at relatively low cost, tested in many versions and which yield to careful analysis. Such methods should be used to the point of exhaustion before attempting any kind of market test, just as the production run should not be started before the possible laboratory tests are exhausted.

The possible objectives for market tests are widely misunderstood. Often overlooked is the undoubted fact that such a test is usually possible only after the seller has committed major funds to the production of a given design. The expenditure required is thus far too great to permit it to be used to test alternative product designs. Market testing is also inherently slow at producing analyzable results, and thus much too cumbersome to test many kinds of alternative promotional designs. Moreover, it is open to the public gaze--and that of competitors. Competitors can learn as much from such a test, with little cost, as the seller who is paying the bill. Thus what Kellogg could observe from the early results of General Foods' Toast-Ems test market caused it to jump in nationally with Pop-Tarts before General Foods' finished its test, and take the major market share. Market tests therefore should never be resorted to in circustances in which a competitor can tool up and produce the product with little time lag.

Nevertheless, only the market test will reveal many of the flaws in the promotional design, just as only a prolonged use test under something like market conditions will reveal physical defects in production or design. Polaroid's initial test market of its SX-70 camera revealed a higher learning requirement than thought and a need for more dealer training. The main purposes of the test marketing operation should thus be to reveal minor flaws in the

promotional design or to test two or three possible variations of
the sales approach, and to learn something about what happens under market-conditioned use.

Test marketing is probably of little use for really high-
learning requirement products. For such, the market development
period itself becomes a kind of market test over a long period of
time, needed to reveal the true nature of the market and of the perceivable product. This market development phase should thus be
as closely monitored as would a normal test market operation. Preparation for introduction is not complete until all desired elements
of the use-system are provided for.

Development of product and of introductory marketing plans
is thus just as much a part of the life cycle of the product as the
gestation period is for any baby, and just as important for future
potential success. A parallel marketing research effort is needed
for efficient guidance of both physical development and of market
plan development.

SUMMARY

1. Because the major profits are reaped during the growth
phase of the life cycle, sellers need to organize the new product
search and development process to insure a steady stream of new
product ideas.

2. Formal responsibility for giving birth to and screening
new product ideas needs to be vested in some managerial group or
person whose main responsibility is the gathering and screening of
possible new product ideas. Generally, the new product effort has
been the responsibility of either committees drawn from relatively
high management levels, or a group or a single person charged
solely with this function.

3. Committees came into being because product search and
development cut across the major organizational functions and requires the compromise of divergent viewpoints and goals of these
functions. However, the committee system bears the usual problem
of all committee decisions and, in addition, is an added duty to the
normal responsibilities of the personnel. Results tend to be restricted and often not venturesome enough.

4. The permanent new product department or executive is
tending to be on the increase. Such executives or groups have no
responsibilities other than the search for new product ideas and
supervision of their gestation into marketable offerings. The basic
function of the new product department is concept review and
screening and coordination of all of the activities implicated from
idea formulation to final market release.

5. Because new products need a champion to insure a healthy gestation, some form of task force is sometimes assigned to see the development process through.

6. The gestation process starts with the collection of as many possible product concepts as possible, because only about 1 in 40 will prove both producible and marketable. All possible sources must be used: employees, officials, sales people, service and technical representatives, distributors and dealers, suppliers, research and development personnel, and customers as well as outside consultants.

7. Ideas originating from marketing sources normally tend to be evolutionary product improvement ideas, with a relatively short life cycle. Ideas from research personnel are often more fundamental, proposing revolutionary ideas which may require learning and have a relatively long product life cycle.

8. Screening must involve far more than estimated marketability, producibility, and profitability. The product must accord with the seller's basic marketing goals, interests and skills, as well as resources. Careful attention must be given to the probable nature of the life cycle, capital outlay needed, legal problems, uniqueness of benefit promised final users, sources of supply, and kind and nature of probable competition.

9. Ideas surviving the initial screening must be translated into a set of performance specification goals for the development process. The degree and kind of innovation involved will determine how specific those goals can be. At one extreme of mere promotional innovation, the aim can be very specific. At the other extreme of true research innovation, even the nature of the physical and perceptual product which can be expected is not foreseeable.

10. Product improvement goals would include such items as simplification of the use-system, increasing the dependability of satisfaction delivery, improved flexibility in the offering package, elimination or at least minimization of such tangible physical product characteristics as have no positive satisfaction value, and bettering the handling, storing, or selling quality of the product, making it more attractive to the intermediate sellers in the chain of distribution.

11. When the new product development involves the finding of applications of scientific knowledge, the goal must be the choice of an area of knowledge ready for exploitation that is harmonious with the known production and/or marketing skills of the firm, and then the development of such specific offerings as are likely to give the most immediately perceivable added value to buyers and require the least amount of learning.

12. The development process is not successful until the prospective offering has acquired some kind of substantial differentia-

tion from other products on the market. Differentiation comes from differences perceived as inherent in the physical product itself or in the associations it cues, differences in the location or other aspects of availability, or differences in the terms of sales, in services accompanying the sale, or in the risk attached to the source of purchase.

13. To succeed, the development efforts must be carefully coordinated and all management efforts needed for final introductory success carefully programmed to insure the right timing. Generally, this means working out a critical path or PERT analysis in advance and the setting of well-chosen mileposts for interim review of progress and modification of plans, or dropping of projects whose probability of success are proving small. Since each succeeding step of the development process is substantially more expensive than the preceding one, such interim reviews are a prerequisite to maximization of development investment.

14. The offering is not ready for commercialization until adequate tests of both production runs and marketing plans have been carried out. Premature launching can endanger the life of the product or severely curtail potential. Laboratory scale or even pilot plant scale production may not reveal dangerous weaknesses in the production-run output--dangerous from the standpoint of market acceptance. The principal value of market tests, when feasible, is to make a final pocketbook test of already well-checked promotional plans. Such full-scale tests are practicable only when competition can enter only after a considerable time lag, or the learning process makes an initial unprofitable market development phase a necessary part of the life cycle.

9

RESEARCH: KEEPING IN TOUCH WITH THE POTENTIAL DURING CONCEPT SCREENING AND PRODUCT GESTATION

Marketing research and analysis are necessary accompaniments of every step of effective product conception and development. New product search and development can have just one useful aim: to find ideas for offerings capable of fulfilling a significant consumer satisfaction gap and to develop these concepts into products which offer a substantial added value for users, at a profit for the producer. Seldom is either the exact nature of such satisfaction gaps obvious in all details of performance requirements, nor the exact acceptance climate manifest at first glance. The buyers and users must be the source of this information, and they themselves can seldom articulate their desires and needs in answer to a simple set of questions.

Research at this stage is not only imperative but requires a high degree of analytical skill. One of the possible research contributions can be the uncovering of unfulfilled satisfactions themselves, of suggestions for product needs. Among the more useful approaches are three important ones--the search for points of wide dissatisfaction with design among many or most users of a product, to uncover a product improvement desired by most of the market; analysis of the common trends in desires and tastes among the fringes of the segments; and the search for problems in the use-systems which can suggest design improvements or new auxiliary products for the system.

Whether or not the original idea came through research, product concepts which survive the initial screening need testing before development to set design performance goals. The form of concept testing needed will depend on the degree of innovation being attempted and the consequent amount of learning involved. Much of what passes for concept testing is concerned only with checking advertising concepts--with evaluating the appeal of different themes for not too different products, because these constitute the vast bulk of "new" products. Some go one step farther--the testing of market concepts--the adaptation of established offerings to new market segments.

Research methods quite adequate for such simple tests of no-learning products are unlikely to be of value where any major learning problem is present. They tend to ignore the problem of use-system acceptability which has tripped up many an experienced marketer. And they are unlikely to predict what the customer's reaction will be to a still unfamiliar type of actual product--the reaction which will be the final determinant of market success. Further user-reaction research is thus needed as development begins to give birth to product in some usable physical form. Finally, it is usually wise to test the product as produced under factory conditions, if possible, to uncover production-run product negatives, before launching any full-scale distribution.

Long before this stage, the organization must have developed an introduction plan which is based on as thoroughly researched a prediction of the learning requirement as can be made. The physical use-system learning requirement can usually be pinpointed by means of a relatively simple comparison of the flow charts of the probable new use-system and the systems it replaces, once we are certain what these will be. Estimating the value perception and role perception learning requires more direct information on consumer and user reaction. Only when all of these information needs are met can we rest assured that we have a rational basis for development of a marketing plan with a high probability of success.

RESEARCH FOR PRODUCT CONCEPTS

Basic research, such as the original duPont work in polymer chemistry, is one valuable source of new product ideas when well managed, but not a source open to many companies nor the source of most new product ideas. Even the end product of such research (a new plastic resin in the duPont case) must itself depend on some further marketing investigations to reveal the useful potential product concepts.

Of course, the search for new concepts should never be restricted to research alone, including marketing research. But when carried out skillfully, such marketing research can be a fruitful source of valuable product ideas. Eloquent testimony to this fact can be seen in such disparate market successes as the Ford Mustang and Maverick introductions, in the original launching of sculptured Wilton rugs, and in the success of the once popular and very profitable snorkel pen. Each of these successes illustrated a different kind of research into product concepts, but all three illustrate the fundamental aim of any research into developing a concept--that aim is the uncovering of some kind of consumer dissatisfaction.

The sculptured velvet weave arose out of analytical research into general customer preferences in rugs. Studies revealed that customers liked the texture of the velvet (Wilton) rugs, but disliked the tendency of such rugs to show foot tracks, leading researchers to pose the question for the designer as to whether a trackless velvet weave was possible. The result was an overnight success in the 1940's. The Mustang and the Maverick grew out of a series of studies into customer desires in small-car styling, looking for dissatisfied fringes of current market segments. These studies led first to the design of the first modestly priced "sporty" car--the Mustang--and later the Maverick.

As in all successful design research, both the rug study and the Ford studies started out with no preconceived design ideas, but with a patient design element by design element test to determine the connotations of specific features to users and their preferences. Rugs were studied in the context of preferences for types of patterns and then of specific basic patterns and color combinations, using designer sketches and then textures, separately. Ford's researchers started with sketches of single hypothetical models with possible variations of a single feature at one time--the fender shape and cutout in one series, the hood line in another series, the deck length and shape in another series, etc. From this emerged a design of a car that could be perceived as "sporty," but also as suitable for a family car by the buyer with a sports car yearning and a young family to transport.

The pen arose out of a different kind of study--a study of the product (a wet-ink fountain pen) in use, looking for substantial negatives in the use-system. This investigation revealed a major irritation--the inking of the nib and barrel end when filling. Designers then developed a retractable filling tube--the "snorkel," which eliminated this problem. In all of these cases, major improvements of products well along in the mature stage of their cycle were uncovered, lifting the developer out of his stabilized niche and giving him a major new product, a product with enough visible growth to stimulate rapid emulation in both the rug and the Ford examples.

Such searches into the customer problems, into the negatives in the available offering bundles, are far too infrequent. They could benefit many companies, revive the excitement in far more industries than they do. Research is far more frequently called in, as it should be but is not always, to investigate concepts which have been accepted for development and to help guide that development into a marketable offering.

194

Research and Review During Gestation

A major reason for special organization of the gestation process is the tentative and relatively unpredictable nature of all research and development and the resulting need for constant guidance as well as support. A continuing interplay of research and product design is needed throughout this period, with very frequent reviews at previously designated milestones to compare progress, actual and expected cost, and opportunities with management objectives and expectations. The kinds and type of milestones chosen will obviously differ so widely between types of R & D projects that no widely applicable checklist is possible.

However, as soon as a specific product concept emerges, the market promise of this concept should be researched to determine development objectives. As development proceeds, immediate information is needed on performance objectives. As realistic product possibilities and alternatives become more sharply defined, the market potential, use-systems, and potential perceived values in the concept will need further refinement to set objectives for succeeding development. Finally, when development seems to have come close to a saleable product, the product should be subjected to as much consumer use-testing and concept-value-perception as is possible in view of product-type limitations and the possible danger of competitive preemption of the market.

When all reviews seem to indicate the probability of a successful product and plans to introduce are developed, such plans should, if possible, be tested on some pilot scale, such as in a test market.

Obviously, a great deal of concept testing of some form seems advisable before spending of development funds. As with every other kind of information, however, concept testing is no routine operation to be used and interpreted without a great deal of judgment. Indeed, much of what is called by that name is often not applicable, and could even be misleading in some kinds of cases.

Coordinating Development and Market Research

The first step in concept testing is the recognition that all new offering concepts have two sides. As seen by the conceiver, the proposed new offering idea is a preconception of what a product should be like or should do, often in very limited physical terms. As perceived by a potential buyer or user, the proposed offering arouses an expectation of what the product may do for him in the way of delivering specific sets of benefits and meeting satisfaction requirements. When properly presented, the offering also involves some possible negative expectations of what getting these satisfac-

195

tions will require of the potential user in the way of learning, risk, or some other price. Uncovering such negative expectations is as important as evaluating the positive values, but seldom as easily carried out.

As previous discussion has already indicated, the extent of possible negative expectations will vary from the insignificant to extremely substantial, depending on the type and kind of concept being investigated. Wood (Walter A. Wood, 1969) has pointed out that much concept testing is concerned with presenting nothing more than advertising concepts--methods of perceiving a product involving no new general or specific physical attributes of the offering. Such advertising concepts are far from being valueless. It was basically an advertising concept which led to Carnation's success with Instant Breakfast. The idea of a breakfast to be drunk rather than eaten had been kicking around the food industry for years, and the General Foods Post Division had previously tried introducing such a product under the label of Brim at the time of the Metrecal boom. However, the presentation had not adequately differentiated Brim from the diet foods and it had not succeeded.

Other concepts are basically marketing concepts--established products presented in such a manner as to position their appeal to new market segments, such as the idea of "teen-age cosmetics," intended to gain acceptance of cosmetic use in a group not previously well covered. One such marketing concept created a spectacular comeback for a camouflage cosmetic originally developed to hide disfiguring birthmarks and scars. The original target market proved too restricted for market success, and the introducers lost their initial distribution outlets. Then some imaginative entrepreneurs, looking for a specialty direct sales item, took it on, presented it as the solution to covering the minor blemishes many women have, and produced a sustained sale which put the product back into the stores.

Both advertising concepts and marketing concepts involve no learning and few negative expectations, because they build on established product forms and established use-systems. Furthermore, the target market is pretty well defined, and the difference between the originator's preconception of product benefit and potential consumer's expectation is likely to be minimal. The analytical skill and imagination needed for testing put little strain on the organization and they thus become the basis for spectacular sounding promotion for rather routine service operations, surveying easily defined respondent groups, requiring little analytical expertise.

The true problems of concept testing come with the introduction of really new product forms with new offering concepts, even with products meeting recognized drives, but in a different manner. Unless the drive is already well recognized, close to the level of consciousness, and perceived as satisfiable by means of an already partly learned system, it may be very difficult, even impossible, to test the concept. In any case, it is extremely important to test the acceptability characteristics of the whole use-system involved if there is even a single minor change in system involved. Bristol-Myers' original attempt to introduce a chewable anti-acid pill foundered because the original consumer panel tests had neglected to investigate reactions to the omission of the drink of water ordinarily needed to facilitate swallowing of other pills. It had been mistakenly assumed that consumers would feel that the need for the water was a nuisance. Post-mortem research indicated the reverse--that consumers felt water to be a necessary part of the remedy,although they probably could not have been able to articulate this perception on any form of structured direct questioning.

Thus, for any new offering concept which is anything more than a mere variant of known offerings, made to establish new market segments, a great deal of interviewing skill is needed. The methods used need to involve much unstructured and exploratory research to uncover possible product perceptions, both negative and positive, not anticipated by those conceiving the product. The more that is really new in the offering and the use-systems, the more is this necessary, and the less precise the result at this initial stage before even a prototype is available, the less useful any standardized testing scheme.

These problems do not vitiate the value of concept testing prior to research and development. With all the problems, well-handled concept research can furnish both negative and positive guidance far outweighing its time and monetary cost, by directing development efforts in fruitful directions and revealing acceptance problems not otherwise foreseen. It can eliminate concepts in which buyers do not see noticeable value, or which are desired, but by too few buyers to make development worthwhile. Development of products without such guidance has often cost more than any possible market would return.

Such initial concept research can also reveal that the really valuable attributes as perceived by the customer are quite a different sort than those perceived by the originator. In these cases, the design emphasis will be far better guided with its help. Obviously, such research should reveal the likely use-system and thus spotlight features which need improvement and those which could facilitate or hamper acceptance. It can also reveal how acceptance may be shaped by preconceptions of what might seem like minor technical aspects of the product. The customer brings all his past prejudices to bear on his initial perception of any new offering.

Among these prejudices, yet, in the U.S.A., is one which considers dehydrated products as inferior in quality and flavor to the original. Thus, the original angel food cake mixes with their important egg content in dehydrated form were easily displaced by the much less convenient mixes which required the housewife to add her own fresh eggs.

An inescapable problem of research conducted before product development is the lack of the product itself. Work is often done with mere typed verbal statements. To translate these, the respondent must fall back on his own personal preconceived translation of the words into personal satisfactions. This is no problem when the concept is a mere advertising one, since the stimulus to which the reaction is being tested parallels that to which the respondent will be later exposed. However, even in such cases, he may need a more elaborate presentation, with much of the artistic skill to which an advertisement for the product would be presented. Coca-Cola thus used professionally prepared storyboards to test the market for a premium-quality orange juice concentrate. This firm was also wise enough to limit the testing to the market segments who could be expected to buy such a premium-quality, premium-priced product. Obviously answers from respondents who would see little added value in a product category are seldom of value.

At best, the reactions to any merely visual or verbal representations are somewhat unreliable unless the offering benefit is largely visual. Experience has shown that tests of new rug patterns, for example, are extremely predictive even when working from crude designer sketches. Pre-tests of these designs, using pictures, have proven to be relatively accurate guides to later relative sales. But visual tests of acceptance of alternate rug textures proved worthless--only a sample which could be felt by the respondent's fingers would work.

At best, a visual and verbal test of a concept tells only whether people can be led to try a product on the basis of a similar description. Once they have the product in hand, the product itself is the major source of perceived value for all offerings whose satisfaction comes from the product itself. Once the laboratory has developed a prototype product, then, this needs testing both on a blind and labelled basis. Blind testing, where possible, is needed to uncover perceptions, both negative and positive, which the characteristics of the product will create. Testing under the labels on which it will or could appear on the market is needed to determine how these labels might change the perceptions of the physical effects or of the use-systems, or both. When a meat packer developed a canned corned mutton, for example, the firm got nothing but favorable reactions from the test panel of users when they were not told the origin of the product. But when put on the market with its correct label, canned mutton gathered dust on the supermarket shelves.

Once development and market research have carried the concept to what seems to be an acceptable solution, it is usually wise to market test the commercial product on a limited scale, with very close monitoring of the movement at retail, of the tendency of customers to repurchase, of any product weaknesses which are being revealed, of the use-systems which are actually developing, of the actual market segments buying, and of any weaknesses in promotional themes, strategy, or execution.

If the product requires minimal learning, every precaution must be taken to make sure that the time taken does not allow competition to observe the value of the product and jump in ahead of the introducer's own planned market expansion. Thus, even at this stage, the firm needs to have made as accurate a prediction as possible of the probable learning content.

PREDICTING THE LEARNING REQUIREMENT

Neglecting to consider the learning requirement and its implications is probably responsible for more of the major product introduction failures than any other factor except, possibly, the introduction of non-products. It is also the least excusable type of failure, since appraisal of the use-systems learning, at least, is a simple analytical objective analysis which can be conducted from a swivel chair or drafting stool, once we know the core desire-set which will be perceived by the user. In addition, we often know quite a little about the kind of role perception learning and the value perception we are requiring.

One spectacular failure in which all three were involved was the attempted introduction of spiced dehydrated Knorr's soups into the U.S.A. by the Best Foods Division of Corn Products. The soups were an established product of the firm's European subsidiary. Their extreme popularity in Europe, particularly in Germany, convinced firm officials that they could duplicate the success in America, and so they were introduced after only preliminary consumer panel testing. That the firm realized that the taste would be strange is clear from the remark of one official who has been said to insist that Americans would "learn to love" the soups!

Few matters of perception take more learning than the question of what is attractive in taste, as any parent with small children could have told him. The firm also ignored the fact that soup is a main item in the major meals of the day in Europe, but is simply a quick emergency meal, largely for children, in America. It is thus astounding to find that Campbell's (who almost own the soup market in the U.S.A.) also entered the dehydrated market shortly after with their Red Kettle line, even though they had long been aware of the emergency role of soup in the American diet.

Both firms ignored the time cost being imposed on the housewife. The canned condensed soups on which Campbell had built its dominance took no more than five minutes from cupboard to bowl. The dehydrated product took a half hour or more of constant work and preparation! It is true that Lipton's, then and since, had a very satisfactory volume in a dehydrated line, but neither Lipton's nor Wylers sold much of their products primarily for soup, and even as soup, they required no more preparation than boiling the water. Studies of which Campbell's, at least, must have been aware, showed that the principal uses for these products were in snack dips and gravies, in which the preparation requirements were minimal. The principal types sold are onion and potato, which work well as flavoring agents in such uses.

Thus Campbell's dropped a reported $10 million and Corn Products a reputed $15 million trying to promote a product which did not fit into a current use-system (the flavors were not well suited to snack use), required learning to perceive a new and strange type of soup flavor as attractive, and which required seeing a dish used primarily in emergency situations as worth an extra time price of about a half hour of constant attention!

The cultural use-system into which an introduction is expected to fit, the desire-sets it is intended to fulfill, and the alternative means of fulfillment are thus major keys to prediction of the difficulty of gaining acceptance. In Germany, as in the rest of Europe, soup is an important component in satisfaction of the desire for a tasty main meal, and spicy soups a desired element in imparting zest. In America, soups are, at best, a very minor element, and families use the meat dish for zest. The kind of bland condensed soups popular in the United States do not fill the German need. The real alternative for them is a soup prepared from scratch ingredients, such a long and complicated process that Knorr's soups constitute a convenience in time cost. In the United States, soups are served in a context in which time, not zest, is at a premium, and the alternative is opening and simply diluting and warming some condensed product. Acceptance of the Knorr product would have required a substantial cultural change in most American households, a complete change in dietary practices. The potential added value was not likely to be there for a high quality meat-oriented culture, one great enough to justify the change after a period of learning.

Predicting Use-System Learning Requirements

The first step in prediction of potential acceptance and its acceleration pattern is proper identification of the target use-system into which the offering is expected to fit and the current alternative use-systems and their alternative ingredients. Often, as in the case of the dehydrated soup fiasco, simply an objective reassessment of the general market information already known is enough to reveal the learning requirement and appraise likely success and failure. Relatively rapid and complete adoption should be anticipated only when any such analysis indicates that all costs are minimal, including time costs, immediately perceived satisfaction values substantially higher, and the use-routine a duplicate or simple abbreviation of those currently in use. Whenever the use-routine is significantly changed in any manner, however, we can generally expect a slow and reluctant changeover and the possibility of rejection by some significant market segment or segments. The best way to assess the use-system is by means of comparative flow diagrams. Figures 9-1, 9-2, and 9-3 outline the procedural systems comparisons for the unsuccessful dehydrated soups, the only partially successful laundromat centers, and the completely successful mechanical refrigerator.

Had Knorr and Campbell analyzed only the use-system and probable consumer values of their products in the context to be used, neither would have spent a cent on product development. In the cultural context of their intended use, the dehydrated products were a much clumsier ingredient than the condensed product and required a much more complex use-procedure as well as more time and energy. The value of the expected end satisfaction of soup in the culture of the American housewife was far too low for such a price. The net satisfaction value of such an introduction was clearly negative.

The common main alternative to the laundromat at the time of its introduction was either the commercial laundry, which was extremely expensive, or the well-established wringer-type washing machine and clothesline in the home. There was also the alternative of the purchase of the automatic for the home, at a very substantial monetary cost. If the family owned no washing machine-- and the burgeoning newly formed families of the 1940's seldom did-- the neighborhood automatic laundry center was unquestionably by far the lowest in monetary cost. Nevertheless, a full generation after its introduction, only a minority of families use it, and even the home version never completely displaced the older style wringer-type washer. To many women, the procedural change involved is an anathema.

The mechanical refrigerator, by contrast, required no change at all in the method of food preservation, only the deletion of the nuisance routines of icing and disposal of the drippings from the melted ice. The latter, of course, would be seen as a positive

201

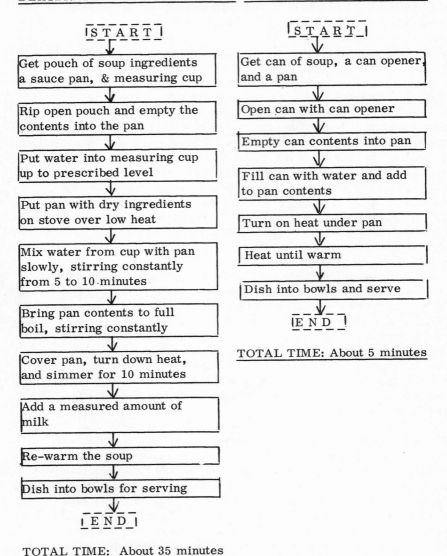

FIGURE 9-1. Comparison of Use-Systems for Dehydrated Soups
and for Established Canned Types

FIGURE 9-2. Comparison of Use-Systems for Wringer-Type Washer, for an Automatic Home Laundry System, and for a Public Automatic Laundry Center

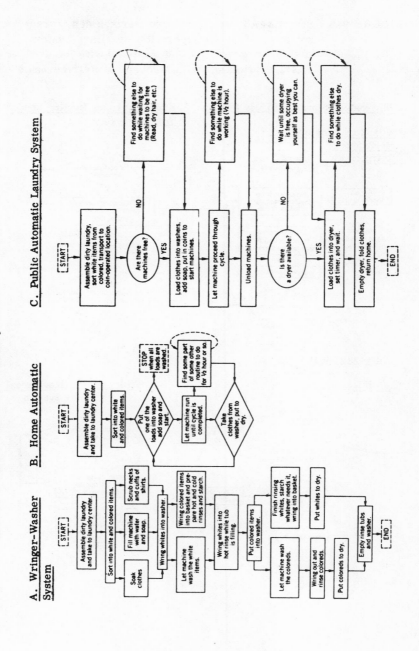

203

FIGURE 9-3.   Simplified Flow Charts and Perishables Storage
System, of Ice Refrigeration Auxiliary System,
and of Beverage Cooling Systems with Ice
Refrigeration and with Mechanical Refrigeration

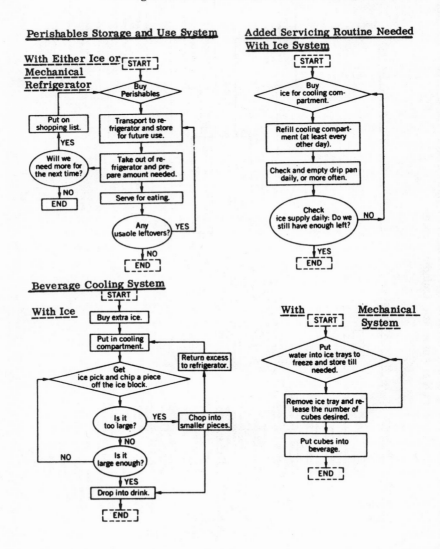

Perishables Storage and Use System

With Either Ice or Mechanical Refrigerator

START

Buy Perishables

Put on shopping list.

YES

Will we need more for the next time?

NO

END

Transport to refrigerator and store for future use.

Take out of refrigerator and prepare amount needed.

Serve for eating.

Any usable leftovers?

YES

NO

END

Added Servicing Routine Needed With Ice System

START

Buy ice for cooling compartment.

Refill cooling compartment (at least every other day).

Check and empty drip pan daily, or more often.

Check ice supply daily: Do we still have enough left?

NO

YES

END

Beverage Cooling System

START

With Ice

Buy extra ice.

Put in cooling compartment.

Get ice pick and chip a piece off the ice block.

Is it too large?   YES   Chop into smaller pieces.

NO

Is it large enough?   NO

YES

Drop into drink.

END

Return excess to refrigerator.

With   Mechanical System

START

Put water into ice trays to freeze and store till needed.

Remove ice tray and release the number of cubes desired.

Put cubes into beverage.

END

204

attribute, and in addition, the mechanical refrigerator did a clearly better job of food preservation. Eventually, of course, both its greater capacity and its food-preservation efficiency brought about a complete revolution in food shopping and food preparation techniques, including the advent of frozen foods and the supermarket. However, neither of these was a condition of adoption, but evolved from an increasing perception of advantageous use-systems on the part of the consumer himself. The mechanical refrigerator thus became accepted rather rapidly for a device which cost, at the outset, two or three months' income, or more. And it put the ice refrigerator in the museum.

Predicting the Perceptual Learning Requirement

Sometimes the perceptual learning requirement is both known and obvious, but its significance merely ignored. In the case of the dehydrated soups, executives even explicitly mentioned it, but brushed off the problem, "Americans will learn to love it!" When a change in taste acceptance of any kind is required, a learning process is always involved, and time for the learning must be allowed for.

Other kinds of learning requirements may only be obvious with thorough analysis and possibly original research. Perception is basically a question of balancing of values, and may require learning that some previous familiar source of satisfaction is really not efficient, is of little value, or that a new one suggested is worth the price it costs.

Those engaged in business research soon learn how strong a barrier to change source perception can be. No matter how irritating and unsatisfactory some previous operating policy has proven to be, from everyone's viewpoint, executives are nearly always extremely loathe to try out alternative ones based on mere research and logic. Railroad managements accustomed to "full cost" accounting were unwilling to accept the contribution-to-overhead system of appraising commuter service, and thus often denied themselves a proven real source of overall profit. The management of a mail order firm stalled for months on the introduction of a new customer sampling operation which had passed every test and was proposed in place of one acknowledged to be virtually worthless. The same executives took four years to abandon a customary catalog circulation policy which repeated tests had shown were actually costing profitable business.

Product adoption frequently requires a change in the perception of the user's role in obtaining the satisfaction. Research has shown that much of the resistance to the adoption of instant coffee was due to the feeling of the housewife that it downgraded her skill as a housekeeper. The automatic automobile transmission has never been completely accepted by that market segment which enjoys driving and has even come to be discounted to the extent that some people pay a premium for a "stick shift."

Appraisal of the perceived value thus must take into account the personal role changes which the new introduction may be perceived as effecting. Some of those role changes may well have positive values. The key to the design and sale of an automatic doffer for textile mills proved to be the fact that the device would eliminate an unwanted job. The mechanism was originally visualized by the designers as simply one of needed last steps to complete full automation of textile mill operations. The task of this device was simply to change bobbins when they were emptied--a relatively complicated task for a machine, but requiring little skill from a manual operator's standpoint. A project engineer assigned the task of completing development was, rather dubious of probable industry acceptance of this rather expensive mechanical substitute for a low-paid job until he lunched with some mill workers during a pilot test of the equipment at a large mill. The girls, as workers often do, were boasting of their prowess at their jobs--of how many spindles they could supervise. Noting a nearby male worker who sat silent during the repartee, the engineer asked the girls what he did. Their reply, loaded with scorn: "He's just a doffer!" This one remark revealed the true design goal: to abolish a job nobody wanted--a job at the bottom of the worker social scale and thus extremely hard to fill. This revelation led in turn to a simplification of the device which made it even more attractive for the purpose.

Every new product confronts the prospective buyer with a risk perception problem. He must be brought to perceive the value of the added benefits which the new use-system promises as noticeably greater than he perceives the risk that the new will not fully live up to the promise. His perception of the value of the old is a well-established reflex based on habit. The purported value of the proffered new benefit is not yet a matter of experience. Risk cost is negligible, of course, if the initial purchase cost can be viewed as small change and a trial attempted on impulse, as it is with a new household detergent. But most important new products involve substantial sums, and adoption hinges on the relative depth of the unsatisfied felt need for the added benefit in comparison with the cost which must be risked to test the validity of the promised benefit to be delivered.

Whenever the cost is substantial, the mere need to learn to perceive the added value prior to use can prolong the rise to acceptance. The 10-year-long delay in development of wide acceptance of color TV resulted in considerable measure from a need to learn to appreciate substantial value in the addition of a color dimension

to the picture on the tube.   True, perceived real service problems
were an added factor, but these merely added to the risk.   Had
there been an initial established felt need of any depth for color,
occasional problems of set adjustment would have been ignored.
Jaguar sports cars, for example, have long had a reputation even
among buffs for high proneness to expensive repairs, yet have lost
none of their glamorous image.

Preparation of a potentially successful introductory plan is
completely dependent of the accuracy of these predictions of the
learning requirements imposed by the acceptance of the introduction.

SUMMARY

1.   Marketing research and analysis of the highest order of
competence has a part to play at every step of the process of product conception and development.

2.   Such research can add materially to the stock of new
product concepts, particularly through revelations of dissatisfaction
with design among large segments of users and prospects, through
analysis of trends in desires and tastes among fringe segments,
and through the uncovering of problems in use-systems.

3.   Product concepts which survive initial screening need
concept testing and other user-oriented research to develop design
performance goals for the subsequent developmental process.

4.   User-reaction research is needed to guide improvement
of prototype products during the development stage.

5.   Before the offering is ready to be released for sale, it
is also best, if possible, to make consumer use tests of production-
run samples, to highlight possible negative values arising from ordinary production run output.

6.   Finally, before introductory plans are crystallized, a
careful analysis is needed of all of the learning requirements acceptance of the introduction will impose: use-systems learning, role-
perception learning, and value-perception learning.   The degree of
use-system learning can usually be rather simply determined through
the comparison of use-system flow charts if we already know the
probable use systems into which the offering will be fitted and the
use systems it will displace.   Determination of role-perception
changes and changes in value perception required normally involves
well-analyzed field research.   The nature of the correct introductory plan is completely dependent on the proper prediction of all
three kinds of learning requirements.

10

INTRODUCING NEW PRODUCTS AND MANAGING THEM FROM CRADLE TO GRAVE

Although regular new product introductions are a prerequisite to profits, the mere introduction of well-conceived and well-designed new products does not automatically guarantee that the pioneer himself will be the beneficiary of those profits. Unless the introduction itself is marketed in accordance with its learning requirement, and the management of subsequent phases of the cycle adjusted to the market conditions of those phases, some more perceptive and more nimble-footed emulator may reap the gains, especially if the introducer does not take full advantage to learn from experience and move fast to reap the fruit of that learning.

Like any other kind of birth, the introductory phase can be critical. If the product be a high-learning one, the resources available and the entire marketing mix must be predicated on the assumption of a prolonged marketing development effort during which constant personal attention must be given to sales and a constant lookout for developing product weaknesses maintained. Provisions must be set up to carry the effort through a long period of dependence on market investment until evidence of growth becomes apparent.

By contrast, if the product is a low-learning one, then the pioneer must be prepared to fend off a rush of emulators eager for a major share of an obviously profitable market. Once the upsurge of sales is clearly evident, the seller, whether pioneer or emulator, must start preparing for the later inevitable slowdown of growth and shakeout of the weaker entrants, hope to be one of those sharing the saturation of the mature market, and in that period prepare for the eventual decline and death of the offering.

Each of these phases of market life involves a different characteristic marketing mix and divergent kinds of management orientation and personnel assignments.

The basic problems of the marketing development period through which every high-learning product must be nurtured are to get trial and approval by key innovators and other early adopters and to support the continuing market investment deficits until these early users legitimize the promise of the offering and the following echelons of buyers start the market spiral upward. The limited demand and the initial attention to the core attributes themselves dictate a limited number of models, high in quality, end-user pricing which minimizes value-perception learning, and high trade discounts to compensate a strictly selected list of sales distributors for the aggressive sales effort needed to reach and convince the limited number of potential buyers to give the product a trial. Promotion needs to concentrate on getting wide awareness of the product's availability through maximum use of publicity and sales made largely through personal means. Marketing research and intelligence needs to devote an intensive analytical focus on identifying product weaknesses for the earliest possible correction and on discovering the exact nature of emerging use-systems. Management should be of the most inquiring and imaginative type, entrepreneurial enough in outlook and temperament to be more interested in building for the long pull than in immediate results.

On the other hand, when introducing low-learning products and when managing the growth phase of any introduction, the main concern must be on forestalling inevitably eager competition. Product design should be as modular and flexible as possible and models multiplied as fast as multiplying market segments can be identified. Price lines must cover every level of taste, from low-end to premium offerings. Trade discounts should be at customary levels for the product category, but no more, since dealer push needs will be minimal. Distribution should be as extensive and intensive as possible, with heavy emphasis on fast service to dealers and constant maintenance of heavy dealer inventories. Mass-media advertising will be the promotional tool of choice, aimed at establishing and strengthening brand position with both dealers and final buyers. Market intelligence will still be alert for product weaknesses but will be focused primarily on market position and on discovering gaps in market and model coverage--on finding opportunities to develop and exploit new market segments. Management should still be dominated by market-oriented personnel, but men of a bent toward mass promotion and dealer relations and inclined to focus on immediate sales volume.

The slowdown in sales growth which marks the entrance of the competitive turbulence phase requires a change of management emphasis toward the defensive stance necessary to profit in the following stage of a saturated market. As unit profits inevitably decline during this period, some competitors will be shaken out. Those surviving will be those who have already established strong distribution and a strong consumer franchise, and have tightened their line to eliminate unnecessary specialties, and have at the same time kept incorporating product improvements. This is the period in which to devise market-broadening pricing tactics and take advantage of promotional pricing opportunities. The promotional emphasis will be on market retention mass advertising intended to keep reminding buyers of the values they are getting and dealers of the organization's market support, plus various kinds of sales promotional devices to attract dealers and hold their goodwill. Distribution will be further buttressed by intensive interest to logistical arrangements which put heavy stress on dealer service and convenience. Market intelligence will watch distribution strength closely and focus ever more strongly on user needs for product improvement, on opportunities to broaden the market, and on possibilities for fresh promotional themes. The kind of manager needed will have a strong bent toward efficient administration, and the more imaginative enterpreneurial types will be of more value transferred to responsibility for newer tomorrow's breadwinners.

The maturity of the succeeding saturation phase brings with it a maturing and relatively stable competitive structure and a need to complete the full turn to a completely defensive competitive strategy, aimed at entrenching product position in buyer usage and strengthening dealer ties. All price moves should be largely defensive and aimed at preservation of the overall product market. A constant alert should be manned for opportunities for incremental pricing to smooth production peaks and valleys and thus further lower costs. Promotional emphasis will be a continuation of the consumer reminder, dealer-loyalty-oriented policy which should have taken over during the shakedown phase. Possible erosion of the market by new up-and-coming offerings of other kinds should be a major concern of marketing intelligence, and a careful watch kept for signs of beginning market decay. Managerial personnel will normally be production minded, aimed at maintenance of profits by cost control.

Once the sales decline becomes obvious, all emphasis should be on marketing tactics aimed at milking the product dry of every potential source of profit. The product line should be stripped down to the major profit producers and prices maintained at profit levels, without consideration for the effect on market share. Promotion should be phased out rapidly, continuing just enough to sustain distribution at a profitable level. Marginal outlets should be abandoned and only enough research attention allocated to identify the point at which the line should be interred.

FORECASTING AND MANAGING THE INTRODUCTION

To note that all individual introductory sales curves start

from zero and accelerate at some pace for a period in some kind of introductory phase is to perpetrate an obvious but meaningless truism. Sales can start from no other point but zero, and the mere process of the spread of awareness through communications is a cumulative process proceeding over time, guaranteeing some kind of accelerating sales rise even for the hottest fad. However, simply creating a general awareness of the existence of an already highly desired satisfaction potential is accomplished much more quickly and easily and with far simpler promotional tools than is required to stimulate sales of a high-learning product whose satisfaction values are not immediately recognized. For the latter, the seller must locate the scattering of buyers anxious enough to undergo a substantial degree of learning new perceptions and revising long-standing habit patterns in order to acquire a new and previously unavailable benefit. If the novelty appeal is sufficiently high and novelty is all that is new, word of mouth and escalating usage may be all the promotion that is really required to put the product over. If the offering is really only a much improved source of a familiar benefit, used in a well-established routine, sales growth will not need a market development period to allow for necessary learning, and the sales success will need only well-planned, strong mass promotion. · By contrast, if new habits of action and thought are part of the price of acquiring the desired benefit, the initial customers must be sought among that small minority of innovators and early adopters, must be ferretted out through patient personal sales contact of some sort and appealed to individually. Those in charge of such aggressive distribution must be protected in their profits by exclusive or selective sales arrangements.

The forecast of the nature of the initial acceptance pattern will thus determine the nature of the introductory sales and promotional plan, and the wrong plan can be fatal or at least extremely injurious. Lack of foresight as to the readiness of the market for an intended benefit has cost many an innovating introducer his right to market eminence, or even a solid niche in that market. Toni was not the first home permanent on the market, but the second. The innovator whose action stimulated Toni's entrance did not understand the character of the needed promotion and has long ago passed from the scene.

Even when a seller survives an initial forecast mistake, a surge of imitative competition for which it is not prepared may wipe out the profit potential. Such was the case with the introduction of frozen orange concentrate. The market was so ready to buy the first cans produced that the introducers did not (possibly could not) preempt the market before a scramble of competitors got into store freezer cases. Within the three years it took to get new groves bearing, the industry became profitless.

Introducing a high-learning product without prevision of the needed market acceptance problem and the consequent proper marketing plan can be just as expensive. Unless the introducer has the financial strength and promotional resources, he is almost sure to fail. Assuming that learning is not needed can trap even the strong. Campbell's Soups dropped a published $10 million and the Knorr brand an estimated $15 million when both misjudged the learning content of dried soup. Just how much RCA lost through its assumption that color TV was just an improved black-and-white set is probably a corporate secret, but the deficits were clearly of the order of millions of dollars per year for ten long years. Manifestly, the most careful possible analysis of the learning requirement should be a prerequisite to the introductory marketing plan. Thus each phase of the cycle has its own unique competitive situation and corresponding strategy objectives.

COMPETITIVE OUTLOOK AND APPROPRIATE STRATEGY AT EACH STAGE

If the product is a high-learning product and thus can be expected to have a substantial market development phase, there is likely to be very little problem of competition, for the simple reason that there is no immediate profit in view to attract competitors. The strategy objectives during this period are to minimize the learning requirements so far as possible, to eliminate possible defects in the product, to get a fix on the use-systems into which the product is being introduced by users, and to develop as widespread an awareness of product benefits as possible and obtain trial by early adopters.

Not until the product market begans to show some real signs of growth and market acceptance are potential competitors likely to leave the sidelines, from which they have been watching, and develop their own entries in earnest. Once some glimmer of profits appears, however, there is certain to be a rush of competitors anxious to get in before it is too late to start to develop a strong market niche. The degree of their eagerness will depend on the apparent speed of market growth and the apparent level of prospective profits in the industry. Since many will already have been watching from the sidelines, any defects in the product or the product line left open will be eagerly seized by them at this time. The competitive situation then is one in which the introducer must expect increasing interest on the part of potential competitors. The strategy objective is to lower the level of this interest by establishing as strong a market and distribution niche as possible and by maintaining as high a level of buyer value as can be done by taking ad-

THE OUTLOOK FOR COMPETITION AND THE APPROPRIATE COMPETITIVE STRATEGY OBJECTIVES AT EACH STAGE OF THE PRODUCT LIFE CYCLE

Product Life Cycle Stage	Outlook for Competition	Strategy Objectives
MARKET DEVELOPMENT	None of any importance likely	Minimize learning requirements, locate and remedy offering defects quickly, develop widespread awareness of benefits, and gain trial.
RAPID GROWTH	Early entrance of many aggressive emulators	To establish a strong brand market and distribution niche as quickly as possible.
COMPETITIVE TURBULENCE	Price and distribution squeezes on the industry, shaking out the weaker entrants	To maintain and strengthen the market niche achieved through dealer and consumer loyalty.
SATURATION	Competition stabilized, with few or no new entrants and market shares not subject to substantial change unless someone gets a new head start with a substantial perceived product improvement	To defend brand position against competing brands and the product category against other potential products, through constant attention to product improvement opportunities and fresh promotional and distribution approaches.
DECLINE	Similar competition declining and dropping out because of decrease in consumer interest	To milk the offering dry of all possible profit, by eliminating any expense or market effort not yielding a provable direct and immediate profit.

vantage of his own increasing accumulated experience to bring prices in line with cost.

At this point, also, it is important that he makes certain that he has eliminated as many product defects as possible and covered as many possible product variations as are needed to satisfy the market, thus leaving few niches for competitors to take advantage of. Only thus will he have prepared himself to weather the coming period of competitive turbulence in which the growing industry capacity and increasing level of competition for shelf space as well as consumer demand will squeeze out a number of the early entrants. He must make certain that he will not be one of those shaken out during this period of declining profits. To do this he must strengthen both consumer loyalty and distributor loyalty to make certain that he has a strong position in the distribution channels, backed up by strong consumer brand demand.

If he continues to take advantage of his accumulated experience, to learn from it and to make use of it, he will then be in a position to enter the saturation or maturity phase of the market with the kind of strong market share position which assures him a major profitable line, due to his volume of accumulated experience. Competition during the maturity phase is normally relatively stable. Market shares are not likely to change greatly unless some competitor from inside or outside the industry develops a very substantial product improvement which the industry has been overlooking. The appropriate strategy objective therefore is to defend the position of brands against competing brands and also to keep a sharp lookout for possible competition from other kinds of products for part of the market.

The most important aspect of his marketing mix during most of this mature period will be his distribution position. It is therefore to his interest to promote ever tighter dealer relationships.

No matter how well the product is defended during the maturity phase, however, sooner or later it will meet competition from some source, leading to a decline. When the inevitable decline becomes apparent, competition is no longer the major focus. There will be a decreasing amount of it within the industry and a declining number of competitors, as one after another abandons the market for lack of profit. At this point, the only wise policy is to trim sales to cut back every element in the marketing mix which is not bringing in a directly provable dollar of profit. The offering must be milked dry of all possible profit, in every way possible: product design variation, extent of distribution, any spending on promotion, and any concern about the effect of price level on the market. All possible resources should be diverted from the declining product to be invested in alternatives which have a brighter

214

future.

Thus at each phase of the life cycle each of the major elements in the marketing mix must be reviewed and the strategy with regard to that element changed. The most important element, of course, is the offering itself.

PRODUCT DESIGN DURING THE CHANGING PHASES OF THE CYCLE

Stage of the Cycle	R & D and Design Objectives
MARKET DEVELOPMENT	Limited number of models with design of both the physical product and of the total offering going to the utmost to minimize learning requirements. Design cost and use engineered to appeal to most receptive segment. Closest possible attention to quality control and to quick elimination of market-revealed defects in design.
RAPID GROWTH	Modular design, if possible, to facilitate flexible addition of variants to appeal to every new segment and new use-system, as they appear.
COMPETITIVE TURBULENCE	Intensified attention to product improvement, tightening up of line to eliminate unnecessary specialties with little market appeal.
MATURITY	A constant alert for market pyramiding opportunities either through bold cost and price-penetration or major product changes. Introduction of flanker products. Constant attention to product improvement and to cost-cutting opportunities. Reexamination of necessity for design-compromises.
DECLINE	Constant pruning of line to eliminate any items not returning a direct profit.

If the initial forecast of the learning requirement indicates a substantial period of market development will be needed to establish the product in consumer use-systems, and this forecast is confirmed by early research, preferably before introduction, the first generation of the introduction should be designed to minimize the required amount of that learning both on the physical side and the side of value perception of price.

It is no accident that the first automobiles were "horseless carriages," in fact as well as in designation. As such, they came at the end of a long period of substituting mechanical power for animal power, long after the first steamboats and railroads and the first steam threshing machines. It is doubtful if the modern sports sedan would have caught on as readily. Similarly, when introducing a new approach to an academic subject, a paperback which can be used as a supplement in an otherwise traditional course will gain much readier acceptance than the same material in a standard-sized text which will require habit-bound instructors to restructure their entire courses (and also their own thinking habits about these courses). The first wave of farm tractors were "one-plow" models, simply putting mechanical power in front of a plow of the same size as previously drawn by a team of horses. Today's monsters which may, in some cases, pull a string of farm tools over 50 feet long, would have required much too radical a shift in habits of every kind, including expenditures. (It should be noted that the first popular tractors cost just about the same as a really good team of horses.)

Product model numbers should be restricted initially, if the product is a high-learning one. Market segmentation will be minimal so long as the core satisfaction attribute is the center of attraction. Only when these desired core satisfactions (such as mechanical transportation, in the case of the automobile) become the old and familiar to many in the market, will a second level of desires in the hierarchy of the set become really valuable. The racy sports cars and the dune buggies can take their time to make the scene, after the basic product has become part of accepted use-systems of buyers. In any case, only after market introduction and completion of much of the market development period will enough be known about actual developing use-systems to reveal the nature of developing market segmentation.

During this period a close watch must be kept on possible defects in the offering and possible sensitivities to the method of use. R & D should also be pushed to be ready with proper model variations to cover as many segments as feasible as soon as sales acceleration of the growth period becomes obvious. Some of these models should be viewed as "stripped" variations intended to trap market fringes who cannot see the value reflected by the going price of the main model. Others will be more elaborate models tapping

segments desiring even more attributes in the offering. Some will
be variations serving special purposes which customers are developing for the product, as shown by market experience in the way
customers are beginning to use that product.

Nearly every product has some built-in defect, if only because of the necessary compromises in any product design. During
this introductory period of market development, it is extremely important that the firm be on continual alert to spot early those defects which users and buyers perceive as having a high negative
value and to correct them as quickly as possible while the firm is
still the only seller on the market. Needless to say, quality control should be as tight as possible. Failure to remedy defects or
deliver consistent quality may spoil introductory sales. Even more
seriously, such failure may leave a wide-open opportunity for competition to take over a considerable share of the market by developing a value package closer to the desires and usage habits of an
important market segment.

Once a customer is lost he is extremely difficult to get back.
One of the weaknesses of the first heavy-duty liquid detergent,
Lestoil, was an odor that many women did not like. When the success of Lestoil became visible to some of their larger potential
competitors, formulations which avoided the odor problem were
able to take over most of the potential and drive Lestoil off the
shelves which its pioneering should have maintained for it. Similarly, General Foods' introduction of freeze-dried instant coffee,
Maxim, was spoiled by its sensitivity to the precision of its use.
Although the product, when properly prepared, quite clearly appealed more strongly to the palates of educated consumers than did
that of some of the competing brands that came on at about the same
time, Maxim was particularly vulnerable to improper measure-
ments. Putting too much coffee in the cup developed a bitter flavor
which aroused a very strong negative reaction among many users.
Competitors, on the other hand, introduced products which were extremely tolerant of the amount the customer used and closer in the
quantity required to their normal usage (a teaspoon per cap, whereas
Maxim required a mere 1/2 teaspoon per cup). The result was that
Maxim was not able to maintain its initial market share. Unfortunately, a later introduction of General Foods, Max-Pak, using a
pre-measured quantity for a potful, met a similar fate for a similar
reason, and General Foods had to reintroduce an improved product
at considerable cost.

It is sometimes forgotten that large numbers of consumers
of all sorts (including industrial) are not always careful in reading
directions and following them and almost never as tender and precise in their use of the product as the experts who design them. It
is extremely important to watch out for such expert-prone problems

in order to maintain the momentum which the accumulated experience should gain for a company. Unless the firm makes full use of possible experience during this part of the introduction, while it is still the only firm in the market, others will be able to jump in and to gain the volume necessary to get the accumulated experience to put them ahead of the originating company during the succeeding rapid growth phase.

Whether the period of rapid growth is the second stage of the life cycle for a given offering, or the introductory stage, makes no difference in any aspect of market strategy. In either case, the introducer will have very little lead time over possible competitors in which to gain an accumulated experience advantage, and it is important that he dominate the market from the first in order that his volume give him the necessary experience lead. Whoever gets and stays ahead of competition for the major market segments and achieves a strong distributive position normally becomes and remains a market leader for the rest of the product life cycle, because of a greater weight of accumulated experience. This can be done only by getting to potential buyers and distribution first with a well-designed product model mix and keeping that design in the lead, covering the bulk of the market segments in the most important price lines. Any weakness opens an opportunity for some competitor, one which he is certain to take advantage of quickly. Ford's 1908 move, with a quality car for its day at a mass market price and design, gave him a lead over the numerous competitors who focused on the high-price market of low volume that was keeping their own factories busy. Ford later lost this lead because he failed to diversify models to meet the growing divergencies of taste during the period of rapid growth of automobile usage and the expanded market--to competitors who were willing to give the customer some color besides black and more than a single body model.

Ford made a similar mistake four decades later when he offered only four spartan models of the 1960 Falcon line to meet the growing "compact" market. This left room for Chevy to recover from an initially cool reception to its competing Corvair by introducing a sporty model. From the very first part of the growth period, therefore, the product design should be as modular and flexible as possible, to facilitate proliferation of model offerings by addition of accessory attributes which could blanket most possible segments. Price lines should obviously include both low-end offerings to penetrate new market segments and premium models to match the attribute desires and value perceptions of those at the very core of each segment.

Timing of an introduction, particularly in this initial market phase of rapid growth is critically important--timing both in the seasonal sense and in relation to the fashion cycle. Naturally, timing in relation to the often parallel R & D efforts of competitors is of paramount concern in not permitting them an experience advantage in the market.

Nearly all product categories exhibit some seasonality of demand, and for some the seasonal pattern is quite marked. Products as diverse as construction and farm equipment, and college textbook adoptions are heaviest in the spring--construction of farm equipment because that is when they are most needed, textbooks because that is when bookstores must order their stocks for the fall before the teaching staffs leave on vacations. Furs and skis sell heaviest at retail in the fall, expensive watches and other gifts best in June and at the winter holidays.

Buyer interest is highest prior to and at the beginning of the appropriate season, and attention rapidly decreases once the season is underway. Decisions have been made and any search for the new largely extinguished. To miss a season is often to miss the year and to allow the luster of novelty to diminish in the interim. Moreover, competitors are frequently working on parallel lines may not be as careless of deadlines and could capture attention and most of the market in the meantime, leaving only crumbs for laggards.

The second place payoff in this kind of race can be very unattractive even when the later introduced product is a substantially better fit to the desire-set. If the first on the market and the first to be perceived comes somewhere near to fulfilling the desired satisfaction-sets, the drive of most buyers to search further is extinguished and late-comers can capture only scattered fringe segments. The texbook delayed until after the April orders are placed is not even examined if beaten by some similar book in March. A new kitchen appliance which is second may not get on to the dealers' shelves and will be the first to be dropped when the shakeout of the turbulence period begins. A survival during the turbulence period depends largely on what has been accomplished before that period.

The lustily booming sales of the rapid growth phase of any introduction tends to overstimulate competitive entries, to bring into the market too many brands, too many models and far too much productive capacity. Once the sales climb slows down, and long before it stops, these surpluses of brands, models and capacities must be squeezed out and eliminated. The market cannot support them all. Surviving sellers will be those whose previously well-executed marketing mix has established preference at both dealer and consumer levels.

Product emphasis during this period normally should be focused on tightening the line, eliminating unnecessary specialties--model variations which are not providing substantial differential value to substantial market segments. This is also the period to start paying more attention to styling and the introduction of other superficial novelty elements which may be attractive to some market segments. This is the time to add more and more novel flavors to the baking mix, more perfume variety to the toiletries offered, more kinds of vehicles if you are in the automobile manufacturing market. It is also a period in which private labelling--manufacturing for others, for sale under their own label--can add a plus to manufacturing volume, and thus to accumulated experience, conferring a cost advantage.

This is also the period to be on the alert for opportunities to broaden the market, to pyramid the cycle by adding new satisfaction elements of a fundamental character, to develop product variations which create or fit into entirely new use-systems or to penetrate into market segments not previously served by previous price lines.

Sometimes the opportunity is suggested by the customers themselves, by adaptations and modifications to the use-systems they have developed on their own. The American automobile industry, for example, did little to furnish the initial stimulus for any of the several developments which have broadened automobile use. Inclusion of cargo and luggage racks to automobiles started with extraneous accessories originally added by individual owners. Sport cars came back from Europe with the veterans of World War II, and Detroit followed slowly and reluctantly. The high performance model was originally the product of back-alley garage modifications. Conversions of pick-up trucks to camper use came from outside the industry, and all original dune buggies were home-made vehicles until well after the sport became popular.

Even when the seller is more alert to buyer attitude changes than this indicates, buyers are bound to find uses not foreseen. The wise seller keeps his R & D effort working to fit such use-systems.

Basically, the product policy during the turbulence period is that of buttressing the firm's position in the market and covering as much volume as can be profitable during the succeeding saturated market. The correct motto for saturated market management is really "more of the same". Research and development should be aimed at continual product development and at elimination or minimization of all product faults.

The necessity for product improvement is a part of the aspect of necessary policy most easily ignored, and the most disastrous to neglect. The stable nature of competition during this period, and the lack of new entries, tends to lead firms to somnolence. Substitutes will eventually bring about a market decline, but that decline will be more certain and sooner if defensive product management is not pursued aggressively and imaginatively.

It is easy to assume that the design possibilities have been exhausted and to believe that design compromises are unalterable. It is never wise to do so. Customers lost at this stage are difficult or even impossible to recapture from substitutes or from new competitors, whenever the improvement possible is substantial enough to bring these in. Detroit's insistence on continual adhesion to a single type of engine design--the 4-cycle reciprocating engine they started with at the turn of the century--left the stage wide open for the invasion by the Japanese Mazda. So long as the customer has not shifted to trying a substitute, the offering need be only enough less worse than a possible substitute to bar incentive to learn some new use-system or to counterbalance the perceived risk of trying the as-yet unfamiliar. Once any substitute is tried, however, the burden of proving extra value is on a return to the old. Thus the steel industry developed a thinner, and thus lighter can stock sheet only after aluminum, plastics and paper had already captured a major share of the container market. The belatedly introduced thinner stock did not win back the lost markets, only saved the market from further erosion.

Because market shares tend to stabilize in mature markets, executives of well-established sellers can easily fall into a dangerous "Don't rock the boat" approach to suggestions for product improvements, adaptive products, or substitutes. They lose sight of the inevitability of parallel invention and also of the truly unstable nature of any market niche and the way such market niches originate.

The long history of invention is replete with examples of parallel invention--indeed, it is a rare discovery which was not paralleled by someone else who was just a bit late in the race to the patent office, his efforts guided by attention to the same problem or built on the same advances in technology. If a firm's laboratories come up with an unwelcome improvement or substitute, it is a practical certainty that some other less well-established entrepreneur has been working along the same lines and has come up with a similar answer. The proper question is always, "Is it better to lose market shares to ourselves, or to someone else?" The advantages of stainless steel razor blades, for instance, were recognized by major suppliers long before the Wilkinson firm invaded the market and captured a share, but were not pushed to final development until the latter had gained a significant niche.

Moreover, any substantial improvement does restructure the market shares, no matter who introduces it. If the established seller is the innovator, his new share comes only partly at his own expense, much of it from others. New market entries inevitably carve their niches from the fringes of other niches, even from other products--almost never from the shares of a single seller or even a single product. Disregard of this fact can be costly, as illustrated by the results of the Chrysler Corporation's toe-in-the-water approach to the imported car market when it acquired the French Simca interest in 1959. The major model then on the market--the Aronde--possessed many attributes potentially attractive to American motorists and drew excellent reviews from the motor magazines. It sold well for a new car in the year just prior to the Chrysler acquisition. Chrysler, however, appeared unwilling to follow up this advantage, perhaps fearing to cut into the possible potential for its soon-to-be-introduced Valiant. The adequate parts and service network was never developed, and the Dodge dealers who were given the franchise showed no interest in their new item. For lack of adequate maintenance backup, the Simca lost its promising foothold and never fully recovered. Nor was this an isolated instance, as the firm's lack of any readiness to counter the GM introduction of its Vega and the Ford entry of the Pinto in the 1971 year proved.

In the absence of possible substantial improvements, market share gains at the expense of closely similar offerings almost always cost more than the possible profit return, once the market achieves full maturity. This does not mean, however, that the opportunities for profitable sales gains are gone like the leaves of autumn. Less spectacular but still substantial profits can be gleaned if useful "flanker products" can be developed, or if the seller capitalizes on information on the various use-systems discovered by different users to increase use frequency among loyal customers.

Flanker products are use-related items bearing the same family trademark designation. Their role is to benefit from the aura of acceptance of the key product, and the sales gains will usually be modest but worthwhile. For example, once Toni had developed the home permanent market and the market had reached maturity, Toni was able to introduce a line of shampoos and hair conditioners and rinses which gained ready acceptance by its market segment. But such a flanker product acquires cheap sales gains only when the product is perceived as use related. When Toni tried capitalizing on its acceptance for hair products by entering a lipstick, Viv, it did not succeed. It was not a useful flanker because not perceived as use related, and it moved by means of a different kind of distribution-communications mix.

Flanker products succeed because they trade on the established brand loyalty of current users. The gains to be made by using flankers, however, are seldom spectacular. An often more rewarding means of capitalizing on acceptance is to increase the frequency of use by getting current users to place the product in more use-systems. Most offerings complete different use-systems for different buyers. Once well accepted into one use-system, buyers or other family members may be easily persuaded to try the product they already have on hand for some other use—systems which other users have found of value. Sometimes the increased total use may be a multiple of the original frequency, and little more is needed than research to discover current use patterns and effective communications to spread the word concerning the added uses.

One spectacular example is the history of "facial tissues," originally sold solely to women for wiping excess cleansing cream from their faces. Some husbands, however, soon found that the tissues made convenient handkerchiefs during colds, and even for everyday use. Advertising capitalizing on this and other discovered uses paid off handsomely, and the market today is many times larger than that originally sought. Moreover, a flanker "man-size tissue" not only succeeded later, but its success was due more to the desire of women for its use than to its purchase by men, and thus to use intensification.

Eternal youth is a vain and even unwise search for both man and his markets. The only justification for production comes when it gives both value to the buyer and profit to the seller. When the buyers' perception of value begins to decline to the level of production costs, there is no economic justification in prolonging the process of product death.

The objective of management during market decline is thus the extraction of maximum productive profit and quiet burial of the dead. The fundamental process should be that of milking the market and withdrawing both physical and managerial resources which can yield greater profits elsewhere, while supplying whatever market remains to be served at a profit. On the product side, this means the withdrawal of all R & D effort and the progressive phasing out of all product model variants which are not currently yielding a direct profit.

Products whose life cycles have obviously passed the point of profit should obviously be dropped. The product should also be dropped or sold to others at other points in the cycle, when getting out would be more profitable than staying. Indeed, for some inventors, the time to withdraw from even a promising product may be as early as a development of the concept and can be at any other time during the life cycle, depending on the sellers resources and his opportunities.

THE WHEN OF GETTING OUT

Up to this point the focus has been on the management of each phase of the product life cycle without regard to who does the managing. The divergent requirements of the different phases of the cycle imply, to some extent, a need for different kinds of

223

personalities in charge, and perhaps even completely different selling organizations at times. This may simply dictate successive shifts in product management personnel if the seller is a large and professionally managed organization. For the small entrepreneurial innovator, however, such shifts in management emphasis may mean that he must assess correctly the proper point in the cycle for him to sell out, or at least unload a major interest onto other shoulders. Even the large organization may not find that staying with an offering from the birth to grave is its most profitable choice. The choice is only more critical for the individual innovator.

History and the bureaucratic logic of any large organization both seem to indicate that the small entrepreneur is more likely to conceive and develop the revolutionary high-learning product than is the large, well-established organization. But the same small innovator is also most likely lacking in the resources needed to see such a high-learning offering through its market development phase into an era of profitable growth or, succeeding in this, to fend off the burgeoning competition once profit is clearly visible. Even if he has or acquires such resources, he may profit more by selling out when the market is booming and market saturation and declining profit margins not yet apparent. It is probably wise to carry an offering through the entire life cycle only when he builds a dominant market position and a relatively large organization with diversified income sources and new generations of products coming along. Even then, he should do so only when he is temperamentally adapted to routine business administration. He should always carefully weigh the value to him of a possible sell-out as against continued personal exploitation of his idea, at every stage in the cycle.

Even the gestation period can demand more resources than those available. Even at the point of conception, the innovator may sometimes do well to consider the alternative of turning the idea over to someone better equipped to develop it if he can get an adequate price, preferably a royalty or other share in the profits. The ideal arrangement, if he has the skills to guide development, would be a sale contingent on his continued direction of those parts of the development process for which he is best fitted, usually something less than total management of the whole process. He may, for example, recognize that he is better equipped technologically than marketing-wise, or the reverse.

Such a sale may not be possible on any reasonable terms, of course, or may not be wisest at this point. Even when the sale is possible, the innovating seller may have the means to bring his idea to a higher and more valuable point of development, one for which the market potential and production feasibility are more clearly visible, and the idea then worth more than the added effort put in to bring it to this stage. The most saleable point may prove to be that just prior to placing the product into commercial production. Such is usually the case, for instance, in most forms of publishing: book and periodical manuscripts, recordings, even movies. At this point, the innovator can usually be assured of retaining some share of the profits, usually on a straight royalty basis. In the case of most books, the author develops the manuscript on speculation, then turns it over to some regular publisher at an agreed-upon royalty.

However, the innovator may find that he can do much better for himself if he chooses not to sell out at this point if he has or can develop the resources to go into production and promote the sale, especially if the actual physical production can be contracted out, as it frequently can and is by firms regularly in the business. Of all the major textbook publishers, for example, only one does its own printing, and the highly successful Polaroid organization contracts out the manufacture of both films and cameras. Advertising design and production is a specialized function done by others for the vast bulk of all business, and specialized independent sales organizations such as manufacturers' representatives and food brokers can often (but not always) be found to carry out the field sales effort.

The innovator need handle only the financing and risk functions and the overall coordination of the management and marketing functions. If he is capable of doing these well, or of learning how in time, and his appraisal of the market reasonably correct, he can usually make more by keeping all rights himself than he would gain through royalties. He will, of course, sacrifice the early returns which royalties assure before the production breaks even, and these can be substantial. But once sales pass the break-even point, his returns will escalate quickly well beyond those of a royalty proportionate to numbers sold. Moreover, he may actually get those net returns earlier and more certainly than if he does sell out. Selling out has disadvantages other than a lesser total return, as well as the advantages of more certainty in getting some kind of return. The innovator could well be more aggressive in developing and getting his product to market than is a well-established organization with other, competing interests. He has no committees to pose hurdles to decision, no other sources of income competing for prior attention. The well-established organization is far more prone than he would be to allocate both production and sales resources in terms of immediately visible sales returns, to place a higher priority on present certainties than on future promising potential. Production of an offering with an unproven potential can be too easily delayed and its vigorous promotion too likely to be held back until after it has proven itself. Such delays in introduction, in making its availability known, and in promoting an appreciation of its benefits can

225

all converge to cost both the innovator and the actual seller a large portion of the potential market to some even inferior production which is handled more aggressively.

It is also true that well-established sellers often hesitate to take on and push the really high-learning product. The innovator may find it impossible to sell the concept or the developed product until after market development has proved its potential. Sales may be possible only after the start of the market growth phase reveals its profitability. At this point, of course, the innovator should be able to bargain for a much better price than he would have been able to get earlier and a larger share of prospective profits and even of the total management, if he is capable of and desirous of taking on the latter. Again, his decision should hinge on careful appraisal of his resources, skills, abilities and degree of interest in marketing administration.

If he has the resources, skills, and interest, he may well profit from carrying the introduction well into the market growth period. The ideal time to profit by selling out a product may well be just at the point at which the rate of market growth ceases to increase and starts declining. Someone has observed that the secret of most large fortunes seems to have been to get in on a fast-rising development, ride it until it approaches its zenith, then capitalize the operation as though the rise were to continue forever and sell out to investors. Much is certainly to be said for capitalizing the innovator's interest and selling out the right to most of the profits before market saturation becomes clearly visible to everyone. The real profits of innovation disappear as the saturation phase approaches. At best, what profit remains is seldom more than enough to give adequate compensation to professional management and to leave enough dividends to satisfy less venturesome investors. The turbulent stage of declining growth, and probably even the early part of this, is a good time to "go public," if the innovator is still the owner.

Once the market reaches the stability of saturation, even non innovating management needs to ponder what part of value it can profitably add to the offering. The organization with well-developed production skills but an inferior brand market position may decide to emphasize contract production for much of the industry, as Gibson has done in the home refrigerator industry. On the other hand, the marketer with a strong niche may find it advisable to let others like Gibson handle the actual physical production and to devote its talents and resources to maintaining its market niche.

Indeed, the decision to drop out may be wise at times even for one of the better-entrenched firms, both in marketing and producing. When early radio sets, just in their growth phase, switched from battery-powered to alternating current, a leading battery producer who had earned a substantial share of the radio set market dropped out because alternating current sets did not fit in with the rest of its business.

Thus the only generalization which can be made about market withdrawal timing is that the move should be done sometime before market decline eliminates the possibility of further profit of a level acceptable to the given seller. Timing decisions of every sort are obviously especially acute in the case of fad cycles.

THE SPECIAL PROBLEMS OF FAD MANAGEMENT

The most important problem of fad management is to recognize that the appeal is that of a fad before any market or production plans are jelled. It is too easy for those giving birth to any offering to believe that their expected offspring has substantial substance beyond that of mere novelty. But such a delusion is not wise unless the buyer is likely to so perceive it. True, the correct introductory phase management of a potential fad bears many similarities to the proper introduction of more substantial offerings destined to enter the growth phase immediately, skipping any considerable period of market development. For both, distribution must be as intensive and as extensive as possible from the very first, with every potential outlet blanketed. Inventory shortages must be avoided like the plague because the obviously heavy sales volume makes all possible dealers avid for a supply, ready to order from any possible source. Promotion, however, should be limited for the fad to that necessary to give the initial lift-off and to get in solid with dealers. Once the growth is well under way, all significant investment in advertising should be dropped, for the short life cycle will not permit recovery of any more than necessary to achieve the lift-off. Whatever product variations are needed to cover all segments should be introduced at or soon after the initial sale.

Similarly, production plans should envision the very minimum of investment, undertaken on the assumption of an almost immediate payoff. If possible, all production should be contracted out. If not, any tooling should be of the least expensive, most temporary kind.

Timely intelligence on sales trends at the point of final purchase is imperative. The moment retail sales growth starts to slacken, production should be phased out and inventories progressively lightened. The aim, difficult to attain, should normally be to have the channels of trade empty just as the demand reaches its peak and dies.

One minor qualifier must be noted with respect to this general plan for fad management. That exception refers to fads destined for a small residual market, and for one or two strong sellers in that residual market who are in a position to exploit the residual demand at minimum cost--for instance, in the case of an adult game fad, some wide-line seller of games and recreational equipment who can distribute the item as a minor addition to his line.

Fad management is something no seller can ignore. Fads, like fashions, permeate every kind of market, not just that for consumer gadgets. The desire for the novel idea or item which exacts no learning price burns just as bright in the breast of the engineer and business executive behind his desk as it does when he is citizen B at home. Fads are just as obvious in politics and private life, as much a part of the investment scene as of consumption. To observe the thousands of dollars which can be involved in a single fad purchase, one need only observe closely the rise to glamor and swift fall from grace of some of the stock groups on any of the listed securities exchanges.

The rules for fad management are thus easy to state but require sharp intelligence analysis and almost a sixth sense to follow properly:

1. Produce with flexible manufacturing facilities which carry no substantial investment commitment to the item, preferably contract manufacture. Be ready for immediate crash volume production as soon as the acceptance of the fad, as such, is confirmed.

2. Introduce with a bang--get substantial stocks in the hands of sellers as widely and as fast as humanly possible.

3. Keep dealer stocks loaded to the hilt so long as actual sales to final buyers are rising at an increasing rate. Expedite all shipments--permit no stockouts at the sales counter.

4. Watch final sales closely. At the first sign of a slowdown, start phasing out production, hoping to stop completely at about the midpoint of the turbulence phase to give dealers time to unload stocks.

5. If not the original producer, be close on his heels and even more aggressive in distribution, taking advantage of every stockout he permits to take over his outlets. If the opening rush of sales is missed, stay out, and look for some other profit opportunity.

The real problems are to recognize when the appeal of an offering is that of pure novelty--when what is offered is destined to be a fad--and then to sense the slackening of demand as soon as it occurs. Like all other elements of product and price management, success with fad management means careful, logical and psychological analysis of product attributes and market reaction, and a feeling for the way customers will perceive things, not just data alone.

An important part of product management is pricing policy. Indeed, since product is simply a set of values from the standpoint of the customer, pricing policy is part of product policy and most strategic pricing decisions are really product decisions, not simply a question of price tags. Thus a careful consideration of various aspects of pricing strategy and tactics must parallel all product moves in every phase of the cycle.

PRICE MANAGEMENT ACROSS THE PRODUCT LIFE CYCLE

Cycle Stage	Pricing Policy Strategy and Tactics
MARKET DEVELOPMENT	To impose the minimum of value perception learning and to match the value reference perception of the most receptive market segments. High trade discounts, and sampling devices advisable.
RAPID GROWTH	Price lines to cover every taste, from low-end to premium models. Customary trade discounts. Agressive promotional pricing with price declines paralleling the drops in costs, induced by accumulated experience. Sampling price devices intensified.
COMPETITIVE TURBULENCE	Increased attention to market-broadening and promotional pricing opportunities.
MATURITY	Defensive pricing to preserve product category franchise. Search for incremental pricing opportunities, including private label contracts, to boost volume and gain an accumulated experience advantage.
DECLINE	Maintenance of profit level pricing with a complete disregard of any effect on market share.

The firm has more leeway in its pricing during the introduction of a high-learning product than it will ever have again, either in that product or with any other kind of product. It is also true, however, that the choice of that price level can be quite critical in positioning a product and so must be done very carefully. The initial competitive aspect of that price is not a major factor. There will be few or no ready buyers at any price and a low price per se will have no discernible effect on demand.

Really new offerings are not normally price elastic, since few are willing to risk purchase at any price until they understand the benefits and receive assurance of their value from early adopters. This does not mean, however, that price planning is unimportant. The initial price should match as well as possible the core market adopter's probable perception of the value of the promised satisfactions. In addition, the phenomenon of imputing value from price will tend to position the product in relation to some specific use system, and where the possible use systems are ambiguous in the beginning, the most valuable one should be the target. Moreover, the initial offering price becomes the value reference point for much of the rest of the life cycle. Setting it too low may not only position the product in the wrong use system, as the makers of plastic dinnerware did, but will certainly limit the room for price maneuver later.

Whatever is done with pricing, it should obviously require as little learning of value perception as possible. It has been noted that the first popular tractors cost just as much as a really good team of horses, and in fact, the first automobiles cost no more than a team of horses and a carriage. This means of course, the price decision must be made long before the point of introduction, since the product must be engineered to sell at this price, but not necessarily at an initially profitable level. Not only will high promotional costs make it impossible to gain any real profit on the sale, but even more important, the price should be one that takes account of the cost reduction which the experience curve will bring some time well after the first items come off the assembly line. Price lines will not be numerous and, in fact, will normally not be more than a one solitary level price to begin with, since the problem initially will be to develop category demand and not demand for individual models. On the other hand, the pricing structure will have to allow for very high discounts for distributors in order to bring forth the heavy selling effort needed to put across any revolutionary new product.

One of the most important aspects of the initial pricing decision is to recognize that the price should not be retained at this level during succeeding phases of the product life cycle. It is extremely important that the prices being charged during the rapid

FIGURE 10-1. The Ideal and the Usual Relationships between
              the Experience Curve, Costs, and Prices during
              the Growth Phase of the Product Life Cycle

A. The Ideal Relationship: Prices decrease in parallel with the

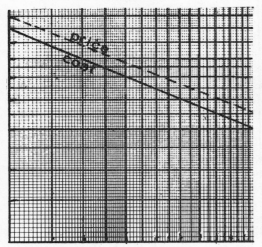

drops in cost caused by
accumulated production
and sales experience.
Unit profits are thus kept
below the level which
might tempt entry of an
excessive number of new
competitors.

B. The More Usual Strategy: Price decreases are permitted to lag

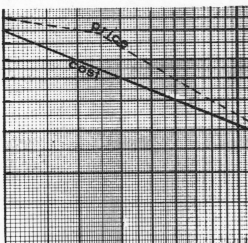

the experience-induced
decreases in cost, thus
providing an extremely
attractive unit profit
and bringing in an excessive
number of new market entrants.
During the ensuing shakout of
the competitive turbulence
phase, prices break sharply,
often below the level at
which they would have settled
under the ideal course depicted
in A.   No firm gains the
sales volume the introducer
might have attained under A.

growth phase of a product life cycle, whether that be the introductory or the second stage of the cycle for that particular product, should be constantly adjusted to take advantage of the declining costs that come with accumulated experience in production and sale. The most important aspect of pricing during the rapid growth stage of a cycle is to keep the margins down to a level that do not bring in an excessive number of new competitors. Unfortunately, the common tendency is to cut prices less than the experience-induced cost decreases per unit, encouraging the entrance of an excessive number of competitors and capacity. The result is a later sharp break in prices when the shake-out comes, and a much lower share of market, resulting in a cost-price relationship over time as shown in Figure 10-1B. Ideally, the policy and results should be as in Figure 10-1A. Under such a price plan, the amount of competition entering will not be zero, but it should be limited to the small number needed to fulfill all market needs.

As already noted, price lines should be broadened during the growth stage to cover as many major segments of the market as possible. Dealer margins should normally be cut at this stage since it is no longer necessary to gain dealer support in order to sell the product.

The introductory price structure tends almost inevitably to not only set the ceiling for the fair price reference points for the rest of the product life cycle, but even to position the offering in a particular use-system. Prices generally obey the law of gravity--climbing up is done with difficulty, falling down is easy, once value is established both for the end price and for the discount structure.

The right price structure and the amount of elbow room for price maneuver depend on the character of the introduction and the point of the cycle at which introduced. The new-to-me-only product, introduced well along in the growth phase or later, must fit into existing price expectations. The only real choice--and it is an important one--is the price niche to aim for--which point between the low end and the premium level. This should always be the one best fitting those market segments least well served so far, the niche which will create its own set of best-fitted segments. The tendency of many later comers is to assume that this is the extreme of the low end--for a product that is made "dirtier and cheaper." Such is not necessarily the case. There are even times when the most vulnerable niche is the ultra-premium level, engineered to appeal to an especially discriminating segment not currently satisfied with the available use values. Thus, while we tend to think of the American automobile industry as made up of four manufacturers, all decades old, a number of new ones came into being in the 1960's and are apparently prospering in the production of specialties such as very expensive copies of classic cars ($75,000 in the case of the

deluxe version of the Stutz Blackhawk). They include an established
truck manufacturer who found a special design niche in the multi-
purpose recreation vehicle market (International Harvester's Scout).

For the relatively low-learning offering with noticeable added
satisfactions, it would seem wisest to aim designs for the premium
use-system (if there be more than one) and at the top of the current
price brackets for that system. The major mistake of the first plastic dinnerware introducers was to position their product, through design and "popular" price, as suitable for the everyday "no-loss-if-
it-breaks" cheap crockery use-system. The introducers of stainless steel tableware were wiser. By careful use of quality design
and original patterns, and by corresponding price bracketing, they
were able to sell a top-grade offering which was seen as the equivalent of the best sterling flatware without the avoidance characteristic of the need for constant polishing. Lower-end versions, with
designs adapted to steel, not silver, were introduced to compete
with cheaper silver-plated ware later, only after the value of the
premium designs were established in prospects' minds as fair price
reference points.

Note that both design and price must be perceived as in har-
mony and be truly perceivable by buyers as paralleled by values not
hitherto available. Mere pricing alone does not position an offering
as of premium quality unless the comparable benefit is there (and
unless a premium distribution channel is used also).

The introduction of the Polaroid camera exemplifies a happy
choice of introductory pricing tactics. Design-targeted to appeal
to the non-professional interested mainly in a single print, the camera was released at the upper edge of the popular camera market
(about $80), with generous retail margins to furnish an incentive
for stocking, and only at special camera outlets and department
stores, where buyers would expect a quality offering. Once well
established in acceptance, it was followed by low-end models to
broaden the market and by precision models even for scientific
work, at higher prices. The design itself was an obvious low-learning design: essentially a quality box camera with the noticeable advantage of a near-instant picture.

The design of any high-learning product should clearly be such
as to minimize the learning cost, but it should also be engineered
to a price and quality mix matching the values being sought by the
most actively searching core market segment which is likeliest to
be the earliest adopters. Almost by definition, this generally means
a high quality product. The learning price minimization will probably dictate, for instance, that the first farm tractor replace a
good team, but not 20 teams. Within this limitation, however, the
design quality should be high, and the price that of a really good
team, both to shape a quality image for the offering and to permit

payment of the generous trade discounts needed to buy a vigorous selling and promotional effort on the part of distributors. If the marketing development effort succeeds, margins can be lowered when concentrated selling effort is no longer needed and low-end models introduced when the pioneer effort has established a fair-price norm. Until then, squeezing down the introductory price is meaningless and robs the innovation of the funds needed for market development. Until adequately promoted, the customer is unlikely to perceive the real value there for him and may judge that value by the price, not the reverse.

If the introduction be a complex of product and supplies (like razors and blades, punch cards and tabulating machinery, cameras and films), the introductory price should be as close as convenient to the total price of previous sources of similar satisfaction bundles previously available, and if the introducer can be reasonably sure of the dominant position in the supply market, the supplies should carry the bulk of the profit. There is far more profit and a much more stable flow of sales in the supply of razor blades than in the sale of razor blade holders, in selling film than in selling cameras, in the vending of punch cards than in the making of machines to process them.

Joel Dean has popularized two pricing concepts that have, unfortunately, been much more widely copied than understood in the meaning he gave them: penetration pricing and skimming prices. As Dean's own formulation of these concepts makes clear, he never viewed these as a matter of free choice, but as correct pricing strategies in quite different circumstances (Dean, 1969). A skimming price--a premium-level quotation intended to get the price willingly paid only by those market segments perceiving the highest value in the new offering--is, as he presented it, the appropriate strategy for the highly differentiated revolutionary product, for the introduction referred to here as a high-learning product for which emulative competition is not an immediate prospect. Penetration pricing--prices set low enough to attract a substantial portion of the fringe market segments--is seen by Dean as the appropriate quotation when the introduction is readily accepted and competition likely to crowd in at the first opportunity to undercut the introducer (a situation characteristic of markets for any low-learning introduction and during the growth phase of any product cycle).

Above all, it should be remembered that the introduction of low-end goods and the quoting of cut prices and thin margins have no significance to buyers until value is positioned. Such tactics can be effective only after experience and promotion have established the value of the main quality product in the expectations of prospects, and they appeal to fringe market segments only, not to core users. Their place is at the beginning of the competitive tur-

234

bulence phase of the last half of the growth period, not during the introduction.

The period when the growth rate begins to slow down and head toward the phase of competitive turbulence is a good time to use market-broadening pricing tactics. The aluminum industry after World War II is a good example of the ways in which an industry can consciously pyramid its own life cycle by successful attempts to add new markets as the older ones become saturated. Promotional pricing was used to get into volume sale and production of aluminum house siding, lowering the price to the level justified by continuous runs before the volume justified such runs. When the steel industry left itself vulnerable by pursuing higher profit margins, aluminum moved into the can market, and when copper prices rose, aluminum captured a substantial share of the wire and cable market.

Life cycle pyramiding is the most spectacular form of market broadening, but not always possible and not the only form. Other market broadening tactics of a pricing nature are very useful. For relatively durable goods, one very common and serviceable price tactic is that of leasing. Sometimes this device is even necessary to gain initial product trial at the time of introduction. At any time, leasing enables prospects to try and to experience the benefits of the offering before they see adequate value in its purchase and helps gain the support of those whose need does not justify purchase of its entire lifetime benefit flow. The proud father may wish a tuxedo to wear for his daughter's wedding but never wear one again. The visitor from out of town may wish for the flexibility of personal transportation granted by a private automobile but not need it for more than three days. The apartment market is obviously one of the oldest and still most outstanding example of the leasing principle of market-broadening sale, but the number of things being leased increases every day. Another especially useful pricing device for high-value items is the installment payment, and a mere lengthening of the terms can give a spurt to the market.

Incremental pricing is often used to fill in slack periods or to improve the production rate. The aim is to sell to segments whose valuation of the offering is less than the current going price. The tactic works best when buyers are from a clearly separate segment and the incrementally priced offering can be so modified that it has minimum attractiveness for the segment being sold at a higher price. The Florida resort thus charges a much lower rate for summer visitors than it does guests during the regular season, attracting people who will not pay for a winter suntan. The seller of a nationally recognized brand of canned peaches may preserve some of the crop under the private label of a major food chain, selling the private brand pack at a lower price than he will sell his own brand to the same buyer. This private brand pack may be similar in quality to his regular brand, or may be slightly lower in quality to sell at a noticeably lower price. The mail order house issues a special in-between-season catalog with very attractive special prices to stabilize its peaks and valleys of orders. In most such cases, the price offered is attractively lower than one which might cover all costs and proportionate overhead, is profitable if it does no more than cover variable costs and makes some contribution to overhead and profit. As the commuter rail lines out of Chicago have shown, such incremental pricing can promote volume business not otherwise available and contribute substantially to overall profit.

Once the product life cycle reaches the plateau of maturity, price policy should turn completely defensive. Every attempt should be made to keep costs down and prices in close concurrence with these costs, in order to leave as little vulnerability as possible to the introduction of new kinds of product substitutes for those now in the market.

No attention whatsoever should be paid to market share once decline sets in. The only rational objective for this period is to make what little money can still be made from the product before it is interred in its final resting place.

Product policy and a well structured pricing strategy accompanying it will not alone guarantee its success on the market. The values being offered the customers must be communicated to them in such a way that they see the price as reasonable for these values.

APPROPRIATE COMMUNICATIONS MANAGEMENT DURING THE
VARIOUS STAGES OF THE PRODUCT LIFE CYCLE

The problem of communications during the introductory phase of a high-learning product is to educate potential buyers to the values being offered them and the benefits they can expect to receive. Only a very small portion of the necessary communications will develop immediate sales, because the innovator and early adopter segments of the market are relatively small in number.

Customers will be few, reluctant, and expensive to sell during this introductory market development period. They must be sought out by personal sales, to whatever degree this is possible, and certainly persuaded with some degree of personal communication. If the size of the individual purchase is too small to justify a personal sales call, as, for example, in the case of the first home permanent kits ($1.75), then some other personal device should be sought, backed up with overwhelming mass communications. In the case of the first Toni home permanents, Toni mounted a true saturation radio and newspaper campaign, one market at a time, and persuaded the girl behind the cosmetic counter to try one herself, so that she

THE VARYING COMMUNICATIONS MIX OVER THE PRODUCT LIFE CYCLE		
Stage of Cycle	Communication Objectives	Most Useful Communication Emphasis Priority
MARKET DEVELOPMENT	a) Create awareness and understanding of offering benefits b) Secure trial by early adopters	{ Publicity { Personal Sales Mass communication
RAPID GROWTH	Create and strengthen brand preference among trade and final users--Stimulate general trial.	Mass media Personal sales Sales promotions including sampling Publicity
COMPETITIVE TURBULENCE	Maintain consumer franchise and strengthen dealer ties	Mass media Dealer promotions Personal dealer selling Sales promotions Publicity
MATURITY	Maintain consumer and trade loyalty, with strong emphasis on dealers and distributors. Promotion of greater use frequency. Keep a lookout for private-brand sales opportunities.	Mass media Dealer-oriented promotions
DECLINE	Phase out entirely, maintaining no more than is necessary to just sustain that distribution which yields an immediate profit.	Cut down all media to the bone--use no sales promotions of any kind.

would become a positive saleswoman.

Although actual sales will result only from some kind of personal contact during any market development phase, publicity and a fanfare of initial advertising are essential elements in the introductory communications mix. Their purpose is to generate a needed wide awareness and interest in the benefits of the new offering, to alert those not yet ready to buy to the possibilities in the new products being tried out by their early adopter acquaintances. Publicity is especially desirable during this phase because it does reach the innovators and early adopters and may even cause them to search, and also because the independence of the source of the message--the publication which publishes it as news--adds credence to the story. And publicity is readily available, if wisely sought, because the truly new product is a news product.

The primary aim of all kinds of communication during the market development period is to create a general awareness of the product category and its benefits and to stimulate trial by early adopters. In terms of the ratio of communications expenditures to dollar sales it will be a deficit operation and basically an investment process--developing an understanding which could lead to future sales.

Once the market development period is ended (or with products that are starting out with no need for any major market development), the general objective of the communications must be to create brand preference among both the trade and the final users. Publicity will be less available and of less value during this stage and personal selling will also begin to be of somewhat less value, but dealer contract and aid will be important. The heavier emphasis will be on mass media, but sales promotions and sampling can be extremely useful. As Figure 10-2A indicates, dollars invested in advertising and sales promotion at this stage should be returned through increased sales and a solid head start in market share.

Too much reliance on personal sales effort at this stage means too little market coverage and allows competitors who choose to dominate the mass communications to get to most of the receptive buyers first and take over the "first" place with large segments of the population, effectively preempting attention. The competitive aspects of this period call for the most aggressively promotional product management possible, administered by those with the most market-oriented imagination available. Only by finishing the growth period well in front of competition, with a greater accumulation of experience, can a seller be assured of the chance for the optimum market and profit position through the remainder of the product life cycle or even of a high probability of survival in the competitive shakeout of the period of turbulence which follows.

Surviving the competitive turbulence phase requires estab-

238

FIGURE 10-2. Results to Be Expected From a Temporary Burst of
Promotional Effort at Various Stages in the Product
Life Cycle

A. During Rapid Growth Period

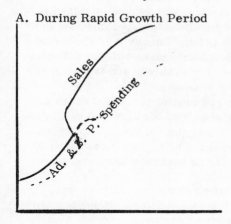

During the period of rapid
growth, an extra burst of promotional spending can be an
investment in future market
share, by attracting and convert-
ing buyers just beginning to sample the product.

B. During Maturity

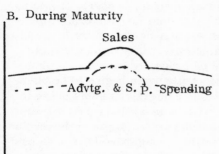

In the saturated mature market,
a heavy promotional compaign may
attract some temporary added
sales, but the gain is seldom
lasting, as most buyers have already made a choice of the brand
they prefer, if any.

C. During the Decline

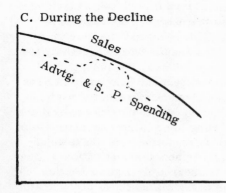

Any apparent gain from added
promotional effort during the
decline phase is more likely due to
coincidence than it is to be an effect.
Most buyers have already lost interest in the product and will tune out
any promotional messages.

239

lishing strong preference at both dealer and consumer levels. With buyers now less avid and more critical, the slow moving brands begin to disappear from the shelves, and dealer ties start to become the major factor in competitive strength.

Whatever brand preference building can be accomplished is already completed and market niche maintenance becomes the main task promotion. The purpose is to remind the buyer of the value of those product attributes which caused him to choose the brand originally but are now coming to be taken for granted, and to find ever fresh ways of doing this, to capture attention.

A parallel problem is to keep reminding the distributors of the value of the seller as a source of a demanded product and to use various promotional means to tie him to the seller. By this time the distributor is as much a target of the promotion as is the final consumer, and with each changing day he becomes more and more important.

Once the product begins to approach the saturation stage, promotion must defend the market share by reminding old buyers of the values they are getting and attracting market newcomers. This is also a period to search for use-systems which, properly promoted, can increase use frequency among established customers. Normally, promotional budgets will be lower during the saturation phase than during the growth phases of a product, but still substantial.

Promotional spending should be gradually phased out completely once the decline in the product life cycle begins to be obvious. Only enough promotion should be used during this phase to just sustain the distribution which will do an adequate job of selling at a profitable volume. All other funds devoted to promotion at this stage will be largely wasted money which could have been used profitably in some other form. One manufacturer of consumer products with a product clearly in this stage found that none of his promotional efforts gained any response whatsoever in terms of a sales difference in his curve. A check on experience with other lines in a similar situation revealed that when no variation in promotion was introduced, an accidental lift occurred one time in five. When extra effort was put forward, the results were essentially the same--a lift one time in four.

Such a lack of response is to be expected. The customer has all the information he wants or needs about this product already, and there is nothing left to communicate. Furthermore, a declining period is one in which there is declining interest and the principle of selective attention would indicate that promotion would have an almost insuperable problem in gaining any necessary attention.

As the need to tie dealers to the source through promotion indicates, the distribution policy is an essential aspect of product life cycle management, and it too must change with phases in the cycle.

DISTRIBUTION POLICY AND THE PRODUCT LIFE CYCLE

As some of the remarks above indicate, distribution policy is just as sensitive to the phases of the product life cycle as any other element of the mix.

Stage of Cycle	Distribution Policy
MARKET DEVELOPMENT	Exclusive or selective, with distributor margins high enough to justify heavy promotional expenses.
RAPID GROWTH	Intensive and extensive, with margins adequate to make product interesting to dealer, but no more than this. Heavy emphasis on rapid resupply of distributor stocks, with heavy inventories at all levels.
COMPETITIVE TURBULENCE	Intensive and extensive, and a strong emphasis on keeping dealer well supplied, but with minimum inventory cost to him.
MATURITY	Intensive and extensive, and a strong emphasis on keeping dealer well supplied, but with minimum inventory cost to him.
DECLINE	Phase out outlets as they become marginal.

Choice of the correct distribution policy in the introductory phase can be critical. High-learning products requiring a market development period must be introduced through a highly selective or exclusive distributor system. Since the initial customers will be few, sales volume will be low, and those selling and distributing the offering will have to expend substantial personal effort for every sale. Such sales representatives must be encouraged in this effort by some form of sales protection, by guaranteeing distributors that whatever volume is developed will be concentrated in as few outlets as feasible without leaving major portions of the potential uncovered.

This usually signifies well-spaced or exclusive or selective distributors who are therefore assured that all their promotional efforts will return home to them in the form of sales prospects. And obviously, also, their efforts must be encouraged by rather large distributive discounts during this period.

It is sometimes true, of course, that a firm which has a long line can get extensive distribution despite the fact that sales volume is low for any revolutionary product. This is unwise even when it can be obtained. Dealers who then discover that the product moves very slowly will often sell against the product rather than sell it under such circumstances. There can be little question that RCA's attempt to make color television available through all its dealers during the first few years of introduction cost them a great deal of sales efforts from the kind of dealers who might have sold it for them. An unpublished shopping study of their dealers showed that customers who came into the store asking for color television were usually switched to the black and white section by most of the dealers. They did not wish to sell and service the color television at the volume at which it was moving.

On the other hand, as soon as demand starts to grow and buyers begin to seek out the product, it is extremely important that the selective policy be modified and phased over rapidly to an intensive system of distribution. Since dealers no longer have to sell the product that customers are actively seeking, a lot of dealers who do not have it will wish to stock it. To use selective or exclusive dealing during such a period will merely stimulate dealers who were denied the product to search for alternative sources of supply and to encourage competitors to come into the market in order to satisfy their appetite for the obvious sales volume. The logistics of physical distribution during this growth period must be heavily biased toward the best of customer service, with any mistakes on the side of over heavy inventories at all levels. The long run effects of any stock-outs can be astronomically and permanently expensive because out-of-stock dealers will start actively soliciting other potential producers to enter competition, approaching a dozen possible sources with promises to buy the same quantities, thus multiplying the apparent demand many fold. The introducer of the Hibachi barbecue grill in the United States made the mistake of permitting his contract manufacturer to run behind in orders and delay deliveries. Stock-short dealers soon developed many other sources, flooding the market and killing any chance for the innovative profit he should have been assured of.

At this stage of the game, of course, dealer discounts can be safely lowered because they no longer are putting out or need to put out the sales effort required for stocking the product because of the demand from customers.

As the growth proceeds and the growth rate begins to level off, intensified attention should be paid to getting and maintaining as intensive and extensive distribution as possible. Continued concern with dealer service is a must. The logistics should now be

weighted toward keeping dealer inventory cost as low as possible.
From this point on, and throughout the saturated portion of the
cycle, distribution becomes an important element in brand differentiation because as the product life cycle proceeds customers begin to see less and less difference between makes. In fact, the
degree of real differentiation between brands, as such, is often
quite low.

The product that is most easily obtained from the most dealers
will get the most attention from the customers under these circumstances. A great deal of promotion during the period of competitive
turbulence, and increasingly during the period of market saturation,
must be aimed at keeping the dealer happy and gaining his aid in
promotion.

There are, of course, circumstances in which the manufacturer
must maintain some form of selective distribution throughout his
own product life cycle. Such is the case, for example, of the specialty manufacturer or the small volume brand which must concentrate its sales volume in a few outlets in order to make it interesting
to that outlet to continue to handle and to work with the manufacturer. This is the policy, for example, of Magnovox in the electronics
field. The dealer becomes not only a selected outlet but handles
solely the one brand, with his margins sweetened by making him a
direct distributor of the product. Such is also true, of course, of
any highly specialized product serving an extremely limited market.

But these are exceptions which are few and far between.
Wherever customer service must be furnished by the dealer and
where it is necessary for some kind of mechanical service to be
widely available, any policy other than the most extensive distribution possible can be fatal, once the product reaches the rapid growth
stage.

For all products distribution policy must be keyed in with all
other elements of the marketing mix, with careful changes at each
movement of the cycle.

BRAND LIFE CYCLE MANAGEMENT

The label, "product life cycles,"has been variously used to
cover both-product category life cycles, and competitive brand life
cycles, no matter where introduced in the basic category life cycle.
As noted earlier, this is not unjustified, since any successful introduction must be differentiated, and thus is always to some degree
a new product--a new category of its own.

There are both similarities and differences between the management of a new beer label, a new frozen pie, or a new hair sham-

poo, and other such food, beverage, and health and beauty aids introductions into obviously mature markets, and the introduction of a new product category such as recreational vehicles, the original instant coffees, and a new kind of food, such as textured vegetable protein.

There are borderline cases, of course, and the distinction between a mere brand difference and a new category of product is not always obvious. The Volkswagen automobile might well have been viewed as merely another automobile brand when introduced commercially to the United States market in 1949. But it was more than that. It was a new category because it did not fit readily into the United States customer's perceptions of what an automobile should be, and had use-system attributes such as size, mechanical attributes, handling, styling--with which the American buyer was not familiar. It was therefore the beginning of a new competitive category which started a new growth curve for a different kind of product, one still growing and penetrating new segments (such as the semi-luxury market) as this is written in the 1970's.

The test is thus: does it fit readily into currently established use-systems, systems not lacking any missing links, with no significant learning required? If so, it will be a brand cycle. ("Our new sugar substitute tastes like sugar, looks like sugar, mixes like sugar, and measures like sugar, but has only 1-1/2 calories per teaspoon.") If not, we are dealing with a new category of offering, however similar it may superficially appear to be to some established category.

Brand cycles are similar to product life cycles in that they must start from scratch and build up sales in growth curve fashion. It is likewise true that the strong brand carves out a strong niche-- a substantial market share--early or not at all, and that its growth attracts emulators quickly. Like any other new offering, the differential value perceivable by buyers must be substantial to gain attention.

But brand cycles normally differ from category cycles in at least three respects. Brand cycles do not pass through any significant initial market development period, objective differentiation is so insignificant that no advantage can be gained through accumulated experience by the seller, and so his profit cycle is brief. And since differentiation is usually achieved mainly by some superficial means such as packaging, fragrance, color, or simply advertising approach, the mature phase tends to be a decline also, but can be "recycled," as shown by Nielsen studies, through "new, improved" product changes ("our towels are now even more absorbent"), new packaging, or even fresh advertising themes. In effect, such "recycling" tends to make a somewhat new introduction of it, since it confers added perceivable differentials. But it seldom brings the

244

product back to the initial peak.

Declining category cycles, on the other hand, are usually immune to such recycling, since the use-system itself is being superseded by a different and more attractive use-system of a competing category, and thus must buck habit change. (Category cycles, of course, are sometimes pyramided, but this is a more fundamental process and derives from the development of new use-systems or the penetration of new markets. Such pyramiding requires more than a mere advertising change or packaging difference.)

None of this is to deny the importance of brand cycles. In the food and drug field from which Nielsen draws its studies, less than one "new product" in one hundred is a category introduction. The rest are all some form of brand introduction, and many quite lucrative for the sellers during their usually (but far from always) brief market reign.

Furthermore the brand cycle phenomenon does not differ so radically from the category cycle that the rules of the latter can be disregarded. Indeed, the correct policies for the growth, maturity and decline stages are largely the same as those for any category cycle. Even the phenomenon of "recycling" is possible only while the category cycle is still in a mature stage, before real decline sets in. Moreover, recycling is carried out by means that should be used by any seller in a mature market: fresh advertising approaches to stimulate flagging attention, packaging improvements, product improvements, and even distribution extensions. And for both category and product cycles, the rules of wise pricing strategies and successful tactics are the same.

Whichever class of life cycle is involved, wise management calls for a complex blend of product, pricing promotion and distribution at each stage. This chapter has looked at each of these separately. The best summary would seem to be to bring together the highlights all together in both dimensions--market stage, and aspect of management.

SUMMARY

THE COMPLETE PRODUCT LIFE CYCLE, MARKETING MIX
MATRIX

THE APPROPRIATE STRATEGY AND MARKETING MIX AT EACH STAGE OF THE PRODUCT LIFE CYCLE

	MARKET DEVELOPMENT	RAPID GROWTH	COMPETITIVE TURBULENCE	SATURATION	DECLINE
STRATEGY OBJECTIVE	Minimize learning requirements, locate and remedy offering defects quickly, develop widespread awareness of benefits, and gain trial	To establish a strong brand market and distribution niche as quickly as possible	To maintain and strengthen the market niche achieved through dealer and consumer loyalty	To defend brand position against competing brands and the product category against other potential products, through constant attention to product improvement opportunities and fresh promotional and distribution approaches	To milk the offering dry of all possible profit, by eliminating any expense or market effort not yielding a provable direct and immediate profit
OUTLOOK FOR COMPETITION	None of any importance likely	Early entrance of many agressive emulators	Price and distribution squeezes on the industry, shaking out the weaker entrants	Competition stabilized, with few or no new entrants and market shares not subject to substantial change unless someone gets a new start with a substantial perceived product improvement	Similar competition declining and dropping out because of decrease in consumer interest
PRODUCT DESIGN POLICY	Limited number of models with design of both the physical product and of the total offering going to the utmost to minimize learning requirements. Design cost-and use-engineered to appeal to most receptive segment. Closest possible attention to quality control and to quick elimination of market-revealed defects in design	Modular design, if possible, to facilitate flexible addition of variants to appeal to every new segment and new use-system, as they appear	Intensified attention to product improvement, tightening up of line to eliminate unnecessary special-product changes. Introduction of flanker products.	A constant alert for market pyramiding opportunities either through bold cost and price-penetration or major product changes. Introduction of flanker products. Constant attention to product improvement and to cost-cutting opportunities. Re-examination of necessity for design-compromises	Constant pruning of line to eliminate any items not returning a direct profit
PRICING OBJECTIVE	To impose the minimum of value perception learning and to match the value reference perception of the most receptive market segments. High trade discounts, and sampling devices advisable	Price lines to cover every taste, from low-end to premium models. Customary trade discounts. Aggressive promotional pricing with price declines	Increased attention to market-broadening and promotional pricing opportunities	Defensive pricing to preserve product category franchise. Search for incremental pricing opportunities, including private label contracts, to boost volume and gain an	Maintenance of profit level pricing with a complete disregard of any effort on market share

247

(table continued from preceding page)

	paralleling the drops in costs, induced by accumulated experience Sampling price devices intensified		accumulated experience advantage	
PROMOTIONAL GUIDELINES Objective of Communications	a) Create awareness and understanding of offering benefits b) Secure trial by early adopters	Create and strengthen brand preference among trade and final users--Stimulate general trial	Maintain consumer franchise and strengthen dealer ties	Maintain consumer and trade loyalty, with strong emphasis on dealers and distributors. Promotion of greater use frequency. Keep a lookout for private-brand sales opportunities	Phase out entirely, maintaining no more than is necessary to just sustain that distribution which yields an immediate profit
Most valuable media mix	Publicity Personal Sales Mass communication	Mass media personal sales Sales promotions including sampling Publicity	Mass media Dealer promotions Personal dealer selling Sales promotions Publicity	Mass media Dealer-oriented promotions	Cut down all media to the bone--use no sales promotions of any kind
DISTRIBUTION POLICY	Exclusive or selective, with distributor margins high enough to justify heavy promotional expenses	Intensive and extensive, with margins adequate to make product interesting to dealer. Heavy emphasis on rapid resupply of distributor stocks, with heavy inventories at all levels	Intensive and extensive, with emphasis on keeping dealer well supplied, but with minimum inventory cost to him	Intensive and extensive, and a strong emphasis on keeping dealer well supplied, but with minimum inventory cost to him	Phase out outlets as they become marginal
INTELLIGENCE FOCUS	Identifying developing use systems and uncovering any product weaknesses	Detailed attention to brand position, to gaps in market and model coverage, and to opportunities for market segmentation	Close attention to product improvement needs, to market-broadening chances, and to possible fresh competition for market	Intensified attention to possible product improvement. Sharp lookout for potential new inter-product competition and for signs of product decline	Information helping to identify the point at which the product should be phased out

11

DYNAMIC MANAGEMENT OF THE AVOIDANCE SIDE OF THE OFFERING: PRICING STRATEGY AND TACTICS

Since price is simply the negative side of product value, product decisions inextricably involve pricing decisions. Indeed, most of the longer range strategic decisions usually thought of as pricing moves are product quality level, product-mix and market niche decisions. On the other hand, the pure price maneuver is the principal tool of competitive <u>tactics</u> at every stage of the product life cycle. As the complexities of price and value perception suggest, pricing is not the simplistic problem of matching an existing supply against a never knowable demand curve, as elementary textual discussions imply, but a variety of kinds of decisions of many dimensions. Those administrative choices we lump together under the common label of pricing decision run the gamut from very long range strategic decisions of whether or not to introduce a product, to the development of temporary tactical price reduction maneuvers to meet an ephemeral competitive crisis. At least nine divergent types of decisions and actions are indiscriminately bunched under this one label:

Decisions as to market entry based on estimated cost-plus and return on investment

Long run decisions as to market niche--the price/quality level decision

Product-mix and merchandise-mix decisions

Distributive discount structure decisions and other dealer-attracting devices

Decisions as to price quotation timing and methods

Tactical price-competitive maneuvers

Bid pricing

Public price regulative policies

Product life cycle related decisions and adjustments: product introductory pricing and price line changes as well as margin adjustments required by the progress of the life cycle.

249

This last point, that concerning life cycle related decisions, has already been discussed in previous chapters. The first three in the list above are basically product-related strategy decisions: cost plus, price/quality and product-mix choices. The distributive discount structure decision, even though a quotation by the seller, is really an offered buying price for distributive services required to complete the product bundle desired by the final buyer. Even tactical price competitive maneuvers are most efficient when they involve some degree of product modification. Only bid pricing is truly a decision on the offering price of a directly competitive offering (and even then, the offerings of different sellers may be perceived as differing).

Both business men and economists tend to be confused about the practicalities, actual purpose and place of cost-plus pricing in business decision. The process should really be labelled price-minus and the choice is made far in advance of production, on the basis of cost estimates that are far from precise. These are really market-entry tests as are also the related return-on-investment and break-even standards. Another extremely important long range pricing strategy decision is the concept usually, but quite incorrectly, presented as the choice between selling "at the market, above the market, or below the market." The actual choice involved concerns the long range market niche which the organization will attempt to occupy--that of a producer of low-end goods, of premium level offerings, or something in between. Such choices unavoidably involve the total design of the offering, the value side of the transaction coin as much as its price quotation side. The price which is obtained always corresponds to the total value customers are willing to sacrifice for the offering as they perceive it--sales are always at the market with respect to the perceived value of the total bundle offered and the circumstances of its offering.

Generally speaking, the most important price strategy decision made by most sellers is the merchandise mix and its related price mix in a multi-product offering. Such decisions are basic, setting the pattern for all later individual pricing quotations. They implicitly or explicitly choose the market segment the seller will be serving and how well he will serve it--where he will fit into the competitive structure. The profit target of such a price-mix decision is a joint profit target, for as many as thousands of items sold at widely different gross margins for profit.

All sellers except those in direct contact with the final buyers must normally concern themselves with a series of prices at the various points in the distribution channel. Along with the final price target the manufacturer must decide on the allocation of the proceeds between himself and those between him and final buyers. The starting point decision must always be a final buyer quotation target and the price-line niche which is thought to correspond to that buyer's perception of value offered. From this must be subtracted various discounts to be available to distribution intermediaries--offering prices intended to pay for services added to the offering value--time and place utilities, services of sales communications, of financing and of product-completing physical operations, as well as feedback intelligence needed for production planning.

MARKET ENTRY PRICE-COST AND RETURN-ON-INVESTMENT STANDARDS

One of the most common arguments between economists and businessmen is over the concept of cost-plus pricing. The business man tends to insist that he must and does price at cost plus some percentage of margin; the economist tends to insist that this does not make market sense. Paradoxically, both are completely correct because they are talking about completely different points in decision time, about a different cost, in consequence, and both are completely wrong as to the nature of the actual decision. And both the economist and the business man are mislabelling the decision. In terms of the way the decision is arrived at, it is a price-minus calculation, not really a cost-plus one (Smyth, 1967). What the businessman does, consciously or unconsciously, is to estimate first the price at which he thinks the offering will sell on the market, to the segment to which he expects to offer it, then subtracts from that his estimated prospective cost at the volume he hopes to achieve, whether he is a merchant confronted by a prospective new item, a manufacturer considering an addition to his line, or a foundryman bidding on a casting. Price, not production, is the initial decision in the sequence, with design following to accord with the price. His decision is then whether to take on the item and enter the market, or refrain because the difference between his estimated returns and his estimated costs are not up to his current standard. If he does enter the market, then he never sells for more than the market price because he cannot, and seldom sells for less in terms of long run considerations. If a manufacturer, he generally starts with a target market price--with the price line of a dress which he can sell, or the price bracket of an automobile, tractor, washing machine, phonograph record, etc. He then designs an offering engineered to be perceived as worth this given price target with some kind of estimated cost which would, at an estimated probable sales volume, yield the desired profit margin. If a merchant, the seller first judges what the market price would be, subtracts his estimated acquisition cost, then decides whether the margin is what he considers adequate for that category of merchandise, as he has designed

251

his merchandise mix. The final decision is thus whether or not to enter the market, given estimated future selling prices and estimated future costs.

The parameters which go into both sets of estimates, he knows, are rough at best, and subject to change over time. The most critical component is the sales, or volume, estimate. This can only hope to be close by accident. Tull (1967) found that advanced sales forecasts ranged in error from 0% to 762%, with a mean error of 128%, for 63 introductions made by 16 firms, and these were probably more carefully made estimates than are usually developed.

The economist, by contrast, is hypothesizing an existing product, already designed and ready for market, and thinking in terms of a known historical cost. Even then, he is thinking of a more solid figure than, in other contexts, he knows cost to be. At this point of time, of course, all costs are irrelevant, since they can be recovered only by sale, and that sale must take place at no more than the market is willing to pay. The businessman, in other words, is talking about a decision in advance of production, made as much as years before the actual market offering. The economist is confusing this with a sales offering in being, at a time when very little room for decision is left. Even as a prospective production decision, cost is never really a firm estimate, and when properly estimated is seldom what the routine expenditure accounts indicate. True decision costs may include many values not on the books and exclude some that are. At times, the costs involved in the decision are for a specific level of production which is below that anticipated, and what is considered is only part of the true cost. As prospective costs at any rate, they are really not closely predictable at the time of decision.

Decision Costs

To the uninitiated, few items of business decision seem more solid than the concept of cost. In truth, even after the fact, cost is such a slippery relative type of quantity that there exists no way of determining its value until we know for what purpose we wish to measure cost. One source of variation arises from the complex structure of any actual cost. Actual unit expenditure cost, even measured historically, is normally a function of at least two and sometimes four parts:

> fixed costs, which are incurred without regard to the quantity produced and sold and which, at the time of decision, have sometimes already been committed (manufacturing plant, official overhead, etc.)
>
> variable costs, expenditures directly proportional to the quantity produced (raw materials, direct labor, etc.)

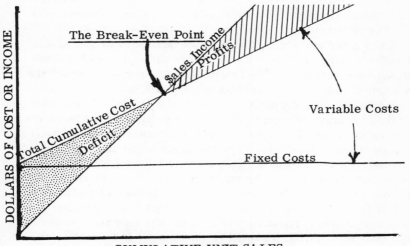

FIGURE 11-1. The Break-Even Concept

DOLLARS OF COST OR INCOME

The Break-Even Point

Sales Income

Profits

Total Cumulative Cost

Deficit

Variable Costs

Fixed Costs

CUMULATIVE UNIT SALES

The break-even point can be determined graphically, as shown above. The break-even concept has long proved a useful means of evaluating possible product and price decisions. The break-even point itself may be defined as that point in the cumulative sales volume at which the total income from sales just matches all costs of production and sales of that unit volume. It is generally a single point. Sales revenues tend to be directly proportional to unit sales volume whereas average unit costs of production and sales normally decrease with each unit sold. The latter occurs, without regard to the normal learning curve phenomenon, because production and sales costs contain two different kinds of costs: costs which are called variable because directly proportional to production and sale (raw materials, direct labor, packaging, manufacturing supplies, sales commissions, etc.) and other costs which are usually designated as fixed because unrelated to the actual size of the sales volume and relatively constant regardless of that volume (plant and equipment investment, administrative overhead, advertising expenditures committed in advance of sales, etc.)

253

> programmed or semi-variable costs, expenditures, such as
> advertising, which may be decided on in relation to pros-
> pective sales, but once committed cannot be wholly sal-
> vaged
> results of forecast miscues, such as unsold overruns or over-
> orders which must be salvaged or sold at a mark-down, or
> order shortages which must be made up at a disproportion-
> ate cost, or timing miscalculations causing excessive in-
> ventory holding costs

Since some costs are related to the quantities produced and sold and others are not, actual unit expenditure cost is clearly a function of the accuracy of the original sales forecast on which the production runs and even plant size were based.

Because the relationship of fixed cost to variable cost is so critical to the cost estimate, decision often hinges on a specific point in this fixed cost, variable cost relationship--the breakeven point (see Figure 11-1). The decision to enter the market may well hinge simply on the estimate that the break-even quantity has a high probability of being sold. Of course, no rational businessman enters the market with an offering which he believes will sell in break-even quantity, but no more. By definition this is the quantity at which there is zero estimated profit. But it is also the quantity at which, theoretically, no loss will be sustained. (As a matter of fact, of course, as usually calculated, the break-even point does involve a minor loss--the imputed or actual interest on the working capital tied up. But this is not really subject to close estimate, since the time element cannot be projected.) The value of the break-even estimate is that it furnishes a benchmark for the rock-bottom sales quantity which would justify market entry. This estimate can then be compared with known market information to decide on the degree of risk involved in the introduction. If the break-even quantity is low relative to expected sales volume, the risk is judged to be low, and vice versa. The rate of unit profit accruing after the break-even point is passed is also a point of attention, and the estimate of this rate can be relatively accurate, for it is simply the difference between unit receipts and variable costs.

Break-even analysis forms the principal basis for market entry decisions and pricing for most enterprises which must continually launch new offerings whose real potential is largely conjectural or intuitive in advance of introduction--products such as newly published books, recordings, etc. In such industries, the seller considers himself very successful if all of his entries break even or do slightly better, and he gets an occasional winner. The post break-even profits can be very handsome.

Estimated return-on-investment decisions are really a variant and extension of the price-minus approach, since they are simply a calculation of the expected return on any necessary added investment over a given period of time, given a specific market volume estimate. When this return is compared with the seller's standard, it too becomes a basis for decision on market entry. Since the sales forecast is just as critical a part of the ROI estimate, such decisions are also subject to a wide error margin.

Quite often, an estimated return on investment forms the basis for decision on market entry at multiple points in the product development and market development process. ROI may be one of the bases for acceptance or rejection of a product concept, then the remaining incremental investment estimated again at various stages such as completion of a prototype, completion of pilot runs, completion of semi-commercial runs, and market test, etc., as market estimates are progressively refined. It should be noted that the only relevant investment costs at each stage are those yet to be committed. Those irretrievably committed and beyond salvage cannot be recovered in any event--they are sunk costs. In any cost-related product and price decision, it is well to understand the concepts of sunk costs, opportunity costs, and of contribution to fixed and overhead costs.

Both in pricing and in product introduction decisions, the only costs which can form a valid basis for logical decision are those actual and imputed costs yet to be incurred. All non-salvageable costs are sunk costs--that is, they are gone no matter what the decision and thus should have no influence on the decision itself. The price decision cannot take such sunk costs directly into consideration. The price quoted must be in line with the value levels which major market segments can perceive in the offering. The latter may allow considerable latitude, depending on the relative sizes of the prospect segments viewing diverse prices as attractive, but are not related to incurred cost. The decision is then reduced to whether the seller views the estimated net returns from the various estimated volumes and proposed prices as adequate return on the incremental investment yet to be made. True, part of that incremental investment may include some of the past investment if this investment can be diverted to some other productive use. The value of the salvaged investment in such a case may then be less than original cost. It will be its opportunity cost--its value as an investment for the other purpose.

Incremental costs and incremental pricing should be important considerations in a stable saturated market. They may add volume and thus reduce costs or share overhead and permit penetrating markets which could not otherwise be reached and do not directly compete with the major segments served. One common form is the production of goods for "private labelling", or distributor-controlled brands.

255

Opportunity cost may also be greater than original cost. An opportunity cost is any net direct, indirect, or imputed cost or sacrifice which will be incurred as a result of a proposed action and which can be avoided if the action is not taken. Opportunity costs manifestly include any variable or direct costs of production and sale. Opportunity costs and opportunity losses also include the difference between returns and receipts which might have been obtained by taking some different alternative action or by using the committed resources in some alternative manner. The merchandise buyer who holds down inventory costs by buying very limited quantities must count as one cost of his inventory policy the lost profits on sales he missed because of stock shortages. The author who publishes his own book must count as part of his publishing cost any royalties he would have received if he had turned the manuscript over to some other publisher. The firm which uses for its expansion land bought at a more propitious time must count the current market value of the land as part of the expansion cost, not the original price paid. The firm has the alternative of selling the land to someone else.

Returns which might be labeled opportunity profits are covered by the concept of contribution to overhead. Any offering which more than covers its own variable costs and other opportunity costs is helping to increase profits, even though returns may not recover a proportionate share of fixed costs if the resources used were not brought into being or maintained primarily to produce the offering. Contribution to overhead is really the obverse side of sunk costs, but the concept has implications for any product line-offering and is basically the philosophy behind all merchandise-mix pricing which uses variable mark-up margins for different categories of offerings. Thus any major freight-carrying railroad must maintain essentially all of its capital and overhead facilities (tracks, yards, etc.) regardless of any passenger business. If the railroad can generate enough passenger revenue to cover passenger equipment costs and ordinary operating revenues, plus some additional receipts, its profits will go up by the amount of this extra. The seller with 100 items for sale will make money on a related 101st item if the added margin returns any more than its related acquisition and direct sales costs.

No estimate of short range average prospective unit costs can be very precise because prospective fixed and overhead costs are a major part of the estimated costs of producing a large portion of manufactured items. The lack of precision prediction would be especially marked in the instance of annual sales estimates for offerings with a highly cyclical demand such as machine tools and automobiles. Unfortunately also, such industries almost always have a long lead time between product plan and market introduction--an

average of three years in the automobile industry--making prediction even more hazardous. The design and production decisions
must nevertheless set a target price at the beginning of this lead
time, based on some estimated average market price, and live with
the estimates no matter what happens to the eventual market volume.
The automobile manufacturer, for example, could not price his
cars higher in a weak market, just because the volume is down, and
is not likely to cut price just because the market is stronger than
expected. The solution to this marketing dilemma has been the development of the standard cost estimate--the estimate of the cost
as it would be if the level of operation were the same as the average
expected over the whole cycle of lean years and good, permitting
the choice of a design target price in advance of knowledge of market conditions.

PRODUCT QUALITY LEVEL DECISION

        Any organization's price-line positioning is unquestionably a
most important dimension of its niche in the competitive structure
and not subject to frequent tampering. In the loose and quite erron-
eous terminology of popular usage, the firm must early decide
whether it will follow a low price, average price, or premium price
policy. Each of these so-called policies involve differences in every
aspect of the marketing mix--in the offering itself, often in the physical product, in the handling of distributive place and time utilities,
and in the promotional mix.
        The correct designations are not low-price, but low-end; not
premium-price but premium-end. Nor does a low-end policy mean
that all costs are necessarily on the economy side. At times the
promotional mix required may call for a much larger advertising
budget than might, for the same kind of offering, be needed for a
high-end offering, for instance. To think in terms of low-end, high-
end, or middle-range offerings is to put the emphasis where market
actuality is--in the perceived quality level of the total offering. Even
were the other aspects besides price truly identical, the very fact
of price-imputed quality would mean that the offerings differed in
perceptive quality for those doing the buying.
        In practice, offerings are far from identical in other objective
respects than price and satisfaction source, although the latter alone
can have substantial significance to the buyer. After all, a product
with a Marshall Field or Nieman-Marcus label carries warranty implications not conveyed by a K-Mart label. Court decisions to the
contrary notwithstanding, the physically identical lower-priced private brand item, made for some customer by the seller of a well-
known and highly-accepted brand, is not necessarily cheaper in the

buyer's eyes than the slightly higher-priced item under the maker's own label. At the very least, it can carry a perceivably higher risk that it does not guarantee dependable quality.

The choice of price-quality level is not a completely open one for any manufacturer or merchant. His own total production-distribution system cost structure must first be favorable to the desired policy relative to his other opportunities. The policy chosen must be the most profitable for the given firm. If an organization wishes to follow a premium end policy, for example, it must be able to consistently design, produce, and deliver an offering which the prospect segment will perceive as of truly prestige quality. It must also be capable of developing a believable advertising, selling, and sales promotional approach which conveys the feeling of quality and prestige. And the firm must be able to get its offering carried by distributive outlets buyers associate with quality. If even one of these elements in the marketing mix is not up to buyer expectations for quality-level offerings, the seller will simply be "pricing himself out of the market." That is, the absence of perceived quality service, the use of packaging or ads which are interpreted by buyers as related to poor quality, reliance on weak distributors or distributors associated with lower-end offerings, or absence of any other single cue to quality will doom it to market failure at a premium price. Stewart-Warner, for instance, found it wise to get out of the television business when that product's life cycle reached the turbulence phase because it had not been able to obtain a quality set of dealers. In general, the choice must be based on the firm's relative experience resources. A successful choice takes advantage of the feel of the particular market and method of operation in which its own accumulated experience gives it an advantage.

Some weakness in the perceivable quality of an offering does not thereby enable it to penetrate the low-end market. Of course, a low-end offering presupposes a favorable cost structure. But the total offering structure must itself be mentally associated with low-end goods by the segment interested in purchasing such offerings. The design itself must appear to be appropriate to this segment. Low-end offerings are not simply items with some of the costlier attributes omitted--they are very specific designs for a very specific market segment. On attributes the buyer considers unimportant, quality may be lowered. The buyer of low-end cut-rate gasoline may not care whether or not the brand has numerous stations, so long as he can find one on the route of his normally heavy travel. The buyer of a low-end dress design may not look very carefully at the stitching and other finer details of tailoring. But the heavy-using buyer of cut-rate gasoline may insist on all-night operation of the stations he patronizes, the buyer of the cheap frock expect much more ornamentation than the user of exclusive designs finds acceptable. Cheap "borax" furniture will be finished in a higher (and less durable) gloss than will the carefully-built pieces.

Basically, of course, a low-end policy concentrates on offerings in which some of the higher-cost attributes are missing because the segment buying such offerings does not value such attributes highly enough. The lower valuation of the attributes derives in some cases from the lack of ability of the less well-informed buyers to discriminate quality details, and such products are generally sold through extensive distribution to a mass market. But low-end goods are sometimes the aim of the better-informed, disciminating market. Typically, cut-rate gasoline sells best to middle-class long distance drivers and to truckers, offering gasoline and oil, but few of the maintenance services of the neighborhood stations, and through much less intensive station coverage.

The choice of quality level is thus as much a choice of target market segment as it is of some specific relative monetary quotation. This is even more true of the parallel problem of product mix or merchandise mix.

PRODUCT-LINE AND MERCHANDISE-MIX STRATEGIES

Single-item pricing is a relatively infrequent phenomenon. Only a very small proportion of all transactions at any level of distribution or consumption are single-item sales. Buyers are normally seeking to obtain an assortment of related items from each seller. They have a very understandable desire to minimize their transaction costs in both time and money by getting as much of each desired assortment as possible from a single seller. Consequently, they buy from those sellers whose offered assortment comes closest to their assortment needs in satisfaction content and value. The seller's real offering is thus his assortment of merchandise and services--what the manufacturer thinks of as his product line and accompanying services and the storekeeper views as his merchandise plan.

Different items in the line will have a high degree of salience for different buyers because each buyer will differ somewhat in the extent of the assortment desired, and in the relative importance of any specific item in that assortment. The importance of price and quality will thus differ from buyer to buyer, and even more from distinguishable market segment to segment. One segment of shopping housewives, for instance, may pay close attention to fresh meat and produce quality in their local supermarkets, and little attention to cold-cut meats and bakery goods. Members of another segment, having more lunches to pack, may seek broad assortments of cold-cuts and breads, and pay much less attention to lamb cuts and produce. The result is the common experience that any business district has heavier customer traffic and prospers more if it has supermarkets under more than one management, and why all of the "competing" department stores on State St. prosper and each has a well-defined core clientele of its own. It also explains why there is no single definable "lowest-priced" merchant except in terms of a particular segment of customers.

Each seller must offer the specific assortment a specific set of market segments desires as perceived by them. He also must make a profit if he expects to stay in business. He will, therefore, offer the quality-price combinations most attractive to his customers in those items highest in the hierarchy within their assortment desire-sets.

In every branch of trade there are some items of frequent purchase which are identical for all customers' assortments and must therefore be carried and promoted by all sellers at approximately the same quality level of goods. Usually, these are also relatively standardized items--sugar and the popular soup brand in the supermarket, women's nylons in the department store, standard carbon steel nuts and bolts in the industrial market, the hamburger at the meat counter. Because perceivable differentiation is low or non-existent for such items and because purchase is frequent, in volume, and therefore important to large numbers of buyers in all segments, sellers must generally "meet the market" whatever their clientele for such items. Because they do bring in customers desiring the rest of the seller's own special assortment, such "traffic items" must be heavily promoted regardless of cost and thin profits because a price which is higher than expectation for such items tends to give buyers the feeling that other prices are out of line, due to the "aura" effect. The profit in such traffic items is thus indirect. They are promoted in order to generate sales of the other items in the product line or merchandise mix.

How, then, does a successful buyer so price a line as to profit, since some goods must be sold at less than a proportionate margin? First he quotes and receives an adequate, but not necessarily high, margin on those items whose quality level, design and price are highly salient for his own specific target segments. With an adequate margin, high turnover among heavy user buyers makes these items profitable. Second, some of the items in assortments bought by his customers will, for them, have a relatively low frequency of purchase and low attention value. He can compensate for low turnover of such items by much higher percentage levels. Finally he may add items which are normally part of the assortment bought by customers in other higher-margin outlets, as the food market has added toiletries, and sell at what, for him, is a very high margin, but average or even low for the other kind of outlet.

The end result of such a policy may make him a lower-cost outlet for his target segments, and a higher-cost one for those whose market basket requires a quite divergent mix.

Product-line and merchandise-mix pricing thus requires a carefully managed price mix which takes account of three factors:

1. The product desire assortment of the target market segment, in terms of items and quality levels, and of the degree of salience of each item to the members of the target segment.

2. The frequency and volume of each purchase, the extent to which it is a part of the desire-sets of all segments, its degree of standardization, and in consequence, the price sensitivity of customers in relation to that kind of item.

3. The turnover of the item when purchased by the target segment.

Traffic items, defined as high turnover, universally bought offerings, will normally be priced very close to or at the same level as quoted by competition and expected to yield minimum margins over cost. Their purpose in the offering assortment is to promote sales for the other items in the line.

Highly differentiated items demanded by and selling in good volume to the seller's own target segments will be priced at a level which yields a good to very good margin over cost, but a price which will be perceived by those for whom the item is salient as giving a high ratio of value to cost. They will form the backbone of the profit structure.

Items which are handled as a convenience for the target segment but not particularly salient to this segment nor bought frequently and in quantity will be priced to yield substantial margins.

Obviously, when a store may stock from 8 thousand to 20 thousand items, and a manufacturer routinely make hundreds for sale, every new item in a constantly fluid mix cannot justify a conference of executives concerning the margin to be asked. What sellers do, in reality, is to classify items by category of margin objective, and use these margins as rule-of-thumb for pricing, adjusting occasionally to temporary competitive situations. The rule-of-thumb margin then becomes a standard with regard to inclusion of the product in the line. If it cannot yield the margin objective, it is not included for manufacture or, in the case of the merchant, for purchase and stocking.

General policy with respect to the margin mix may be so infrequent that no current executive in an organization may ever have given any thought to it, so long as it works. Thus even though the margin-mix decision is a price-oriented one in the first instance, it becomes a product-acceptance standard in its operation.

A single-item purchase such as an automobile, a home, a

printing press, insurance, and the like requires a similar policy. Most sellers of such large-ticket purchases must also offer an assortment, a choice among partly competing items, in order to serve well a large enough segment of the market. Such sellers also have to devise a price mix which will both be attractive and ensure the possibility of a reasonable profit. In this case also, some of the possible choices must be offered at very modest margins in order to attract segment fringes, and others can sustain a more robust markup. Experience has taught that in the case of the internally competing assortment, the rules for successful pricing seem to parallel those for the supplementary-item assortment.

Generally speaking, such single-choice assortments are composed of a broad range of perceivable quality levels. Generally, also, the cost range of producing the disparate models is much narrower than the perceived quality range, at least for those buyers interested in the higher quality ranges. These latter, of course, are those prospects constituting the core of the market segment, buyers who seek and see high value in more of the possible product-differentiating attributes than do those at the fringes of the segment. Because those in the fringes perceive significant value only in the core product attributes, the seller is in more direct competition with other sellers for their business than he is with respect to the business of those seeking the higher-level models with the differentiating characteristics. These become his "traffic-attracting" items, although not in the sense of sales volume.

The low-end buyer, in other words, is seeking what the trade has come to call the "stripped model": the replacement tire or the replacement automobile battery which will keep the car on the road for another year of relatively moderate service, the automobile which will give good dependable transportation service but not necessarily any of the aesthetic satisfactions which go with decoration and various special accessories. Such a buyer does not see any substantial value in and will not pay even a price proportionate to cost for accessory attributes. Since he is interested mainly in the core attributes, he also perceives little value difference between the offerings of different sellers.

Most possible buyers, on the other hand, do perceive real value in the differentiating attributes of the products of one or another of the sellers and will pay a reasonable price to obtain them. Some smaller proportion see even higher value in added attributes and will pay a very good price to differentiate their purchase even more.

In pricing the internally competing line, therefore, the seller usually aims to:

    1. Offer a relatively unattractive low-end line with a highly competitive, very thin margin low-end price. The effect

on his average profit is minimized by means of "plain-Jane" design.

2. Offer a middle-line group designed to be the best compromise in relation to the desire-sets of the main body of his target market segment. The margin between price objective and design cost is aimed to give him his target margin objective on the average.

3. Offer a premium line with all of the accessory options for those valuing highly the maximum satisfaction package, aimed to yield a very high margin between target price and design cost.

While the low-end line should be designed to be relatively unattractive to the main body of the market segment, it is seldom wise to treat this design as a stepchild. It should attract the fringes of the same segment as does the main line.

Sellers sometimes miscalculate the nature of the market to which what they think of as their low end is appealing, and have been known to repel possibly attractive business. Ford Motors seems to have made such a mistake with its 1960 introduction of the Falcon to meet the growing foreign car competition. Assuming that the small car demand was solely for economy, the firm offered the Falcon in an essentially Spartan context. Although the research on which the design was based is reported to have indicated a potential demand for a wide set of options among some of the target market segments, no engine but the tamest was offered, only four basic body styles, and few other options which would increase sales value. The result was a basic design which proved to be the most attractive of the 1960 compacts, but which had a very brief design life. What had seemed to be a market for a stripped-down model was really a different kind of segment.

Structuring the prices of any type of product assortment thus requires a complex balancing of target market value perceptions against profit margins. The process starts with the choice of a feasible average profit margin target, then balances low-end offerings of traffic items yielding thin margins, to gain customer attention and patronage, against main-volume items at or near target margins and high-end items with robust contributions to profit. A main consideration must be the content, proportioning and salience of the desire-set assortments sought by target market segments.

Margin-over-cost calculations also form the basis for a different aspect of the pricing decision--the discounts to be offered the distributive agencies in return for their contributions to the final satisfaction bundle purchased by the ultimate consumer.

DISCOUNTS AND OTHER DEVICES FOR BUYING DISTRIBUTIVE SERVICES

One major aspect of most producer price decisions is the choice as to how much discount or commission to allocate to those who link the factory to the final user and who must, in the process, add some of the most costly services necessary to the final satisfaction bundle.

The offering becomes complete and capable of delivering on its perceivable promises of satisfaction only at the point of final satisfaction. The aim of all price quotation is to match the value perceivable by the final buyer, and all other prices must work back from this figure. Much of the value perceived by this final user is the result of services contributed by those in between the first maker and the end buyer. Since most of the intermediaries are normally independent business men, these services must be purchased by offering an attractive slice of what the consumer is expected to pay: through what the merchant thinks of as his mark-up and the manufacturer quotes as a discount. (These terms are exact synonyms and are calculated in the same manner: both are the result of dividing the total margin over buying price by the price at which sold.)

Distribution discounts are thus really purchase prices--an offering of a given portion of the customer-perceived value in return for a number of value additions to the satisfaction bundle.

Generally speaking, distributors add four basic types of user-perceived value to the manufacturer's product, and contribute also to his intelligence input. Services added to the product by distributors include:

Time and place utilities: maintenance of inventories where most convenient to most buyers, at the times buyers desire them, in the unit quantities needed by buyers

Communications services: local advertising, attention-getting displays, personal selling services

Financing services: by paying for the inventories they carry and by assuming credit risks

Objective production services: assembling of use-related items and services desired by their customers and matching their needs; performing fitting, altering, and other services designed to adapt the physical product more closely to the customer's needs; provision of parts, repair, and maintenance services; furnishing of instructions for use and maintenance; adding a close-to-the-buyer warranty of value

In addition, the distributor's orders and other information feedbacks provide intelligence services valuable both for planning and for administrative control.

The product as it leaves the factory lacks many high-value attributes of considerable importance to the consumer. Gasoline in the storage tanks of the Indiana refinery is not much good to a motorist whose tank is running dry in the middle of Iowa. Stockings at the hosiery mill in North Carolina do not appeal to the New York secretary who has snagged her last pair of nylons and has a date for the evening. Steel bars in carlots at the mill in Youngstown, Ohio are no help to the Peoria machine shop who has a rush order for a special repair part for an impatient contractor. The buyer needs ready inventories near where he is, in the quantities and sizes that fit his needs, in the styles or colors matching his requirements. It is the job of the distribution system to foresee those requirements and position stocks in literally tens of thousands of locations ahead of demand, in just the form, sizes, colors, etc. likely to be needed by local buyers.

The communications function of distributors adds to value for the consumer as much as it relieves the manufacturer of this effort. The customer needs to know where to find what he needs, learn what it can do for him, and have it so displayed that it is brought to his attention.

Since mass manufacture presupposes production ahead of orders, the financing made available to the producer through distributor inventory policies should have such obvious value as to require no discussion. During the growth phases of the auto industry, entry of new makers was facilitated by the fact that much of the working capital was furnished by dealer deposits.

The assortment assembly function of the distributor--assembling related items from unrelated sources to match the desire assortments of his clientele--is as much a form of objective production as is the assembly of a television set from components bought from various suppliers. However, distributor contributions to objective production are not limited to assembly of merchandise assortments but extend to even more visible kinds of production operations. Men's slacks can seldom be manufactured economically to the size and exact leg lengths needed by all the customers in the market, so the dealer must perform the final fitting and alteration operations. The steel mill cannot afford to run small lots of every possible width of steel strip needed by the myriad of small machine shops, so the steel service warehouse buys sheet stock and slits it to order. Bulky furniture is much cheaper to ship to the dealer unassembled ("knocked down") and assembled at the point of sale. In such matters, each distributor becomes an extension of the manufacturer's production department, fitting the product to the needs of local buyers much more efficiently than could the central factory.

In many kinds of durable items, the customer expects also to

265

get an adequate service network, often instructional service, and usually local adjustment of complaints as part of the package he purchases. Generally, only the distribution network can satisfy these attributes of the satisfaction bundle adequately.

Deciding on the correct discount structure is a relatively simple problem in the case of many established types of offerings: the seller accepts the general trade practice for that category of goods, as it is followed in each channel through which he distributes his output. Very commonly, distributors and dealers in any one kind of channel follow a standardized basic mark-up practice for each of a few broad categories of goods which they handle, one established as workable through long years of experience and capable of yielding an overall margin objective with wise management of merchandise assortments. So long as the flow of goods through the various channels and the relative strength of these channels remain roughly stable, sellers are not tempted to tinker with this accepted practice. Periodically, however, distributive structures are upset by the entrance of new types of sellers--sellers creating new types of assortments, new merchandise practices, and even appealing to new types of market segments.

Such new types of sellers often start out, at least, as low margin sellers, and their entry can, as did that of the appliance discount houses of the 1950's, change the channel flow and restructure the whole channel system. When this occurs, older distributors often tend to press the seller to keep out of the developing channel, and if this proves impossible (as it usually does), to make use of legalized price maintenance devices, setting a minimum price level below which no distributive outlet may sell.

Such "fair-trade" arrangements have been a recurrent legislative and commercial aim of established dealers at various periods of history, at least as far back as the medieval guilds. In the United States, the first major push came during the 1930's, when the retail druggist organizations succeeded in getting a number of states, and then the Federal government, to pass enabling legislation permitting retail price maintenance, hoping to cripple the developing cut-rate drug chains. Reluctant manufacturers were, trade gossip said, forced to take advantage of such laws by retailer boycotts in some cases. "Dealer protection," in other words, became part of the price which had to be paid to retain the services of these established channels. And it was and is a price which carries a considerable cost: enforcement of retail price maintenance without restricting outlets is at the expense of the manufacturer.

Fair trade has always proved far more expensive than it was worth when enforcement was conscientious. Invariably, also, it has broken down because this form of dealer protection seeks two incompatible ends.

Dealer protection in the form envisioned by so-called Fair Trade legislation has never succeeded in driving out the new channels or even crippling their operations because it does nothing to take the profit out of selling the items by these newer outlets. When really prevented from selling below the fair-trade price, such outlets can use the price to highlight the savings to be had in buying their own similar "private brand", which may yield even greater margin. Even if they do not resort to this tactic, they can use the generally lush margin the fair-trade price engenders to offset deeper price cuts elsewhere in the assortment they offer, and thus make the whole assortment more attractive. It is, after all, the price of the total assortment which interests the buyer. The low-price aura may even cause some buyers to feel that they were getting even the price-maintained items at a bargain.

Furthermore, those proposing such arrangements are asking for the economically impossible. They are asking for intensive distribution to every seller who wishes to handle the pre-sold product, at margins far in excess of those necessary to pay for the type of distributive service rendered or even needed for an established popular brand.

Really effective dealer protection is possible and often a justified price for the services rendered during the market development phase of the product life cycle or even, at times, during later phases for manufacturers with a relatively narrow consumer franchise. In the latter case, the distributor may and usually does also get a larger monetary discount than he would from a more entrenched brand. Both the monetary discount and the protection are prices he needs to justify the aggressive selling he must undertake to develop brand acceptance which is necessary to move an adequate volume of product. A seller that is as well entrenched as RCA is in electronic appliances, for example, can depend on his own mass advertising and sales promotion to establish consumer preference and, because that acceptance is high, will be able to get close to complete distribution, so that local advertising may be a relatively minor element in success and personal selling not important. Indeed, the wholesalers and retailers may need such a line to bolster the adequacy of their own assortments more than the manufacturer needs any one of them. By contrast, a smaller, specialized producer such as Magnavox may have to concentrate its sales through a few carefully selected and widely spaced aggressive outlets who can draw trade to themselves with hard-hitting local advertising and personal sales effort. A firm in this position will have to grant larger margins and pay the price of selectivity in its outlets, giving each a practical monopoly of a sizable territory, or lose out in the market.

Since discount structures are the price paid to get distribution

services and since distributors tend to follow stable rule-of-thumb
margin policies because of the very multitude of items they must
handle, discount structures need periodic review but infrequent
changes.

Actual total prices, on the other hand, require constant review because of the constant flux of direct and indirect competition,
because of constant changes in customer evaluation of the contained
satisfactions, because of fluctuation and trends in cost factors of
many kinds, and because of changes in the value of money itself.
Prices are so inherently unstable that any organization which can
exercise any degree of discretion in either the level or timing of
its price quotations relative to those of competitors must decide
whether to be a leader or follower.

PRICE CHANGE TIMING: LEADER OR FOLLOWER?

There is nothing static about the forces determining the value
perceived by buyers or about the costs of producing these values.
Even were all other forces static, the history of the industrial
world has taught that the value of money itself is subject to change,
mostly downward. Since most prices in an industrial society are
necessarily the result of forward quotation, those who do the quoting
must consider the quotations made by those marketing other similar
or even dissimilar competing products and the reactions of these
others to whatever quotations they decide upon. Periods in which
price increases seem both necessary and workable can thus be the
cause of a relatively high level of anxiety among those who must
make the price decisions. One method of reducing the anxiety
level, and one many businessmen would feel most comfortable with,
is for all to get together and agree on the amount and timing. Such,
indeed, was the approved practice in many countries for a long time,
with legal blessing for the cartels. Since the 1890's, however, such
collusion has been outlawed in the United States, and most informed
economists approve of at least the intent of such antitrust legislation,
if not the specific court decisions in every case. Even formerly
highly cartelized European industry is beginning to have to learn
the ways of a more rugged competition. As Adam Smith long ago
observed, such price conspiring is not likely to be in the interest
of the consumer.

Nevertheless, costs do move widely, both up and down. If
the consumer is to be assured of a continuous supply of the things
he desires, upward-moving costs must sooner or later be offset
with price increases. And if industrial profits are not to be raised
to the point that invites over-expansion of capacity and the head-
aches these bring on, downward-moving costs must be met with

lower prices. The problem becomes: who makes the first move, with the attendant chance that others may not follow, us or the other fellow? The leadership sometimes tends to rotate, as in the automobile industry, and when it does, some interesting maneuvering can ensue, each endeavoring to get another to assume the aura of high price. In most industries, however, some one dominant seller tends to set any upward trend, and others quickly follow. When this is the situation, a firm must consider whether it is better suited to the role of leader or of follower most of the time. Only a firm with a strong market position can assume such upside price leadership. Any firm with a substantial market share can lead downward moves.

The role of price leader does not thereby give a firm a great deal of freedom. In fact, it imposes a form of responsibility for the competitive health of the whole industry which many in that position may overlook. The leader must resist with all of its strength any temptation to set a price umbrella which automatically covers all costs with a comfortable margin. To do so is to endanger the market position of both the leader himself and of the whole industry.

The history of the pricing policies of Standard Oil Company of Ohio (Learned and Ellsworth, 1959) well illustrates the effects of both shortsighted and well-considered price leadership policies. At the time of the breakup of John D. Rockefeller's trust in 1911, Ohio Standard had about a nine-tenths share of the petroleum products market in the territory left to it--the state of Ohio. For nearly 17 years, the officers attempted to hold the prices at levels guaranteeing what they felt was a fair profit. The inevitable happened: new competitors flocked in under the shelter of the profit umbrella so thoughtfully provided, and by 1923, Sohio's share of the gasoline market was down to 11%. Sohio then shifted to an attempt to adjust its statewide price to conform to current conditions in the general petroleum market and pulled back to a 30 per cent market share within two years. The market share dropped again in the 1933-36 period, to 20 per cent, when Sohio abided by the national NRA regulations assuring wide dealer margins. After the death of NRA, Sohio's share began to recover, and in 1938, the firm shifted to an even more flexible policy, responding to local competitive pressures in various parts of Ohio. By 1941, its market share was back to 30 per cent, and has largely remained above that level ever since. One of the apparent results of Sohio's close attention to leading the industry in its area to pay close attention to competitive pricing has been a relative freedom from the kind of endemic price wars which have sprung up in areas just outside its sales territory, where less foresighted price leaders have attempted to price at lusher margins in between price wars. In addition, cut-rate marketers have consistently penetrated only about one-tenth of the market, in contrast to most metropolitan regions where cut-rate competition has taken over as much as half of the volume. When price wars do break out, Sohio follows the price down but does not attempt to lead the drop at any time.

In the case of Standard of Ohio, the dangerous potential competition has come from inside the industry. But quite often in the case of mature products, the greatest threat of competitive erosion and over-expansion comes from the outside and thus is often less visible to the pricing executives. The menace is often in the form of new product bundles fulfilling many of the desire-sets of those served by the established products, by products on the edge of their rapid growth phase, just waiting to take over new markets. One of the insidious dangers of such newcomer competition is the ease with which it can be overlooked or even blatantly ignored. Because the new competition is usually much smaller at first, the established industry may look only at current relative volume and delude itself that no real problem looms. When the aluminum industry started challenging the steel market after World War II, steel executives were inclined to sniff, "Aluminum a threat? Their production is still measured in pounds, steel has to be counted in tons!" Unfortunately, once the invading industry gains the extra stimulation of unwise "fair profit" price leadership, the experience curve would guarantee that the extra volume gained would confer additional cost advantages and thus gain more new customers permanently. The extra growth stimulus can launch the newcomer into an area of lower-cost production.

Moreover, both the customer learning barrier and the ordinary inertia which normally hinder adoption of the new have been hurdled, and the new is now in use. Regaining old customers for the old product now requires that the old prove to be a substantially better value than the new--something not necessary before. Thus the copper producers have always been loathe to raise prices in the last two decades because of the potential loss to aluminum of many of their customers for copper cable. In terms of unit electrical conductivity, the newer metal had an edge already in price, but the need to learn somewhat different techniques of application had hindered its spread. Once a major utility customer was lost to aluminum, however, the industry had learned that it could not retrieve the business.

The steel industry was not as wise in its price leadership following World War II. Feeling that wartime price controls had squeezed profit margins too much, steel officials apparently decided to bring prices back to a profit level they considered fair. With every change in labor contract costs, prices were increased to a substantially greater degree (Silverman, 1960). Sales never-

270

theless boomed for a while because of the materials famine. Within the rising sales curve, however, steel was steadily losing markets to both the foreign steel makers and to competing materials. By 1957, it was clear that major markets had been lost to prestressed concrete structurals, to plastics, and to aluminum and even paper, which took possession of a considerable part of the important liquid container market.

Not all price changes are up, however, the long-term inflationary trend notwithstanding. Almost any industry experiences recurrent periods when demand eases below the current supply level. Even in shortrun periods, a neat balance between production and consumption is rare. Given free rein, prices on the market can fluctuate from day to day and even hour to hour, as the commodity and stock markets have long demonstrated, in the case of undifferentiated sellers.

Buyers, however, do not always view such freely fluctuating prices with unmixed satisfaction, particularly in the instance of commodities which are important raw materials or components in their cost structure. Most manufacturers must give firm quotations of their prices well in advance of delivery or sales, and often in advance of materials purchases, often months and occasionally years in advance. Since the maker must engineer his product to sell at the quoted price at a profit, he manifestly is eager to be certain of the level of his future costs when he makes such an advance quotation, and would also like to be sure his competitors will have similar costs.

Where the actual delivered price of the commodity does fluctuate frequently, most manufacturers have attempted to control costs by long term contracts, or by hedging through purchase of futures--that is, of commodity exchange contracts for future delivery. The risk reduction by such hedging operations long ago proved so substantial that flour millers, for example, could reduce the allowance for manufacturing margins as much as three-fourths.

Even organized exchanges and hedging through futures are no perfect answer to erratic and frequent price fluctuations. Hedging itself requires a high degree of skill and thus the diversion of executive resources. So much skill is required, for example, that the profit in the production of mixed agricultural feeds long depended more on the purchasing skills of the manager than on his skills in any other aspect of his business--marketing or physical production, or even financial. Thus any manufacturer who can choose between such a freely fluctuating cost element and one whose average cost is about the same, but fluctuates very little, will inevitably choose the latter. For this reason, when producers are so few that the seller has some latitude in price quotation and can allocate supplies, they usually find it wise to avoid frequent quotation changes, particularly in industrial goods. The very fact of price stability can be an attractive added value to prospects for whom the offering is a very substantial item in their cost structure.

When major producers really control a substantial proportion of the potential supply, they must therefore consider seriously whether or not to quote prices in line with the day-to-day demand situation or follow a policy of relative price stability. If they choose the latter, they must make infrequent changes, announce price changes well in advance, and adjust in accordance with the longrun trend in demand, supply, and costs.

Probably because of the administrative problem of attempting to make frequent quotation changes when production is relatively concentrated, as it generally is in most of industry, most industrial pricing follows some kind of relative price stability policy. Whenever this is done, the industry must, of course, adopt some provision to allocate supplies when demand temporarily exceeds current supply. In the case of some industries, this is done by changing actual monetary price through some form of subterfuge. The steel industry, for example, seems to have done this often through fluctuations in the actual application of its somewhat complex price structure. Steel is quoted on the basis of a specific amount per ton, base price. But this base price applies to a very few standard forms, in a few sizes, in carload lots. To determine the quoted price of any of the multitude of other sizes, compositions, special metallurgical treatments, and different-sized lots, the buyer must consult a thick book of "extra" prices applying to specific specifications. During periods of slack demand, the mills have often ignored some of the extra charges. During periods of high demand, conversely, the mills have often charged all extras, even in the case of odd lots sold to buyers, like steel service warehouses, who bought overruns at a discount in normal times, of items not necessarily desired at the specification to which produced.

Obviously, such a policy of subterfuge tends to somewhat vitiate any policy of relative price stability, although it does recapture some of the profit potential of the high demand period. The alternative is to institute some system of private rationing, and such a policy is also widely followed. Usually, the rationing takes the form of alloting available supply, in times of shortage, on the basis of previous purchases from the supplier during periods of slack demand. Such has tended to be the custom of the producers of primary aluminum. The degree of price stability this has granted aluminum buyers is implied in the comparison of the prices of primary and secondary aluminum ingot--physically identical items, differing only in the identity of the suppliers. Primary ingot is manufactured by those selling primary ingot from their own production. Secondary ingot is made of the same mixtures of primary and

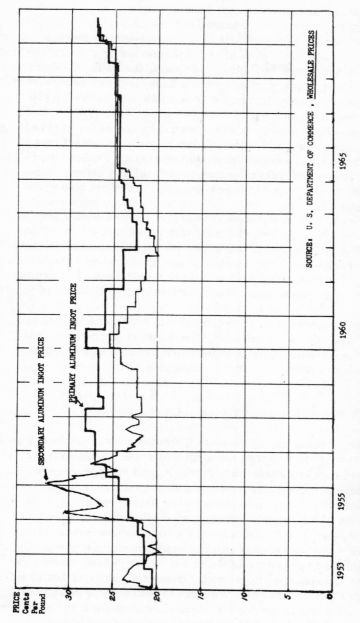

FIGURE 11-2. Prices of Primary Aluminum Alloy Ingot and of the Physically Identical Secondary Ingot, 1953-1969

273

secondary metal, but by those with no facilities to produce the primary metal. The secondary sells on a freely fluctuating market at prices which are above the primary in times of scarcity, well below at other times. (See Figure 11-2).

The method of raising prices is all important. Occasional price changes are inevitable, if only because major cost and demand fluctuations are always with us. Obviously, the seller hopes to get major attention to every price cut he makes, and just as fervently hopes to have his price increases draw little notice. The j. n. d. effect permits achievement of just such objectives, if downward changes exceed a noticeable difference and "salami tactics"--a little slice at a time--are used when raising quotations. Merchants of all kinds have always recognized this when trying to clear over-stocks or launch special promotions: "1/3 off and more," "your second tire at 1/2 price with the purchase of the first tire at the regular price."

It should be clear that most price policy decisions such as those discussed above call for relatively infrequent executive decision. The quality-level, product-price-mix, discount structure, price leadership, and price stability decisions are not subject to frequent reconsideration, and thus these major aspects of pricing do not land high on the executive agenda, as Udell discovered (Udell, 1964).

Many industries, however, must pay constant attention to a different type of pricing decision, the decision on price tactical maneuvers--temporary price maneuvers intended to gain a competitive edge or defend it, or to open up new markets.

PRICE-COMPETITIVE TACTICAL MANEUVERS

Most of the time, price-setting would be a relatively low level clerical concern for a large proportion of sellers if general policy and market conditions were the only principal stimuli for price action. That the price decision for offerings other than new introductions lands even as high as it does in the list of executive concerns is due to its use as a tool, not of general strategy, but of competitive tactics--as a means of response to day-to-day competitive pressures which are largely product oriented. Price is the only element in the marketing mix which can be put into effect on a moment's notice--changes in product, promotion, or distributive arrangements all require some substantial lead time to effectuate. Product changes require tooling, materials procurement, and time to fabricate. Advertising takes time to work out and produce and must be submitted hours ahead, at the minimum, often weeks ahead of publication and exposure to an audience, and often takes considerable repetition to take effect. Distributive arrangements are seldom easy to change at all, and even when they can be, take months of planning and more months of hard work to put into effect. But a direct monetary price change can be made with a simple telephone call.

Unfortunately, a direct monetary price change—a mere difference in the quoted asking price—is not always the most useful form of price change. The advantage, first of all, tends to be extremely evanescent. As soon as the seller (the corner gas station, for example) posts the new price, the competitor down the street can counter with a new quotation matching it or going one better. Moreover, if the aim is that of temporary advantage, it is usually wise to make certain that it is temporary and understood as such. Otherwise, the effect may be an induced change in the buyers' expectation and perceptions of the price he can expect to pay which locks the seller into an unacceptable price level. It is always easy to lower price, but not always so simple to raise one when necessary. The tactic must therefore be done in such a manner as to emphasize the temporary character of the quotation or handled in such a manner as to be difficult to follow immediately.

Price reductions which are safely perceivable as temporary take many forms. The simplest is the "cents-off" deal or the bargain pack ("four bars of face soap for the price of three"), prominently labelled on the package and in the advertising to make sure the outlet passes on the reduction. Such deals are self-restricted to the run of packages so marked, or to a specified time in the advertising. When the reduction involves a specially printed package, as is common, it also gains some time over competitors, who must, if they meet it in the same manner, themselves order and have printed a similar run of packages—a time-consuming operation. A variant is the price allowance coupon which is, of course, a money substitute limited to the quantity printed and distributed, either directly or by publication in some print medium.

The useful purposes of these forms of temporary price reduction is largely confined to the tapping of a new segment of customers by temporarily lowering the avoidance reaction, or to hold customers for a while in the face of an extra-attractive new competitive offering or heavy competitive promotion.

However, such promotional pricing is also useful at times in getting buyers to absorb an otherwise unwieldy inventory or to increase consumption. Generally such a promotion takes the form of specials for multi-unit purchases. When the target customer is a dealer or distributor rather than the final buyer, such a deal is called a "free-goods offer" ("one extra carton free with each order of 10") and is aimed to stimulate the dealer to load his inventory in order to realize a wider profit margin. It is generally expected that if he buys, the dealer will promote the product more heavily in order to reduce his own inventory and will tend to pass on part or all of the price reduction. Such a dealer gains an indirect sales advantage when he does pass on the whole saving because the attractive price itself has an aura effect, helping him to be perceived as price-aggressive, and thus a source of bargains.

Large food processors often use seasonal free goods offers in order to avoid storing the output of a six-week tomato canning season, for example, for the other 46 weeks. The end result is usually to transfer a considerable portion of the output into kitchen cupboards and quite possibly an increased total consumption because of the ready availability of the product in the home.

On the basis of cold economic calculation, all of these forms of temporary price reductions might appear identical in effect--the consumer spends that much less money to acquire his purchase. The basic results can differ significantly and are also usually much greater than the effect of a simple price reduction. When Florida orange growers were faced with a swollen hang-over of the previous season's frozen concentrate, for example, they found that a "one free with six" offer moved far more added product than experience had indicated that a straight price reduction of the same amount would have accomplished. Studies and carefully controlled tests made by Kenyon and Eckhardt have shown that 85 per cent of mailed coupons were redeemed by new buyers as compared with only a 35 per cent new buyer proportion among purchasers of a "cent-off" pack (Advertising Age, 1962). The difference is accounted for in part by the divergent attention-getting potential of the mailed coupon as opposed to the package sitting on the shelf in the store.

One interesting and apparently effective variant of the ordinary store or mailed price-reduction coupon is the refund offer--a coupon prominently attached or distributed independently, which entitles the buyer to a very substantial refund (sometimes as much or more than the product's price) if submitted to the original seller with some proof of purchase such as a label. Those who have used this device seemed to have experienced a substantial sales stimulus with only a relatively few refunds actually requested.

Some of these temporary price reductions really entail some modification of the offering itself. The coupon good only for a multi-unit purchase is a change in the size of the basic unit being proffered. Sometimes this is done by means of the package itself--banding together the four cakes of soap offered for the price of three, for example. Sometimes it may be a combination pack of a large unit with a smaller "sample size" with the offer: "try the sample and if you do not prefer it, return the big package for a full refund."

A combination deal may also tie two disparate but use-related items together in a single offering: "Free: 65 gallons of our premium grade gasoline to everyone who buys a set of 4 of our tires during the sale." The purpose may simply be to impart drama to a simple price reduction by combining the gift of a certain-to-be used item (gasoline) with the one being promoted (tires). Or it may also serve as an incentive to non-buyers to sample the "free" product (our premium gasoline). In fact, the gift may be the main purpose of the offer, a method of sampling (a free package of our new superedge blades with our new super-adjustable razor at the low introductory price of the holder alone).

Any combination deal is some form of a price differential less vulnerable to matching than would be a simple change in price. Another form which is difficult for customers to compare directly is the use of outright premiums with each purchase of a specified value. This may take the form of a specific physical premium of value directly given with the sale, such as the toy in the box of Crackerjack or the set of cocktail glasses with each tankful of gasoline. It may sometimes be in the guise of a reusable container for the product (a plastic refrigerator storage container filled with our brand of tea bags, for instance, either at the same price as the product in the usual container, or for a price differential which is much less than the customer could ordinarily obtain a similar container through ordinary channels. At times, the premium may be available only if ordered from the original seller with evidence of purchase of product (a space compass with 10 cereal box tops, or perhaps with one box top and 25¢, for instance). If a charge is made for the premium, the price is usually a "self-liquidating" one--it fully reimburses the seller for his direct premium cost, but gives the customer a perceivably higher value than he would get by direct purchase through usual channels.

A major problem with the specific physical premium is the difficulty of finding premiums with a truly universal appeal to potential buyers of the main product. Even when widely acceptable, buyers' needs for the specific premium may be subject to early satiation, and the premium thus loses all value to them. A family needs only a small number of cocktail glasses, sewing scissors or kitchen canisters. When only a very short-run effect is desired, this simply involves the problem of finding a very widely acceptable premium. Sometimes, however, the aim is to establish and maintain a perception of substantially lower price for some indefinite longrun period, and do it in such a manner that the move is not easily matched because the value is viewed by buyers as "something extra," not that of the product for less money, and also because valuation of the premium itself is difficult. A common means of avoiding the difficulty of premium selection is to offer, not a specific premium itself, but a whole catalog of possible premium merchandise which the buyer can obtain by use of some form of blocked currency given him with each purchase--cash register receipts, coupons, or, commonly, stamps.

All of these forms of apparent indirect price reduction can succeed for a considerable period because they are not initially perceived by the customer as quite the equivalent of a simple price concession and also because, like all other changes in the total offering, countering them takes time. If they do offer a competitive advantage however, they will be countered sooner or later in some manner. Thus, whatever the intention, their ultimate effect is temporary. Because the premium becomes part of the offering, abandoning it may be difficult, moreover, as the makers of some coupon brand cigarettes discovered.

Price may also be changed by changing the size of the package contents. In the case of popular candy bars, this is the only method normally open to adjust to significant changes in cost because of consumer price-line expectations. It is used on other occasions, however, when no necessity exists to use such a subterfuge. Sellers of goods commonly sold in relatively standardized sizes of containers sometimes take advantage of the principle of the just noticeable difference to substantially reduce contents offered without seeming to. A relatively imperceptible difference applied to all three dimensions of a container can effect a very substantial reduction in total contents without the notice of the unsuspecting buyer, and thus give a higher price return without the buyer's immediate awareness of the stratagem. Toilet paper, for example, was long sold in rolls of 1,000 sheets each by most makers, with only a few selling clearly smaller 500-sheet rolls. Then the fluffier types of paper were developed, and some corner-cutting seller apparently discovered that, in this form, the 625 sheet roll would appear equal in size to the 1,000 sheet roll to most customers, despite the printed count on the label. The result, eventually, of course, was that the 625 sheet roll became very near to be the standard for most sellers, and the customers absorbed higher distribution costs occasioned by the waste space in the roll center, which did not change. Can sizes have undergone a similar degradation through lowering of the size by overanxious sellers trying to appear to be selling at a bargain they did not offer. A major firm that desired to invade the cooking oil market apparently used a similar ploy to gain an advantage. At the time, nearly all salad and cooking oils were offered in standard quart or pint containers. The new firm developed a wasp-waisted bottle which did offer the customer some advantages in terms of unslippability. But it also was as tall in the pint-and-one-half size as the standard quart bottle, and was introduced in this odd size. Soon, of course, the pint-and-one-half size became the standard, with no benefit to anyone except for the foothold which had been gained in part by the deceptive container.

A knowledge of psychological perception can also be used to emphasize a price drop, however. In this case, only a single dimension of the container is changed, to emphasize the difference. Thus one scouring cleanser maker produced his packages one-third higher, with one-third more contents, and advertised the difference aggressively. This can be an effective device when the cost of raw material is a relatively minor part of the cost of putting the final offering in the final consumer's hands. Standing close to a competitor's offering on the same shelf, it can attract attention even without heavy promotion, and if the quality of the offering is already established in the buyers' perceptions, proclaim greater value in a dramatic manner. Again, this form of price move is not easily countered immediately because, like all product changes, meeting it directly takes time and the buyer is not likely to perceive a simple price reduction counter as the same thing. Unit-cost calculations take time and effort not worth expending on what is usually a relatively minor buy for the final user.

Even though all of these indirect temporary price-competitive maneuvers gain time because they are imbedded in some kind of product change, the product difference gained and the value difference perceived is more ephemeral than would be a substantial perceived difference in the satisfaction content of the offering bundle. Moreover, as stamp-givers have discovered, all of them are subject to some kind of more or less effective countermeasures and are inclined to lead to much the same kinds of relatively destructive escalation as are mere changes in price quotations. Stamp wars and sales promotion wars do not differ in kind from ordinary price wars and are just as burdensome in the end. None give the customer what he really desires--offerings better fitted to his desire sets than are those currently available. Furthermore, even if escalation does not ensue, what starts out as a temporary tactic can sometimes be impossible to discontinue because the tie-in gets to be the main product and the core item in the offering an unappreciated premium, as happened with children's cereal box-top offers.

There may be occasions, of course, when the apparent price reduction is not intended to be temporary, nor is the sale ever expected to yield a profit directly. At times, the product being sold is basically aimed at the sales promotion of something else which does yield a dependable profit. Thus razor holders have always been sold to promote the sales of blades, Polaroid cameras priced to create users of the special film required. Card tabulating equipment was long rented at levels ridiculously low for high precision machinery, to create markets for the large volumes of tabulating cards they needed. Such moves are never intended to be temporary, and profit from the item itself no factor in the pricing strategy.

279

In the end, any marketing strategy based on price appeal alone is self-defeating because price has meaning only in relation to the value being offered. Value comes from offering something fitting the desire-sets of a considerable segment of prospects. In one very important kind of pricing decision, of course, the producer has no choice but to design the core of the product according to the very exacting specifications of the buyer--in the case of major sales on the basis of competitive bids.

BID PRICING AND COMPETITIVE BIDDING STRATEGY

All of us probably think of both product specification development and of the following design development as primarily the function of the producer, who must generally guess at the performance desires which will later be most important of fulfillment to that market segment at which he aims. But a very substantial part of the GNP consists of products whose specifications are first formulated by the buyer and often even designed by him, then produced by someone else at a price determined by competitive bidding. The seller usually develops his bid by some procedure similar to the following:

Decide first whether or not the product is one which the seller is well fitted to produce and thus whether he should even develop a serious bid

If he decides to make a serious bid, determine what his objective should be in attempting to land the business--optimum immediate profit, maintenance-in-being of his going organization, or indirect future profit, for example.

Estimate his probable cost to produce

Estimate the probable aggressiveness of the other likely bidders and the probable sizes of the bids each is likely to make, based on the present state of the market for the services of the industry and on what is known about their past bidding practices

Decide on the profit margin best fitting his current bidding objective as well as current market conditions, and submit a bid based on this estimated margin

When bidding promises to be brisk, each knows that bids from the various competitors may be relatively close to each other and that he must calculate carefully, yet never lose sight of his objectives. The decision can obviously be conducive to the development of stomach ulcers.

A very useful technique for appraising alternative bid possibilities in a relatively objective manner is the Bayesian decision tool known as competitive bidding strategy. The input data for competitive bidding strategy computations are much the same as those most bidders normally use, but the calculations reveal the quantitative implications of that data for the future profit structure of the organization and thus permit a calm appraisal of the value of each alternative in the light of the sought-for objectives.

The basic principle of competitive bidding strategy is the essence of common-sense simplicity: bids are compared on the basis of the estimated profit they yield, discounted by the estimated probability of their success. The profit position thus estimated is a single number for each possible bid, permitting a dispassionate comparison of bid consequences which simultaneously takes account of both the estimated profit and the degree of uncertainty in landing the business.

The calculation itself requires the development of an estimated distribution of the probabilities of success of all bids within the range being considered, using the same information about past bidding he generally uses and considers as relevant. This probability distribution is developed from past bids on jobs considered equivalent to the current one, under similar market conditions, by considering each as an equally likely type of bid in the current situation. This computation thus contains the implicit assumption that the estimating and bidding procedures of each possible competitor are relatively consistent and therefore an indicator of future bidding behavior. Another implicit assumption is that the cost estimating procedures of the various competitors tend to yield parallel (but not necessarily equal) results. These are, of course, the assumptions the prospective bidder must always make under any logical process of bidding competitively.

Calculating the profit position proceeds as follows:

1. Assemble the available information on past bids made by each prospective competitor.

2. Choose from this list those n number of bids which are judged to have been made under circumstances and on jobs comparable to the present one.

3. For each one in this list of n bids, list the bidder's own estimate of cost at the time the bid was made.

4. Using this bidder's own cost estimate as his estimate of his competitor's cost estimate, estimate each competitor's percentage margin objective in the case of each of these past bids.

5. Rank each competitor's margin objective values according to size, thus producing an initial array for each competitor of the estimated values of his percentage margin objectives (m).

6. Convert this array into an estimated cumulative probability distribution of $n + 1$ bids, composed of the known n bids plus the next, unknown one by plotting these at the midpoints of $1/(n + 1)$ fractions of a 100 per cent probability distribution, starting with the highest at the low end.

7. Graph this cumulative frequency, preferably on normal probability paper, and draw a smoothed cumulative frequency curve which seems to best fit the plotted points. Repeat this process for each competitor.

8. Develop a set of tables showing cumulative probabilities for each competitor by interpolating the data plotted on these first estimate curves at the same convenient round number bid levels (for example, -10%, -5%, -2%, -1%, 0, +1%, +2%, +5%, etc.).

9. Develop a combined cumulative probability table for all competitors together by multiplying the probabilities of all competitors together at each point in these tables. That is, if the cumulative probabilities of three possible competitors, at the point of a 10 per cent margin or better, has been estimated separately at .19, .20, and .18, respectively, the probability that a bid of 10 per cent profit margin will win over all three bids will be estimated as (.19 x .20 x .18), or .00684. (This value is so much lower than the chance against any one bidder because the bids of each of the other three must be assumed to be independent.)

10. Develop a cumulative probability curve for the win probabilities in the bidding by plotting a smoothed distribution of this table.

11. Determine the profit position of each of a number of bids within the range meeting the firm's objectives by multiplying the absolute profit estimate by the probability interpolated from this last curve.

12. Plot these profit position values on another graph to learn the optimum profit position value bid, and get a depiction of the distribution of profit position values (Wasson and McConaughy, 1968, or Wasson, 1969).

The optimum profit position is, of course, not necessarily the figure for the bid which best fits the organization's objectives. The bidder may aim instead to obtain as large an absolute profit as seems feasible, given the probabilities. Such an objective would generally suggest a bid with a somewhat lower probability of success than the estimated profit position optimum bid would have. Or the difference in profit positions may not be very great in the vicinity of the optimum, and the organization may decide on a somewhat lower bid with significantly higher chance of success.

The competitive bidding calculation, in other words, does not point out which bid is best to make. That is determined by the firm's objectives. The computations, however, do accomplish all that any mathematical tool can do--furnish a dispassionate analysis of the consequences, in quantitative terms, of the results of different alternatives, and thus permit a better comparison than one which does not develop these quantitative implications. The result is likely to be a bid which comes closer to optimizing profits on those which are won than is a bid less firmly based on the quantitative aspects of past experience.

An unpublished study by one of Donald S. Tull's students, of an actual set of bids made in the ordinary manner by an oil drilling company, indicated that had this mathematical model been used, "the same bids would have been won and lost, but, for each one won, a higher price would have resulted." (Letter to author from Donald S. Tull.)

As with all other kinds of pricing, bid pricing is one element of the total marketing strategy, and as such, is the obverse side of the product decision. These two strategy elements are inseparable and basic to the decision on all other aspects of the marketing mix.

All pricing decisions require the use of the carefully analyzed and digested information best labelled as market intelligence, as do, indeed, any competitive plans.

SUMMARY

1. Pricing is a complex of at least eight different kinds of marketing decisions, some of them strategic in nature, some of them merely tactical.

2. Two of the most important strategic decisions are essentially product policy choices: the price-quality level of market niche to be sought, and the price-product or price-merchandise mix to be followed.

3. Any organization in competition with others making similar offerings has to determine which price-quality level of offerings it is best qualified to develop and market effectively--high-end, average, or low-end. Although sometimes described as high, average, or low price policies, each of these levels designates a perceivably different offering design and different kinds of promotional and distributive strategies. The choice is partly forced on the seller by his own skills and cost structure, or by his available market potential.

4. Most sellers must also price a line of products or an assortment of merchandise, not each single item at a time. Prices within the mix are partially interdependent, and the pattern of profit margins sought will reflect the priorities and expectations of the market segment served. Some items in the line will be priced to yield relatively thin margins because the salience of these products and their relatively undifferentiated character help impart an aura of good overall line value to buyers. Other items specifically designed to sell well to the target market segments will be priced at overall target margins to yield high total profits through heavy turn-

over. Some items especially appealing to the core of the segment
served will sustain very high margins and thus balance off the low
margins of the traffic-inducing items at the other end of the margin
structure. These same general principles apply to both the internally supplementary line and to the product line which is internally
competitive.

    5. Trade discounts and other devices such as price mainten-
ance offered to attract distributors are really offers to purchase
distributive services essential to completion of the satisfaction bundle intended for the final buyer. These services include the time
and place utilities such distributive agents are best equipped to furnish, local communications functions they perform, financing of inventories awaiting sale, and even actual objective production services, including the assortment-assembling service, fitting the
product to the final buyer's needs. The distributor also furnishes,
directly and indirectly, marketing intelligence needed for management planning. Some of the price offered for these various services is normally in terms of a monetary discount, a division of
the payments expected from final buyers. Some payment may be
in terms of other arrangements desired by distributors--a price
maintenance policy, for instance, or some form of selectivity in
distribution.

    6. One important aspect of price policy which must be given
attention in many organizations is the timing and degree of initiative
taken in price changes, relative to the actions of sellers of similar
offerings: shall the firm lead or follow when changes in price seem
necessary? Choosing the leadership position on the upside is assuming responsibility for the relative position of the whole industry
with respect to potential and actual substitute satisfaction packages,
as well as for the immediate profitability of the whole industry.
The leader must always avoid the temptation to assure a strong
short-term profit position for the industry without respect to possible outside competition, particularly when the product has reached
maturity. Ignoring the threat of such potential external competition
can result in premature and permanent loss of markets.

    7. Whenever, as is normal, the major part of industry pro-
duction is concentrated in a few organizations, sellers must decide
whether or not price quotations will be permitted to vary with every
fluctuation in demand or held relatively stable and allowed to move
only in relation to the long run trend. A policy of relative price
stability is probably best whenever the item is an important component of the cost structure of other industrial buyers. Such a policy of relative stability, however, requires sellers to forego possible temporary extra profits during times of high demand relative
to supply and to institute some form of private rationing in times
of such supply shortages. When well managed, such a stable price

and intermittent rationing system permits the seller to offset some of the foregone profits by maintenance of customer loyalty during periods of easy supply.

8. The temporary price reduction is a useful tool f tactical maneuver because price can be changed with a minimum of lead time, in contrast to the advance planning needed to accomplish changes in the other aspects of the marketing mix.

9. The competitive advantage gained by a direct price reduction tends to be very ephemeral, however, just because competition can usually follow in no more time than it takes to place a simple telephone call. Consequently, most of the more effective forms of temporary price reduction involve some modification of the offering itself, modifications which require lead time for the user to effect, and additional time for competition to catch up.

10. Among the more common types of such temporary price reductions are the familiar "cents-off" deal, the bargain multi-unit offer, and the combination deal. Another form is the offer of some sort of premium with each purchase--either some specific premium item, or some sort of substitute money such as coupons or stamps which can be used to select from an assortment of premiums.

11. Care must always be taken to ensure that the intended temporary reduction is clearly labelled as temporary, in some convincing manner. There is always some danger that the premium will become perceived as the main product and the core product perceived as a mere premium attribute in the offering. Using the premium approach as a basic element of longrun policy is subject to the same sort of burdensome escalation as are straight competitive monetary reductions. No mere price reduction is as effective competitively as a noticeable product improvement granting some substantial market segment a better fit to its desire-sets.

12. Bid pricing, the common practice when the buyer specifies exact product performance and even design in advance of production, involves a careful estimate of possible profits and of the size of competitors' offers, and an equally careful assessment of the bidder's own objectives in seeking the award. A Bayesian decision tool, competitive bidding strategy, can be helpful in facilitating a dispassionate comparison of the probable effects of alternate possible bids on the longrun profit position of the bidder.

12

INFORMATION MANAGEMENT AND CONTROL OF THE MARKET LIFE CYCLE

It should be obvious that planning and execution of the kind of changing marketing strategy needed to adapt to the shifting phases of the product life cycle makes urgent a constant flow of well-analyzed intelligence on where the offering is relative to that cycle, on the kind and degree of acceptance the offering has achieved, and on the opportunities which can be exploited. Plans must always assume some kind of prediction, and information is needed on how well the predictions are being met and what is needed to bring plans into line with reality. Mistakes are bound to be made in product design and in marketing strategy and tactics, and the seller needs to make repairs early and quickly. The fact of the cycle makes market withdrawal inevitable at some point, and the proper point for a given firm may come at almost any stage of the cycle after the start of product development. Consequently, the success, market position, and profitability of all items in the line must be under regular review from the moment of conception to the point of final deletion. Continuous feedback is needed on whither consumer tastes are trending in order to get ahead of both the customer and the competition, and to stay ahead.

Nothing is automatic about the product life cycle except its general existence, nor are profits an automatic consequence of any successful product introduction. The biological analogy is very useful but not a perfect parallel. Financial success involves much more than the launching of a well designed product in the right market with the correct strategy. Management must be aware of the precise nature of that success and foretell near future demand and competition correctly and provide for them. Since the perceived nature of the product and its value shift throughout the cycle, constant feedback is needed concerning the changes in customer perceptions, customer use-systems, actual and potential competition (both direct and indirect), and promotional and distributional requirements. Successful management of product and pricing is best assured when full analytical use is made of the kinds of marketing research and intelligence appropriate to each phase of the product life cycle.

If the product is expected to be a high-learning introduction, field research and intelligence during the introductory period should focus on a close check of sales experience against prior expectations. In what use-systems are customers actually positioning the offering? Are the learning requirements at the level anticipated, and if greater, what can be done to ease them? Are previously unexpected weaknesses and faults showing up in the design or in production, and how must they be remedied?

Management of the market intelligence operation needs to be geared to the phase of the cycle just as much as must the other elements of management. The only difference is that the information flow must always be looking forward to the next phase:

Stage of Product Life Cycle	Marketing Intelligence Emphasis
MARKETING DEVELOPMENT	Identifying developing use-systems, uncovering any weaknesses in any aspect of the offering, and identifying the target market segments
RAPID GROWTH	Detailed attention to brand position, to gaps in market coverage, distribution, and model coverage, and to opportunities for market segmentation
COMPETITIVE TURBULENCE	Close attention to product improvement needs, to market-broadening opportunities and to possible fresh promotional means and themes
MATURITY	Intensified attention to possible product improvements. Sharp look-out for potential new inter-product competition and symptoms of decline
DECLINE	Information helping to identify the point at which the product should be phased out

As the first signs of a speedup in sales herald the start of a period of rapid growth, attention should shift to collecting intelligence needed to forestall competition that is certain to appear quickly. Among the now ready or almost ready buyers, do some desire model variants? Are new modified use systems developing, and what design variations can thus create new market segments? Are there segments on the market fringe who could be attracted by low-end models, or others by premium offerings? Are there newly interested dealers to whom distribution could wisely be expanded? What attributes in the offering appeal to fringe market segments, and how can this interest be exploited? As competitors become a reality, what segments are they capturing and what are they doing to distribution and to our share of the market? What market niche are we carving out and what can we do to entrench ourselves in it?

When a slowdown in the rate of sales growth heralds a coming shakeout, research and information attention should phase over to a search for ways to increase product value both to distribution and to consumers. Management needs to ask, What is our position with distributors and dealers, and with what quality of each? What can we do to strengthen that position? What is our real market niche, and what refinements in our offering will firm up our position with final users? What fresh advertising themes might draw renewed attention to the differentiated values we are offering? What kinds of market broadening opportunities can be discerned? Is our position strong enough to survive the shakeout well, and if not, what is the best way to withdraw before we begin to lose?

If the offering survives the competitive shakeout of the turbulence period with a healthy share of the now mature market, attention should be shifted to finding opportunities for capitalizing fully on the market niche achieved. Can the offering be substantially improved in a way which yields a better cost/benefit ratio for our buyers? Does our brand acceptance provide opportunities for use-related flanker products? Does the offering include attributes no longer worth their cost to users and which should thus be eliminated? What is our market share, and if changing, what is the reason for the change? Is the product category beginning to suffer market erosion from outside the industry, from the growth of new kinds of products better fulfilling some of the desire-set? Is an inevitable decline foreshadowed?"

Once decline seems on the way, the entire attention of management should focus on the best way of milking the profits from the decline and the timing of deletions. Are there models no longer needed? Are there distribution channels no longer worth serving? What means of phase-out, and what timing, will maintain customer goodwill? Such product deletion questions should not necessarily wait for the decline of the product category cycle. Sick and dying products are valid candidates for deletion at any phase of the cycle, and formal reviews of every item in the firm's offering should be a routine procedure, aimed at identifying the sick, the dying, and even healthy products which could be more profitable to other sellers than to the originating firm.

All of these questions assume that someone, somewhere in the firm is conducting a continuing life cycle audit of each major line.

PRODUCT AND MARKET RESEARCH DURING THE INTRODUCTORY PHASE

Because of the substantial investment required for even the simplest introduction, planning should be based on the best volume estimate available intelligence permits and on the most careful analytical appraisal of the acceptance climate. But neither product development nor market intelligence attention can safely be relaxed at introduction. Indeed, the initial introductory period probably calls for the closest kind of real-time feedback on target accomplishment, on offering design, on markets being reached, on the type and degree of acceptance, and on developing use-systems.

Until actual introduction, we have only estimates concerning market reaction, and such estimates are subject to a high level of forecast error. An immediate determination must be made of actual learning requirements being revealed and of the actual market segment being reached, and a reassessment made of the size of the market potential and of the necessary introductory market strategy. Have the learning requirements proven much less than expected? Then the entire production and marketing strategy must be shifted into high gear to capture and retain a substantial lead over quickly developing competition.

Product weaknesses, quality control slips, gaps in marketing coverage must be identified immediately and a crash research and development program instituted to remedy the vulnerable aspects before competition takes advantage of the opportunity.

By contrast, perhaps the use-system actually developing involves an unexpected learning barrier to adoption and the offering a much more protracted market development period than was forecast. Then market strategy needs to be turned around in the other direction--the promotional mix emphasizing the personal approach rather than the mass tools of advertising, distribution cut back to the selective use of a few aggressive outlets, proliferation of models held in abeyance and the product design scrutinized for possibilities of simplifying the required learning, signs of perceivable product weakness searched for with a microscope.

A major justification of most test marketing operations is the uncovering of product effects and planning and promotional misconceptions, to permit remedy before full commitment to the market. Polaroid's initial Florida test of its SX-70 camera revealed that displays were not realistically planned, that more dealer instruction was necessary than originally thought, and that customers needed much more extensive instruction helps than had been foreseen. Plans were accordingly revamped before full introduction.

Even when the learning requirement appraisal seems to have been reasonably correct, the customers actually attracted by the offering may prove to belong to a different segment than anticipated, requiring changes in the promotional or media mix. Ford's Mustang was originally thought to be aimed to convert buyers similar to those buying the Corvair. Sales proved to be to a different group of segments, and, fortunately, to a much broader market.

Clearly, the introducer needs a great deal of up-to-the minute, relatively objective market intelligence during the introductory period:

1. Who are the buyers? Are they innovators only, or do they, even at the start, include some members of the usual early majority? What characterizes the kind of people in the market segments most interested? Do they belong to the segments originally targeted, or are they a somewhat different group of buyers?

2. What are the purchasers buying? What values do they really perceive in the offering? What does this imply for offering design improvement? What does it mean for promotion? What does it forecast as to the duration and shape of the product life cycle?

3. Into what use-systems is the product being fitted? What do these imply for product revision, for product promotion, for distribution?

4. If the product is one of several competitive entries being introduced at about the same time, is it really succeeding, or is it simply getting trial by a rotating group of buyers, then rejected as really not offering a noticeable added value? If so, can the product be repaired, or should it be phased out immediately? (Even at this point product failures are common and to be expected as much as half the time.)

With answers to such questions as these, the seller should be in a position to evaluate the kind of life cycle he faces and to revamp his initial marketing strategy to fit. He should know to what market segments his messages need to be directed, what kinds of communications are needed to convert prospects to buyers, and what values and satisfactions they can perceive in the product and in the use-systems into which they have fitted them. And he will be in a position to improve the immediately noticeable product weaknesses before competition can take advantage of them.

GROWTH PHASE RESEARCH NEEDS

As market acceptance progresses, research needs to concentrate on any developing segmentation of potential demand and on
the kinds of product modifications useful in meeting the diversifying
desire-sets.

Analysis of the segmentation achieved needs to be far more
than a formal tabulation according to demographic factors. Nor do
some of the fads for personality measurement help much. Both
means are too indirect. In essence, what is needed is an insightful
probing into the kinds of satisfaction packages different buyers are
seeking by their purchases.

Newly developing use-systems need to be identified and product development as well as communications pushed to take advantage of these developments. The changing attitudes of distributors
must be closely attended to, and potential competition identified before it develops, if possible, and forestalled by the correct diversification of models and price lines as well as distributive enlarge-
ment.

Once sales are well into the growth phase, market intelligence
should be increasingly concerned with a close watch on the rate of
growth and the changing composition of the market segments, as
well, of course, as with competition. An especial alert needs to
be mounted for the first symptoms of a slowdown in the rate of
growth, especially to the slowdown in the number of new customers
being brought into the market. Increasing attention needs to be devoted to low-end offerings and to a stabilization of new distribution
outlets.

SHAKE-OUT PHASE INTELLIGENCE

A levelling off of the rate of increase in sales and new customers or other signals of growth slowdown and impending shakeout suggest another turn in product development emphasis and in
market tactics--a turn toward a defensive stance, to entrenching
and making less vulnerable any market position already won. Product emphasis requires increasing attention to information concerning product weaknesses and to finding improvements which will
render the offering more valuable to market segments already won.
At this point, the line should also be examined to determine whether
all models are justified, and increasing attention paid to production
and marketing costs, to finding ways to keep price down to the now
beginning-to-lower perception of value and yet maintain profit.

As the approach of the saturated market is presaged by a
levelling off in total sales of the product category and a stabilization

of the number of competitors and their market shares, there should
be an intensified search for unsatisfied market fringes, an increasing alertness to possibly remediable product weaknesses, and an
even closer look at advances in general technology or in customer
use patterns which could give the cycle a new spurt of growth to
pyramid it to even higher levels (as the switch from electronic
tubes to solid state devices did for radio).

RESEARCH ON MATURE MARKETS

Unless such opportunities are uncovered, management is
forced into a purely defensive stance. Market shares will be relatively stable, and any gains in market share at the expense of competitors are likely to cost more than they return in profits. Gains
from outside the industry (at the expense of other products, that is)
can come only from moves which broaden the market, either by
getting the product into new systems by pricing moves or demand
pyramiding through use of new technology, or by designs which
capitalize on newly developing use-systems among users. This is
the period for intensive product-in-use studies, aimed at discovery
of negative attributes in the offering which designers may be able
to detour, at finding unfulfilled desires giving positive direction to
design which will widen usage, or revealing the existence of use-
systems which, if adequately publicized, will increase frequency
of use by loyal customers or their associates. Eliminating the
negative attributes can give a lift to the whole market, as the introduction of textured velvet weave rugs proved, or at least restructure the market shares to the advantage of the introducer. At the
least, they can reveal useful fresh promotional themes and help
prolong the mature market, delay the onset of the decline, during
which all efforts must be directed to phasing out the sick and dying.

TREATING SICK PRODUCTS AND ENDING THE AGONY OF THE
DYING

Quite a few have written concerning the identification of sick
and dying products, and much of what they have outlined is valuable
(Alexander, 1964; Berenson, 1963; Kotler, 1965; Talley, 1964).
Most of the approaches outlined, however, implicitly assume that
death is preceded by a more or less successful life cycle, yielding
sales records for easy diagnosis. But infant mortality--and a rather
high rate, at that--is a fact of product as well as animal life. Products, like all mortal creations, can sicken and die at the moment
of birth or at any other point of existence for any of a number of

reasons. Only a minority of potentially valuable market entries lives a long and profitable life and survives to a period of slow and graceful decline. Periodic product health checks are a wise precaution from the moment of introduction, and like all health checks, those reviewing the evidence must have some norm against which to measure the state of health.

One important reason for advance estimates of probable initial acceptance is to provide a benchmark against which the degree of introductory success can be judged. If the sales exceed the expected, the seller needs to learn why quickly in order to revamp his production and promotional plans before competitors take advantage of a vacuum. If sales fall short of expectations, the introducer needs to investigate the reason, to find out whether the product was ill-conceived and really not destined to live, whether it has some specific curable weakness in need of immediate repair before the market is irremediably damaged, whether the product is being incorrectly positioned by buyers and needs a change in the promotional approach, or whether the product is being taken up by a different market segment than that visualized and promotion needs redirection.

Even when sales seem to be on target, the seller still needs to learn whether the result is fortuitous or due to a correct forecast. Moreover, sales, especially initial sales measured at the factory level, sometimes seem to start out as well as or better than expected, then suddenly lose momentum because of a product or promotional weakness which should have been discovered immediately and corrected before too many customers had bad experiences. One such instance was that of a well-designed coal stoker brought out by a manufacturer at a time when the market for these was on the upgrade, replacing hand feeding of home furnaces. Unfortunately, in use by actual customers, the stokers developed some irritating minor defects, a fact not discovered until a relatively large number had been sold and put into use. The defects were such that they could have been eliminated easily by minor redesign, but after careful review of the problem, the firm reluctantly came to the conclusion that the bad reputation engendered by the substantial number in use left no wise alternative but to withdraw the product and abandon the market--that from a market point of view, the knowledge of the problem came too late for correction. Likewise, the initial waterjet small boat propulsion systems took off on a very satisfactory growth curve when first introduced in the early 1960's, only to lose sales and nearly die before the makers learned that their bearing designs were faulty and that the means used for steering was inadequate. Most sellers dropped out, but the stronger introducers stayed on and developed a satisfactory product. Unfortunately, when they tried their comeback, a rival high-power propulsion system--the inboard-outboard motor--had come into the market and captured much of the segment the waterjet might have had.

Success that is much greater than expected needs just as careful investigation as problem situations. An extremely rapid initial sales growth needs researching to find out the nature of the benefits being perceived and the permanence of their demand pattern. Any such early surge of sales should always raise the suspicion that the demand has a fad-like character, and this hypothesis should be discarded only on the strongest of evidence that the acceptance is that of a true missing-link product. As already indicated, the production and market management implications of these two cycle types are exactly opposite. Any residual suspicion of fad demand requires the closest attention to movement at the ultimate consumer end to detect the first faint signals of sales slowdown. Production must be phased out, in such a case before the peak of the market unless there is a known residual market which the introducer is in an especially favorable position to serve profitably.

Products may be deleted from the line at any point after the moment of conception. Many offerings are normally dropped at one or another of the milestone review points during development, either because they cannot be built to desired performance and cost specifications or because the market does not look profitable. But recognizably viable products may properly be abandoned because they do not fit the seller's normal operation. When General Foods bought out S. O. S. steel wool scouring pads, they thereby acquired also some promising developmental work in fiber metallurgy. After careful consideration, the firm spun off this physical development stage offering, simply turning it over to Armour Research Institute as a gift. The Institute almost immediately found two purchasers for the rights--firms operating in industrial markets, for whose operations the product could be valuable, as it was unlikely to be for a grocery products firm.

All established products, at any stage of the cycle, should be subject to formal periodic health examinations to permit early detection of sickness, of a need for possible changes in the product line or marketing mix appropriate to advances in the life cycle, or for euthanasia as they show signs of advanced decline. The review should also weigh whether each item might not be of more value to some other seller or have a better chance in life under hands better equipped to market it. When Monsanto proved with its "All" that a significant growth market existed for a low-suds detergent, it suddenly found itself in rougher competitive company than it felt equipped to handle. With only 100 salesmen to cover the market, it could not hope to match the effort of Procter and Gamble's force of 1,000, nor expect to trade advertising dollars with the latter. They decided to turn sales and responsibility for the brand over to

Lever Bros. , while an exploitable market for the brand remained.

Product reviews should probably be divided into two stages. Responsibility for identifying weak products should be delegated to some lower level of management, or even to a routine computer program. Kotler (1965) has suggested that this mechanical review should apply previously decided on-yardsticks, looking for such items as:

consistently declining share of company sales

consistently declining trends in total sales, after due allowance for cyclical and seasonal trends

consistently declining share of market

consistently declining gross margin (but note that this alone
could happen during the shakeout period as well as during
the decline)

consistent inability to cover a minimum share of overhead

Those products which are spotlighted by this mechanical check should then be reviewed by a higher level product review committee drawn from the topmost echelons, officials who could bring to the decision information necessary for appraisal of the present and future value of the offering in the firm's total strategy. A logical composition of such a committee would include representa-tives from the following, with the type of information indicated:

Marketing, with information on basic strategy, customer relations, competitive developments, future sales expectations

Manufacturing, with data on scheduling, and manufacturing
and inventory problems

Purchasing, with knowledge of future material costs

Accounting and Finance, to provide information on past sales,
costs and profits and develop implications of product aban-
donment on cash flow and corporate rate of return

Personnel, to outline the feasibility of reassigning any affec-
ted personnel

Research and Development, to tell what replacement products
under development might use the physical and human resources now devoted to the products under consideration

Such a review committee would also be able to make judgments about trends toward increasing drain on executive time by the prod-ucts in question--important data in itself, since sick products nor-mally take more than their share of executive attention. They could also testify regarding the degree to which returns from development and product improvement were diminishing for each item under con-sideration. No product is ever completely free from possibilities for improvement, but such improvements contribute less and less to market gains as the cycle ages. Some point is finally reached at which the improved product does little more than shift sales volume from one brand to another, or one model of the same make to a different one.

The review committee's task is just started when it gets the list of really sick products. Its job is to decide which ones should be repaired and which dropped. Judgments must be made with respect to the value of the offering in the total profit picture. Direct profits from sales is seldom the sole criterion for retention--the effect on the total product mix must be considered. Some sort of formal retention index should probably be devised for every review, with some agreed-upon standard for the overall score to retain some semblance of objectivity and avoid decisions based on emotional commitment. Each item in the index would carry a specific weight, depending on the industry and on the firm's objectives, and a subjective judgment score assigned by each participating executive. Such items as the following should certainly be included in that index:

1. Outlook for the trend in future gross margin
2. Estimated future sales potential
3. Contribution of the product to overhead
4. Value of alternate opportunities for the resources being devoted to production and sale
5. Value of the item in aiding sales of the total line--its importance to the total product mix
6. The amount of executive time which would be released by product deletion
7. Possibility of resuscitation of the product by design repair or marketing strategy modification

If all other items seem to indicate deletion, but the product is a valuable element in promoting the rest of the line, it may be worth looking for an outside manufacturing source which is more efficient and maintain the item in the marketing mix as long as needed. SCM (typewriters and other office equipment), for example, sold out its carbon paper manufacturing operation but retained sales rights, and Westinghouse still sells a complete line of home refrigerators, but gets them from a contract manufacturer.

The reality of the costs used in appraising individual product profits always deserves the closest of scrutiny. They must always be evaluated on the basis of the alternate opportunities open for the use of the resources which would be released: capital used in production, both circulating (inventories, etc.) and fixed (equipment, plants, etc.); employees; executive time; limited material resources; distribution facilities and manpower.

Even when the decision to drop a product from the line is clear, the timing of the phase-out needs careful planning. One major factor in such timing, one affecting the productivity of the resources employed, is the availability and the appropriate timing of any replacement product currently in research and development or otherwise planned for introduction. The human factor must be taken into account--the problem of timing necessary shifts of executives and other employees to other useful tasks. The handling and phase-out of existing inventories at all levels of distribution is an obvious consideration of the timing of any deletion plans. Care must be taken to avoid damage to distributor relationships by causing dealer losses, and thought must be given to methods of compensating distributors and taking care of final customers and their service needs. In the case of durable goods, provision needs be made for continuing service and parts on models already in use, for as much as decades, at times. A manufacturer of heavy trucks, for example, always produces a "life-time supply" of spare parts when phasing out a model, and will make parts to order if needed to keep models in active use that have been out of production for 25 years, if the owners desire. Such thoughtful policies add materially to the value of new products to be sold later.

Timing needs to be planned also in relation to the salvaging of as much as possible of the capital involved in production. If demand has a significant seasonal pattern, planning the phase-out for the off season can substantially mitigate the impact on both production and distribution and lead to the least market disturbance for everyone.

Thought should be given to whether the product goodwill has enough residue that some smaller maker, able to operate on limited value, might not profit by it, and if so, a buyer may be found.

Product deletion can clearly be as complex a process as product introduction and requires the same thorough planning and programming. Critical path analysis may often prove as valuable for planning and control of the process as it is found to be for product introduction planning. Any mourners will be left with a better feeling when the burial is well planned, as such an analysis permits.

AUDITING THE POSITION IN THE CYCLE

Perhaps one of the most difficult problems in adapting plans to the phase of the product life cycle is that of making a continuously, coldly objective audit of just where a product line is in its cycle.

The difficulty arises from two sources. First, those in charge of day to day direction of the marketing effort tend to lose perspective. The changes which do come are mostly gradual, and often less over a short period than the fluctuations of season and competition. Just as important, booming current success or the past history of a product line's success tends to create a degree of emotional attachment to an assumption of product line immortality,

sometimes long after the decline is clearly visible to outsiders.
In any case, today's breadwinner is likely to get more attention
than one that has its sales volume ahead of it.

When a firm is strongly committed to the product manager
system, the problem of the personal empire can raise another barrier to objective appraisal and sound action. For all these reasons,
there needs to be some formal arrangement, with communications
lines leading to top management, for a continuing audit of the position of the firm's product lines. This may also be a place where
the outsider can render a signal service, if thoroughly experienced
in product life cycle analysis.

However it is doing what we know about product life cycles
does permit an objective and accurate analysis in experienced hands.
The symptoms of each stage are measurable:

Product Life Cycle Stage	Symptoms
MARKET DEVELOPMENT	High degree of awareness when pub-licity and other promotion is ade-quate, but a reluctance to buy. A high degree of potential added val-ue to major market segments, as perceived by them, but obvious learning requirement problems slow market growth, with heavy promo-tional expenses. Buyers from early adopter groups well satisfied after trial and ready to recommend to friends. No visible rush to enter market by others. Dealers not eager--must be sold on taking on the line and need high margins. Buyers secured only by intense sel-ing or advertising.
RAPID GROWTH	Sales beginning to grow more rapidly and becoming profitable. Promotion of all kinds returning a profit over cost. Dealers beginning to seek to carry the line. Other firms showing strong interest in market entry. Personal selling or saturation ad-

advertising no longer so necessary.

COMPETITIVE TURBULENCE   Numerous competitors in the market and more building capacity.
Some of them trying to buy distribution and sales with price cuts.
Rate of growth in sales still good,
but beginning to slow down.
Dealers beginning to trim back on
brands carried.
Production capacity on stream and
in process of building assumes
market will continue to expand at
previous rate for the indefinite
future.

MATURITY   Industry dominated by a relatively
small number of major producers.
Few or no new entrants interested.
Market shares tending to be stable
and due in part to distribution
strength. Changes in market
shares normally more costly to
achieve than the effort is worth.
Customer interest in the product
no longer at a peak. Brand
differentiation tending to be as
much psychological as physical,
and not sharply perceived by
many buyers.
Effects of extra promotion relatively temporary.

DECLINE   Many producers dropping the line.
Other products have displaced
the line in important use-systems.
Extra promotional effort largely
ineffective.
Dealers not very interested in
the line, and tend to carry a
single brand when possible.

All of these symptoms are, of course, corollaries of what
has been said of the cycle earlier. Like symptoms in any field,
however, the total pattern must be analyzed. They are not some-

FIGURE 12-1. Abbreviated Summary of a Life Cycle Audit of the Offerings of a Major Research Services Firm

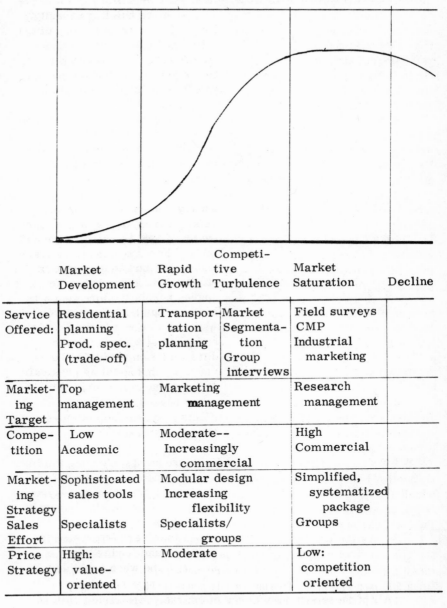

	Market Development	Rapid Growth	Competitive Turbulence	Market Saturation	Decline
Service Offered:	Residential planning Prod. spec. (trade-off)	Transportation planning	Market Segmentation Group interviews	Field surveys CMP Industrial marketing	
Marketing Target	Top management	Marketing management		Research management	
Competition	Low Academic	Moderate-- Increasingly commercial		High Commercial	
Marketing Strategy Sales Effort	Sophisticated sales tools Specialists	Modular design Increasing flexibility Specialists/ groups		Simplified, systematized package Groups	
Price Strategy	High: value-oriented	Moderate		Low: competition oriented	

300

thing that a computer can automatically spot or prescribe for. This is particularly true of products in the introductory stage, whether that seems to parallel a market development phase or hit a period of rapid growth early.

Difficult sales growth is the primary visible symptom of the market development introduction. This may be due to the fact that the product is not really viable, or it may be due to a high learning requirement and the need for extensive trial by early adopters. Or the same symptom may result from improperly directed promotion or a minor product defect, which, if corrected, could lead to relatively good sales growth.

Likewise, extremely rapid sales growth can be true of either a very solid introduction, destined for long life, or it may be due primarily to a fad reaction, or a mixture of the two. The answer lies, again, in the nature of the perceived use-system, and this is not likely to be discovered by simply knocking on a few doors.

In other words, as anyone knows who has ever observed amateur medical diagnosis, skilled analysis of the symptoms is as important as a knowledge of them. And as in medicine, it is wise to let this be carried out by someone without a potential emotional attachment to the patient. Executives deeply involved in the success of a product line are likely to have a distorted perception of the import of the sales results.

Given an objective viewpoint and experienced analytical skill, however, accurate analysis is possible, and plans based on it can lead to a profitable competitive position.

SUMMARY

1. Successful adaptation of marketing strategy to the product life cycle and proper implementation of the strategy clearly demands a constant flow of appropriate information feedback and critical analysis of the intelligence.

2. The most important information needs during initial introduction concern identification and analysis of the use-systems which are developing, of the learning requirement types and levels being imposed, of the market segments being attracted by the offering, and of the offering design strengths and weaknesses.

3. As the market develops, attention should be focussed on the discovery of possible market segmentation opportunities, on identification of differentiating desire-sets relative to both price lines and use-systems, to ensure adequate market coverage.

4. As the growth rate slows down, the focus should shift to closer attention to indentification of the market niche achieved and to strengthening it, and also to identifying possibilities for broaden-

ing the market.

5. Once market maturity has arrived, even closer attention should again be paid to identifying avoidance characteristics in the product design and finding ways to overcome them.

6. All offerings at every stage of the cycle should be reviewed regularly to identify sick products in need of repair or euthanasia and dying products whose withdrawal from the line needs careful planning of a phase-out. Every deviation from expected sales growth, whether favorable or the reverse, needs careful analysis to determine the possible need for changes in strategy and tactics.

7. Profitability or prospective direct profitability are important considerations in product retention or deletion but by no means the only standard, and products may be candidates for disposal at any point in the entire life cycle, including the product development stage.

8. Every organization needs some kind of formal review procedure to identify the sick and the dying and a two-step analysis of information on the relevant facts on competition, sales, and profits of every existing offering in the line.

9. The first step in such a formal review should be a regular initial routine analysis of every item in the line to select candidate products for consideration. Lower echelon personnel should spotlight items with consistently declining share of company sales, declining share of the total product market, declining gross margins, or consistent inability to cover a significant share of overhead.

10. Such candidate products should then be reviewed by some higher level management group or committee representing all major functional areas of management, to decide which offerings should be scheduled for deletion. This group should apply such criteria as the drain on physical resources and management attention and on the opportunities for product repair or alternate use of the human, financial and physical resources committed to its production and sale.

11. Once the deletion decision is made, planning for the careful phase-out should be as meticulous as the planning should be for any introduction, with a carefully programmed time schedule based on close attention to preservation of human and distributive resources involved and of customer goodwill.

12. An objective audit of the place of each product line in the cycle is needed for successful competitive strategy plans. The symptoms of each stage are reasonably obvious corollaries of the descriptions of the cycle phases previously described. Analysis of the symptoms is not necessarily simple, however, in part because of potential emotional attachment of executives involved. For this reason, analysis of the cycle position needs to be in independent hands.

References

Advertising Age, "General Mills Scores Gains as Venture Units
    Proliferate," Advertising Age, December 29, 1969, p. 3

_____, "Couponing Grows, Gives Boost to New Products, Repeat
    Purchases, Kenyon and Eckhardt Study Shows," Advertising
    Age, February 12, 1962, pp. 63-68

R. S. Alexander, "The Death and Burial of 'Sick' Products,"
    Journal of Marketing, April 1964, pp. 1-7

Conrad Berenson, "Pruning the Product Line," Business Horizons,
    Vol. 6, (Summer 1963), pp. 63-70

Booz, Allen and Hamilton, Management of New Products, Booz,
    Allen and Hamilton, Feb. 1968

The Boston Consulting Group, Inc., Perspectives on Experience,
    The Boston Consulting Group, Inc., 1972. (Boston, Mass.)

F. E. Brown, "Price Image vs. Price Reality," Journal of Market
    Research, May 1964, pp. 185-91

Business Week "Tanera Tries to Fill Leather's Shoes," Business
    Week, February 17, 1973, p. 26

_____, "Scripto Starts Writing in Black Ink," Business Week,
    February 17, 1973, p. 46

_____, "Magnavox Tries for a TV Comeback," Business Week,
    April 14, 1973, p. 49

_____, "Tektronix: Where One Product Isn't Enough," Business
    Week, August 4, 1973, p. 65

Brooks Carter and Kenneth Berkowitz, "Rats Preference for
    Earned in Preference to Free Food," Science, Feb. 27, 1970,
    pp. 1273-4

Edward H. Chamberlin, Toward a More General Theory of Value,
    New York, Oxford University Press, 1957

J. Maurice Clark Jr., Competition as a Dynamic Process, Washington, D. C., Brookings, 1961

Joel Dean, "Pricing Pioneering Products," Journal of Industrial Economics, July 1969, pp. 180-7

Fortune, "Great Hopes from Ovshinsky's Little Switches Grow," Fortune, April 1970, pp. 110-124

Winfred B. Hirschman, "Profit from the Learning Curve," Harvard Business Review, Jan.-Feb. 1964, pp. 125ff

Samuel C. Johnson and Conrad Jones, "How to Organize for New Products," Harvard Business Review, May-June, 1957, pp. 49-62

Philip Kotler, "Phasing Out Weak Products," Harvard Business Review, Mar-April 1965, pp. 107-118

Edmund P. Learned and Catherine Ellsworth, Gasoline Pricing in Ohio, Division of Research, Graduate School of Business Administration, Harvard University, Boston, 1959

Herbert F. Lionberger, The Adoption of New Ideas and Practices, Ames, Iowa, The Iowa State University Press, 1960

J. W. Lorsch and Paul Laurence, "Organizing for Product Innovation," Harvard Business Review, Jan.-Feb. 1965, pp. 109-122

J. D. McDonnell, "Experimental Examination of the Price-Quality Relationship," Journal of Business, October 1968, pp. 439-44

Albert J. Melberg, "How to Get Successful New Products from the Laboratories," The Professionals Look at New Products, Michigan Business Papers No. 50, Bureau of Business Research, Graduate School of Business Administration, University of Michigan, Ann Arbor, 1969

James E. Myers and William H. Reynolds, Consumer Behavior and Marketing Management, Boston, Houghton Mifflin, 1967

The Nielsen Researcher, "New Brand or Superbrand?," The Nielsen Researcher, No. 5, 1971. The A. C. Nielsen Company, (Chicago, Ill.)

_____, "The Changing World of HBA," The Nielsen Researcher, No. 2, 1973. The A.C. Nielsen Company, (Chicago, Ill.)

Opinion Research Corporation, "America's Tastemakers, No. 1 and No. 2," The Public Opinion Index for Industry, Princeton, N.J., Opinion Research Corporation, April 1959 and July 1959

Everett Rogers, The Diffusion of Innovations, New York, The Free Press, 1962

C. E. Silverman, "Steel, It's a Brand New Industry," Fortune, December 1960, pp. 122-27 ff

R. L. Smyth, "A Price-Minus Theory of Cost?," Scottish Journal of Political Economy, June 1967, pp. 110-17

Walter J. Talley Jr., "Profiting from Declining Product," Business Horizons, Volume 7 (Spring 1964), pp. 77-84

Alexander Thomas, Stella Chess, and Herbert G. Birch, "The Origin of Personality," Scientific American, Vol. 223, No. 2 (August, 1970) p. 102

William T. Tucker, "Development of Brand Loyalty," Journal of Market Research, Aug. 1964, pp. 32-35

Donald S. Tull, R. A. Boring, and M. H. Gonsler, "A Note on the Relationship of Price and Imputed Quality," Journal of Business, April 1964, pp. 186-91

Donald S. Tull, "The Relationship of Actual and Predicted Sales and Profits in New Product Introductions," Journal of Business, July 1967, pp. 233-50

Jon G. Udell, "How Important is Pricing in Competitive Strategy?," Journal of Marketing, January 1964, pp. 44-48

George W. Van Beek, "The Rise and Fall of Arabia Felix," Scientific American, December, 1969, pp. 36-46

Chester R. Wasson, "What is 'New About a New Product?," Journal of Marketing, July 1960, pp. 52-56

_____, Understanding Quantitative Analysis, New York, Appleton-Century-Crofts, 1969

305

_____ and David H. McConaughy, <u>Buying Behavior and Marketing Decisions</u>, New York, Appleton-Century-Crofts, 1968

Walter A. Wood, "Developing and Measuring Concepts," <u>The Professionals Look at New Products</u>, Michigan Business Papers No. 50, Bureau of Business Research, Graduate School of Business Administration, University of Michigan, Ann Arbor, 1969

Index